TRANSFORMING THE FIELD EDUCATION LANDSCAPE

UNIVERSITY OF CALGARY
LCR Publishing

TRANSFORMING THE FIELD EDUCATION LANDSCAPE

Student Handbook on Field Education

Julie L. Drolet and Grant Charles

EDITORS

LCR Publishing Services
An imprint of University of Calgary Press
2500 University Drive NW
Calgary, Alberta
Canada T2N 1N4
press.ucalgary.ca

LIBRARY AND ARCHIVES CANADA CATALOGUING IN PUBLICATION

Title: Transforming the field education landscape : student handbook on field education / Julie L. Drolet and Grant Charles, editors.
Other titles: Student handbook on field education
Names: Drolet, Julie, 1971- editor | Charles, Grant, 1953- editor
Description: Includes bibliographical references.
Identifiers: Canadiana (print) 20240528344 | Canadiana (ebook) 20240528379 | ISBN 9781773855585 (softcover) | ISBN 9781773855592 (Open Access PDF) | ISBN 9781773855615 (EPUB) | ISBN 9781773855608 (PDF)
Subjects: LCSH: Social service—Fieldwork—Canada—Handbooks, manuals, etc. | LCSH: Fieldwork (Educational method)—Canada—Handbooks, manuals, etc. | LCSH: Social work education—Canada—Handbooks, manuals, etc. | LCGFT: Handbooks and manuals.
Classification: LCC HV11.8.C3 T44 2025 | DDC 361.3071/55—dc23

The University of Calgary Press acknowledges the support of the Government of Alberta through the Alberta Media Fund for our publications. We acknowledge the financial support of the Government of Canada. We acknowledge the financial support of the Canada Council for the Arts for our publishing program.

Alberta Government   Canada   Canada Council for the Arts   Conseil des Arts du Canada

Cover image: Colourbox 8837818

Contents

Introduction: Student Handbook on Field Education

Julie L. Drolet and Grant Charles

The Student Handbook on Field Education is designed to accompany social work students in their field education journey. Field education or practicum is the site where students prepare themselves for their professional practice and transform into social workers. We are reminded by many of the contributors in this *Handbook* that "learning is at the heart of field education" (Chapter 1). For many students, it is in the field where one can integrate classroom learning and personal experience with real life situations.

For many years, social work education has brought together classroom learning and field learning—in equal importance—together contributing to the development of required competencies for professional practice. Students attend classes to learn practice principles, values, and ethical behaviors that will inform their future practice. Field is the place where students get to integrate these practice principles, values, and ethical behaviors into practice. Field education is an integral and valuable component of the social work curriculum for students (Drolet et al., 2012). Indeed, it is recognized as the signature pedagogy of social work education (Council on Social Work Education [CSWE], 2015). Field education is systematically designed, supervised, coordinated, and evaluated. Students engage in "hands-on" learning with the supervision of a field instructor(s) in a setting that is affiliated with the social work education program. Student learning is structured through a learning agreement, or learning contract, that identifies the goals and objectives into specific practice and learning tasks for the student. Social work education programs use a variety of approaches to facilitate the integration of theoretical content into practice, and there is increasing awareness of the need to also integrate research into practice and in field education. Field education programs bring together students, faculty, field instructors, and practitioners. Field instructors provide ongoing evaluation of the student's progress through formal and informal supervision and by providing feedback regularly to the student. A midterm and final evaluation of the student by the field instructor(s) occurs prior to the end of the term.

There is an urgent need for social work education programs to re-vision how field education is conceptualized, structured, and delivered, and ultimately how the profession prepares the next generation of social workers (Ayala et al., 2018; Drolet, 2020). Many of the contributors in this *Handbook* would agree that the landscape of the social work practice environment is dramatically changing, and this is having a direct impact on field education (Drolet et al., 2021). Many social work education programs are facing increasing challenges in delivering quality field learning opportunities to students around the world (Drolet, 2020). There is an urgent need for new resources to inform social work field education. New practices, insights, and approaches to teaching and learning are urgently needed for social work education to thrive in evolving and increasingly demanding social contexts, educational landscapes, and labor markets (Drolet, 2020; Walsh et al., 2022). Numerous studies call for the integration of research in social work practice, specifically in field education (Hewson et al., 2010; McConnell et al., 2023; Traber et al., 2021). In social work field education, students are immersed in both academic and practice settings, and these environments influence their professional development. The concept of Research As Daily Practice is used to understand this integration of research and practice, through which practitioners reflexively consider how to improve their practice (St. George et al., 2015). Because social workers work with vulnerable populations, such as children in need of protection and adults living in poverty, among many others, it is critically important to create new knowledge for better practice in complex situations (Drolet, 2020). The integration of research in field education will improve social work practice. This will contribute to micro, mezzo, and macro system improvements in social and health services for all.

Since the COVID-19 global pandemic, social workers are increasingly involved in remote service delivery (Drolet et al., 2020; Ossais et al., 2021). Technology continues to expand social services with e-counselling, e-therapy, and videoconferencing options. Many social work students have experienced and will continue to experience practicum placements that involve remote or hybrid models of field learning and/or service delivery. Students are being called upon to address complex realities in social work practice (Drolet & Todd, 2020). By integrating diverse practice experiences, this *Handbook* contributes to equipping students with a better understanding of social work practice and policy in the field.

We strongly support an open-access book publication for students to serve as a guide during their practicum experience, a key requirement in social work education. It is our hope that this *Handbook* will serve as a resource to stimulate new ideas and thinking in preparing students for placement. This is the first Canadian open access *Handbook* in social work field education for undergraduate and graduate level students and will also be available in print. The *Handbook* is edited with contributions from members of the Transforming the Field Education Landscape project (TFEL) that brings together diverse theoretical, geographic, practice research, and sites of learning in field education. The *Handbook* reflects the diverse sites of learning that students experience with respect to practices, policies, procedures, and strategies in field education.

The TFEL partnership, funded by a Social Sciences and Humanities Research Council (SSHRC) partnership grant, brings together social work academic researchers, field educators, students, professional social work associations and partners who share concerns about the state of field education in Canada and internationally (Drolet, 2020). TFEL research is focused on identifying innovative, promising, and wise practices in field education that can inform the development of sustainable models of field education in the future. TFEL is actively engaged in the training and mentorship of students through qualitative and quantitative research and partnered research training activities. Our research findings identified the need for open access resources to support student learning in field education. TFEL members offer this *Student Handbook on Field Education* to students in the field, as well as social workers, field educators, practitioners, academics, and researchers, to share insights, knowledge, strategies, and innovations that will facilitate student learning in the field.

The *Handbook* shares practices, tips, and strategies to support the field education journey of social work students as well as social work practitioners, academics, and field educators. The *Handbook* is structured into 14 chapters and includes several features that will appeal to diverse learning styles, including activities, exercises, short case studies, reflections, practice research, discussion questions, assessments, suggested readings, and web links to videos, webinars, podcasts, and other media resources. A workbook is included at the end of the book to allow students to reflect on their learning using a journaling format. The content can be integrated into field seminar courses and student field learning agreements and can inform self-directed practicum activities to transform students' learning and experiences in field education.

The *Handbook* focuses on anti-racism, anti-colonialism, equity, diversity, inclusion, health placements, interprofessional practice, remote field instruction and supervision, self-care and wellness, trauma- and resilience-informed practice, practice research, spirituality, and student transition from school to work. These topics need to be urgently incorporated into social work field education.

It is important for students to learn about the history and current trends in field education. Without an awareness or knowledge of the Canadian field education context, there can be little appreciation of the importance of field education in social work. When students engage in practice, they often find their values challenged. It is in the field that students will learn about people who have a variety of needs for support and intervention in their lives; in the process, students will learn more about themselves The *Handbook* will assist students in identifying their strengths, values, beliefs, knowledge, and skills through a variety of self-assessment activities and what they bring to their field placement. This is particularly important for student wellness and self-care (Drolet & McLennan, 2016; Drolet et al., 2017; Samson et al., 2019).

Undergraduate and graduate students develop a learning contract with their field instructor(s) in the first few weeks of practicum. The learning contract includes the learning goals, objectives, assignments, tasks, and activities that will provide the context for the learning and inform how the student will be evaluated. To be effective, social workers need to base their work on a variety of theories and approaches that are applicable at the individual, family, community, and society levels. Social work theories are essential for good practice, from social cohesion theories to empowerment theories, social change, and development theories. Theories guide and direct social work practice in diverse contexts, and it is important that practitioners be able to explain why they engage in the strategies they use and why they need resources to support these strategies. Students are often encouraged to begin to develop a theoretical framework for practice that is congruent with their personal and professional values in the field placement.

The *Handbook* begins with Kelly Allison and Antoine Coulombe's "Tips for Starting a Field Practicum" (Chapter 1). This chapter is written for students who are about to begin their placement and provides students with guidance on developing relationships with service users and colleagues, making ethical decisions, and considering how social context shapes individual and collective realities. The authors discuss some of the uncertainties experienced by students who are starting a new practicum and acknowledge that students may feel anxious or worried about their ability to meet the challenges. As a new learning context for students, the chapter guides students in navigating the practice environment at the start of practicum such as participating in orientation and onboarding activities. Allison and Coulombe identify one of the most challenging aspects of beginning a practicum as the difficulty students have accepting the vulnerability of being a learner. Students are encouraged to proactively take responsibility for their own learning and to understand the diverse ways they can learn in a placement. The field placement provides an opportunity to engage in concrete activities and requires time to intentionally reflect on these experiences and connect these experiences to theories and concepts that they have been learning about in the classroom. Students are reminded about the importance of meeting the people and building relationship in their organizational context or workplace, guided by their interests and curiosity. The chapter also points out that students learn about the practicum organization's structure, policies, and legislation, and how various teams work together. Students are encouraged to set up a learning agreement contract for a successful placement in consultation with their field instructor supervisor. Each placement offers a variety of learning opportunities and activities, and these will inform their learning objectives. The authors explain that students may encounter challenges in their practicum placement and provide guidance based on their experience in facilitating communication while considering safety issues. The chapter introduces the need for practicing good self-care and identifies the field placement as an excellent opportunity to begin to explore self and collective care strategies.

Practicum is an entry point for students to consider self-care skills and wellness plans. In Chapter 2, "Making Space for Wellness in Field Education" Sherri Tanchak, Patricia Samson, and Julie L. Drolet consider the relevant literature. The chapter begins by explaining that there are multiple ways of understanding well-being. For example, from Indigenous perspectives, wellness is embedded in teachings of the Medicine Wheel that integrates physical, mental, spiritual, and emotional well-being (Nabigon & Mawhiney, 2011). Similarly, the mosaic approach, which includes diverse perspectives, contributes to supporting holistic self-care, health, and wellness in ways that are culturally relevant. The field placement creates opportunities for students to become practitioners that work to support and promote well-being in others, which calls for social workers to consider themselves and their own sense of wellness.

In the literature, Grise-Owens and Miller (2021) describe social worker well-being and organizational wellness as complementary. This is an important consideration for field agencies and organizations as they prepare students as emerging practitioners and promote a culture of wellness among those in the profession. Further, the authors discuss how organizational wellness has a direct impact on the field supervision process; both individual and organizational wellness are important to the overall health and well-being of social work students and field instructors. The chapter provides examples and resources that students, field instructors, and faculty can utilize as they embark on a reflexive journey to establish their own self-care plans as they navigate their professional and educational paths throughout their careers. The authors encourage students to reflect and respond to questions based on their lived experiences and understanding of well-being and present students with opportunities to use their reflections and awareness as a foundation for developing and practicing well-being. The chapter also discusses the role of emergency self-care, which can supplement well-being plans after a negative event that has dysregulated one's thoughts, emotions, and body.

Chapter 3, called "Trauma- and Resilience-Informed Practice for Self-Care among Social Work Students," by Evalyna Bogdan and Elaine-Miller Karas, builds upon Chapter 2. This chapter presents the community resiliency model that aims to strengthen individual and community resilience by teaching biology/body-based wellness skills that bring the nervous system back into regulation after stressful and traumatic events (Miller-Karas, 2015). The authors discuss the role of social workers in helping clients and communities build resilience and argue that to build the resilience of others, social workers first need to practice and demonstrate resilience skills. The chapter introduces wellness skills with brief descriptions and accompanying activities that can help students manage stress during their social work education and when transitioning into one's career. The functions of the nervous system are presented along with four wellness skills for self-regulation/stabilization, and self-care. The iChill app is a resource that can assist in this process. The chapter introduces the Resilient Zone, which is state of well-being in mind, body, and spirit. The authors demonstrate the biology of the stress response and the ways it assists in adopting non-judgmental responses towards everyone who is struggling with stress and trauma.

Chapter 4, titled "Remote Field Instruction and Supervision" is written by Eileen McKee, Jenna Nieves, Kelly Allison, Cyndi Hall, and Shella Zagada. This chapter presents resources to support students with e-learning and supervision in their field education. With the increased use of technology in remote social service delivery, students are developing technical competencies in remote field education, including how to develop effective field instructor–student relationships. The chapter discusses how the onset of the COVID-19 crisis has fundamentally shifted our thinking about ethics and standards in this unprecedented era. Important ethical considerations need to be addressed in remote field instruction, as well as strategies and approaches to enhance the education of social work students. The authors articulate considerations for equity and diversity in remote field education and recognize the importance for racialized students to have access to online spaces to talk about equity, diversity, inclusion; to provide counternarratives; and to offer and seek resources. The authors argue that remote service delivery, and thus remote social work learning and field practicums, will continue to some degree post-pandemic. Students, therefore, need to be equipped with the skills to thrive in their field learning with flexibility and accessibility for both clients and students.

"Integrating Research into Social Work Field Education—Beginning with your Learning Contract," Chapter 5, by Sheri M. McConnell and Melissa Noble, presents how research and research activities can be included in field practicums. Students are encouraged to add their own research-based learning objectives and activities in their learning agreement contracts. The authors highlight the need for students to develop applied research skills and make connections between research and practice. To effectively engage in research and research activities in field practicums requires field educators, agencies, and students to integrate research activities into direct practice or community-based field placements or in research-focused placements. The chapter provides practical, concrete examples of how to include research and research activities in field practicums through Bachelor of Social Work (BSW) and Master of Social Work (MSW) learning objectives and research activities and skills.

In "Research As Daily Practice as an Agency Asset" (Chapter 6), Sally St. George and Dan Wulff describe daily research practice for students, field instructors, and field agencies. The authors consider an approach to research that happens in the daily activities of practitioners and agencies, creating new possibilities for student involvement in any practice or organizational context. The authors explain that as practitioners attend to questions and issues that arise in their daily work, they often work with their colleagues to figure out the best ways to systematically inquire into those questions. This approach provides a venue for integrating research into field education by recognizing that research is already being done in social service agencies and with social workers.

Chapter 7, titled "Maneuvering the Macro: A Guide to Macro-Level Field Placements for Social Work Students, Field Instructors, and Field Liaisons" is presented by Julie Mann-Johnson, Anne-Marie McLaughlin, Brenda Vos, and Maddie Wandler. This chapter shines a spotlight on the importance of macro-level placements in social work education and in generalist practice. Policy development, research, analysis, advocacy, administration, organization, and mobilization that aim to influence systems captures the macro-level social work discussed by the authors. Macro-level competencies and skills are presented with a focus on learning and growth, reflexivity and relationships, leadership, critical thinking, professional communications, and values and ethics. The chapter concludes with a reminder of the important contribution of macro practice to social change and the pursuit of social justice.

In Chapter 8, titled "Developing a Theoretical Framework for Practice" Heather I. Peters discusses the need for students to bring theories into their social work practice and develop a theoretical framework for that practice. While many students recognize the need to integrate theory into practice, it is not always clear how to make these connections. Historical influences from the late 19th century that have informed social work practice are identified. By exploring various theories, students can distinguish between different levels of theory (such as grand theories and practice theories) and related skills.

"Striving for Equity, Diversity, and Inclusion in Social Work Field Education: From the Personal to the Political" (Chapter 9), by Emmanuel Chilanga and Jill Hanley, focuses on providing students with the knowledge and skills they need to understand and implement equity, diversity, and inclusion (EDI) principles in their field practicum. The authors discuss the meaning of equity and equality, and the need for students to develop a strong understanding of the systematic barriers faced by service users from underrepresented groups in accessing social services. Dimensions of diversity are presented using a diversity circle scheme (Gardenswartz & Rowe, 2003) that considers intersectionality and diversity attributes that give advantages and disadvantages to some members in society. Students are advised by the authors to think about EDI when working with populations and reflecting upon the organizational culture and practices in the field setting. Students are also encouraged to reflect on how EDI applies to them, and to ensure that EDI principles are present in their emerging practice skills.

Saleema Salim contributes to the conversation about EDI by centering Chapter 10, "Addressing Discrimination Against Minority Groups in Social Work Practice and Field Education," on educating students about the pervasive discrimination experienced by minority groups and provides tips and strategies for addressing discrimination in field education and social work practice. The author explains how diverse people experience difficulties due to discrimination and outlines the role of social workers in addressing institutionalized discrimination and oppression in their social work practice. The chapter invites student to reflect on their own self-identity and purpose to gain a deeper understanding of their own perspectives and biases. The author calls for students to increase their engagement with diverse groups and to address institutionalized discrimination and oppression against minority groups in their practice. The field practicum can provide an opportunity for students to develop practice skills that encompass respect for human individuality and the richness of diversity through compassionate, empathetic, caring, and to improve the well-being of minority groups.

Chapter 11 offers a spiritual practice model for integrating spirituality into one's professional identity and practice. Heather Boynton and Indrani Margolin's chapter, titled "Becoming a Spiritual Influencer through The Heart and Soul of Field Practice," presents spirituality as a dimension of social work practice. Drawing from the authors' work, students are guided to understand and conceptualize spirituality while developing a greater awareness of their own spirituality. The chapter includes spiritual assessments and guidance on how to approach spiritual questions using a holistic strengths perspective. The authors consider students as change agents in the field as well as learners who can become spiritual influencers in their practicum sites and in their future practice.

In Chapter 12, "Advancing Social Work Field Education in Healthcare," Patricia L. Samson, Janet McFarlane, Debra Samek, Hilary Nelson, and David B. Nicholas, discuss social work in healthcare and how the shifting context influences field education opportunities for students. The chapter provides background and context to social work in healthcare with a focus on patient-centered, or person-centered, care in the healthcare system. The gaps in healthcare are presented, including disparities and inequitable access to quality healthcare due to factors such as race, gender, ethnicity, social supports, geographic location, and income, as well as systemic challenges embedded in the healthcare system. New models and innovations seek to advance social work field education in healthcare and to create more potential placement opportunities. Rotational models, co-teaching, interprofessional collaboration, and a community of practice for social work students are among the new practices to consider in field education. The COVID-19 pandemic amplified many challenges in the delivery of health and social services, and this chapter highlights the need to re-envision how field placements are delivered given current realities.

Chapter 13, "Interprofessional Education and Practice in Social Work Field Education," by Kelly Allison and Grant Charles, demonstrates why social workers should engage in interprofessional and collaborative practice. The authors discuss how the complexity of social and health issues led to the creation of multiple health professions and a complex system for service users who often interact with team(s) of professionals for effective interventions. Interprofessional education and practice is needed to improve interactions among health and human service professionals, including social workers, and to ultimately improve the quality of care and service delivery for service users. Drawing from their practice in British Columbia, the authors define key terms, explain concepts, and identify competencies for interprofessional practice and education. Some core skills identified in the chapter include cooperation, assertiveness, effective communication, working collaboratively with other professions and autonomously within one's own profession. A model for optimal learning that focuses on exposure, immersion, and mastery is laid out for health and human services students and practitioners; the model identifies optimal points of learning based on stages of professional identity development, readiness to learn, and new perspectives on professional interaction. Practicum students are encouraged to articulate their role and scope of practice and to understand the role of other professions.

The final chapter, "The Transition from School to Work, From One Work Setting to Another: Guided by Curiosity" is a student reflection from Karen Lok Yi Wong. As students learn in their field placements, they also prepare for social work practice. This chapter documents one student's transition from school to work while remaining curious about new practice contexts. The 'curiosity' approach is explained and considered in three practice sites—working in a senior community centre, a long-term care centre, and a hospital. While adopting a learner stance through curiosity, the author shares her strategies for observation, searching for answers, asking questions, and reflection.

The *Handbook* provides a conclusion, and additional pages for student reflection through journaling or memoing.

Sharing innovative, promising, and wise practices in field education is of interest to Canadian and international academics, field educators, researchers, and practitioners. The *Handbook* supports students who are seeking to develop new understandings and practical skills for their social work practice while living in a highly interconnected and complex world. This is the first open-access book that focuses on building students' capacity in social work field education. The book is written for students and is of relevance to field educators, field education directors and coordinators, and faculty members and liaisons who support student learning in field education. We also expect that academics and researchers interested in work-integrated learning, experiential education, internships, and preceptorships in the health and social sciences will be interested in this *Handbook*. Field instructors and supervisors in field agencies may wish to use this resource to guide the development of field learning agreements and to inform student evaluations. Other parties in field education may be interested in this *Handbook*, including but not limited to professional social work associations, academic institutions (and libraries), government institutions, non-governmental organizations, health and social service organizations, social policy institutes, activists, social planners and policy makers, and social program officers.

The book will be of particular interest to the fields of social work and human services, and we anticipate that many professional programs and disciplines that offer experiential learning, internships, and work-integrated learning opportunities may be interested in the book. This may include disciplines such as nursing, education, social policy, health studies, geography, planning, sociology, international development, criminology, and others.

The TFEL partnership is contributing to the development of talent through partnered research training initiatives that integrate research and practice in social work field education. This *Handbook* brings together diverse perspectives on field education to support student learning during field practicum. Social work scholars, students, field educators, collaborators and practitioners in the book offer new insights, practice experiences, case studies, and reflections that offer the potential to transform student learning in social work field education. This *Handbook* is being published to advance a transformational approach that will enhance student learning in practicum by accompanying students in their field education journey and creating new understandings of field education that is of relevance to the current and future generations of social work scholars, practitioners, and policy makers.

REFERENCES

Ayala, J., Drolet, J., Fulton, A., Hewson, J., Letkemann, L., Baynton, M., Elliott, G., Judge-Stasiak, A., Blaug, C., Tetrault, A., & Schweizer, E. (2019). Restructuring social work field education in the 21st century in Canada: From crisis management to sustainability. *Canadian Social Work Review, 35*(2), 45–65. https://doi.org/10.7202/1058479ar

Council on Social Work Education. (2015). *State of field education survey: A survey of directors of field education on administrative models, staffing, and resources.* Council on Social Work Education. https://www.cswe.org/CMSPages/GetFile.aspx?guid=05519d2d-7384-41fe-98b8-08a21682ed6e

Drolet, J. (2020). A new partnership: Transforming the field education landscape: Intersections of research and practice in Canadian social work field education. *Field Educator, 10*(1), 1–18. https://doi.org/10.1080/02615479.2022.2056159

Drolet, J., Alemi, M. I., Bogo, M., Chilanga, E., Clark, N., Charles, G., Hanley, J., McConnell, S., McKee, E., St. George, S., Walsh, C., & Wulff, D. (2020). Transforming field education during COVID-19. *Field Educator, 10*(2). https://tspace.library.utoronto.ca/bitstream/1807/107218/1/Bogo_Transforming%20Field%20Education%20During%20COVID-19.pdf

Drolet, J., Alemi, M. I., & Collins, T. (2021). Beyond the challenges: New insights and innovations in field education. *The Hong Kong Journal of Social Work, 55*(1/2), 39–52. https://doi.org/10.1142/S021924622100005X

Drolet, J., Clark, N., & Allen, H. (Eds.) (2012). *Shifting sites of practice: Field education in Canada.* Pearson Canada Inc.

Drolet, J., & McLennan, C. (2016). Wellness and relational self-care in social work field education. *The International Journal of Health, Wellness and Society, 6*(4), 9–21.

Drolet, J., Samson, P., Tanchak, S., Kreitzer, L., & Hilsen, L. (2017). Self-care and well-being in social work education: Creating new spaces for learning. *Journal of Educational Thought, 50*(2/3), 200–215. https://www.jstor.org/stable/26372404

Drolet, J., & Todd, S. (2020). Community practice and social development themes and implications. In S. Todd & J. Drolet (Eds.), *Community practice and social development in social work* (pp. 457–472). Springer Nature.

Hewson, J., Walsh, C.A., & Bradshaw, C. (2010). Enhancing social work research education through research field placements. *Contemporary Issues in Education Research, 3*(9), 7–15. https://doi.org/10.19030/cier.v3i9.230

McConnell, S.M., Noble, M., Hanley, J., Finley-Roy, V., & Drolet, J. (2023). Integrating practice research into social work field education. *Journal of Teaching in Social Work, 43*(1), 1–19.

Ossais, J., Drolet, J., Alemi, M. I., Collins, T., Au, C., Bogo, M., Charles, G., Franco, M., Henton, J., Huang, L. X., Kaushik, V., McConnell, S., Nicholas, D., Shenton, H., Sussman, T., Walsh, C. A., & Wickman, J. (2021). Canadian social work field education during a global pandemic: A comparison of student and field instructor perspectives. *Journal of Comparative Social Work, 16*(2), 113–140. https://doi.org/10.31265/jcsw.v16i2.406

Samson, P., Tanchak, S., Drolet, J., Fulton, A., & Kreitzer, L. (2019). The contribution of clinical supervision to wellness in the workplace: Implications for social work field education. *The Field Educator*, *9*(1), 1–24.

St. George, S., Wulff, D., & Tomm, K. (2015). Research As Daily Practice. *Journal of Systemic Therapies*, *34*(2), 3–14. https://doi.org/10.1521/jsyt.2015.34.2.3

Todd, S., & Drolet, J. (Eds.) (2020). *Community practices and social development.* Springer Nature.

Traber, D. K., Collins, T., Drolet, J. L., Adamo, D. J., Franco, M., Laban, K., McConnell, S., Mi, E., St. George, S., & Wulff, D. (2021). Integrating practice research into social work field education. *Field Educator*, *11*(1), 1–12. https://fieldeducator.simmons.edu/wp-content/uploads/2021/05/20-272-1.pdf

Walsh, J., Drolet, J. L., Alemi, M. I., Collins, T., Kaushik, V., McConnell, S. M., McKee, E., Mi, E., Sussman, T., & Walsh, C. A. (2022). Transforming the Field Education Landscape: National survey on the state of field education in Canada. *Social Work Education: The International Journal*, *42*(5), 646–662. https://doi.org/10.1 080/02615479.2022.2056159

Tips for Starting a Field Practicum

Kelly Allison and Antoine Coulombe

Congratulations! You are about to embark on a social work field education experience, deemed our profession's signature pedagogy (Council on Social Work Education [CSWE], 2008; Shulman, 2005). Field education offers opportunities for real-world experiences where you can begin to enact social work values and ethics and integrate the knowledge and theories you have been learning in the classroom into the complexities of practice. You will have the chance to develop relationships with service users and colleagues, observe ethical decision making, and analyze how social contexts shape individual and collective realities. Practicums are exciting learning opportunities! In order to help prepare you for this experience, in this chapter we offer some suggestions for planning before you begin and helpful tips for getting started in your practicum.

Before You Go

Understand That Nerves Are Normal

Despite field learning being a much-anticipated experience for students, it is normal to feel nervous about starting your practicum. Learning about a new agency or organization, meeting new colleagues and professionals for the first time, and beginning to engage with and provide services to people can sometimes feel overwhelming. There are many uncertainties about what lies ahead, and some students worry whether they can meet the challenges. It is helpful to be patient and kind as you enter this new learning context and allow yourself the time and grace to adjust to this new environment. Accepting the uncertainties that go along with a new experience is essential to your learning. Allowing yourself the vulnerability of being a learner is also a vital part of managing anxious feelings. With time, experience, and support, you will likely become comfortable more quickly than you anticipate.

Do Your Homework

Before your first day of practicum, taking a few steps to ensure a successful start can be helpful. You have likely learned a bit about your practicum site while preparing for your interview or

Tip: To learn more about why students feel anxious about starting field placements and ways to use your field anxiety as a motivator visit this website *Field placement anxiety.* https://www.fieldanxiety.com/field-placement-anxiety

during your matching process. Having a general understanding of your agency's services and knowing about the client population they serve is a valuable foundation for the start of practicum. This information can be gathered from your agency's website and research regarding the client population being served (e.g., journal articles from your library). It can also be helpful to review recent news and to become informed of events that may impact this population. Although you will learn a great deal more about your agency and dive deeper into its organizational processes, this general overview can be a helpful starting place.

Consider How You Will Learn in Field

One of the most challenging aspects of beginning practicum as a student is allowing yourself the vulnerability of being a learner. You are not immediately expected to know how to be a social worker. You are a student, and a practicum is meant to be a learning experience. Although you have learned a lot in the classroom, there is still a lot to learn, and that is okay! You will make mistakes, and that is expected. It can be uncomfortable to acknowledge that you don't know something and that you will need to ask a lot of questions and sometimes need help. This vulnerability is all part of the learning process. Being honest about your limits and approaching your learning with a lot of curiosity and a willingness to risk making mistakes will help you maximize the learning opportunities in your field setting.

Learning is at the heart of field education. To proactively take responsibility for your own learning, it is essential to understand the diverse ways you can learn in a placement. This skill is also vital to being a social worker. As we often face new and complex situations, we must continually learn new things. To ensure that you have the best possible learning experience, it is crucial to consider your approach to learning, your needs as a learner, and how field learning differs from classroom learning.

Determining how you learn best can be important information in a field setting. Does it help you to write down instructions? Do you prefer to observe first before jumping in? It will be helpful to think about how you learn best and discuss this with your field instructor. You may have an issue that may impact your learning in field education. In that case, it is essential to talk with your field team about possible accommodations needed in the environment, the curriculum format, or any specialized equipment you require to ensure your field learning is optimal for your needs.

Experiential learning is a theory that believes we learn best from the interaction of concrete experiences, reflection on those experiences, and then adjusting our understanding and experimenting with new ideas (Kolb, 1984). Although students are often keen to actively "do" social work in a placement (such as conduct an assessment or assist in running a group or program), it is essential to take the time to intentionally reflect on these experiences and connect them to theories and concepts that you have been learning about in the classroom. Experiential learning theory helps us understand the ways we can learn in field settings.

Plan for Day One

Knowing some of the logistics of your first day of the practicum will be helpful to ease nerves. Do you know how to take transit to your site or where to park? Have you and your field instructor agreed on a start time and meeting place within the organization? Will you pack a lunch, or have you inquired about options for purchasing food on-site or near your agency? Having answers to these types of questions will help you feel prepared for your first day of practicum. It may be useful to identify your questions for your first day and reach out to your field instructor by email or phone.

Get Oriented to Your Practicum Context

Your first few weeks at practicum will be focused on getting oriented to your placement site and learning about your placement context: the organization and its structure and function, the people within the organization, and specifics regarding how they work. As all this learning might seem overwhelming initially, it can be helpful to focus on learning about your team or unit first and then expand your learning to the broader organization. As you learn about the organization/agency, you should develop a good understanding of the policies, procedures, and legislation that guide the work of your agency, how various professionals within an organization work together to fulfill their mandate, and how your agency fits with other social services to provide service to clients or the community.

Before you can move into this deeper learning about your organization, you will need to learn some day-to-day routines quickly. Here is a list of key questions for your first day that will help you get comfortable and situated within your agency or organization.

- Where can I leave my belongings to keep them safe while at practicum?
- Is there a check-in procedure, or how and where will I start each day?
- Do I need identification, keys, passcodes, etc., to move throughout the organization?
- How do I access a computer, telephone, and/or email if that is available?
- How do I access paper, pens, agency forms, etc.?
- Is my schedule set for me, or do I need to let someone know my schedule?
- How do I access client files? What are the policies on accessing client files?
- Do I need to keep statistics on how I use my time?
- Where is the washroom and break room?

Meet the People

The strength of most organizations lies in their people. Getting to know the people in your organization is an important early step in orienting to an agency. As your field instructor is your main point of contact within an organization, developing a strong, working relationship with them is a great place to target your energy. Interest and curiosity are good relationship-building tools. Don't be afraid to ask your field instructor questions about their role and job. Where appropriate, learning a bit about your field instructor as a human being can also be helpful; however, it is important to consider what kind of questions are appropriate for your context and the initial stages of your relationship.

Ask your field instructor if you can initiate meetings with other members of the team or other professionals in the organization. One-on-one meetings can be an effective way to learn about various roles within the team or organization, and how different professions interact in your organization. These meetings with other staff in the organization can also help you begin to build relationships within the agency.

Lastly, it is important to learn about the people served by your agency. This can be done in different ways and will vary for each placement. Discuss how you could best learn about clients with your field instructor. Here are a few questions you may want to explore:

- What word is used in your agency to describe people who attend services (client, service-user, patient, etc.)?
- How do clients begin to engage or receive services with your agency?
- What is the best way to engage with clients in your organization?

Learn About the Organization Structure, Policies, and Legislation

One aspect of learning about an organization is understanding their structure. Organization charts that outline the different units and the reporting structure within an organization can be helpful to get a bird's eye view of how various teams fit together. Ask your field instructor if the agency has an organization chart or other tool (such as websites) that will help you get a broader sense of your context.

Policies and procedures are an organization's guidelines and protocols for carryout out their work. They can cover everything from how professionals work together respectfully (i.e., a code of conduct or discrimination and harassment policies), how information is gathered and safeguarded (confidentiality policies and documentation policies), how decisions are made (referral policies, risk assessment policies), and how to ensure safety for clients and staff (health and safety policies, procedures for handling an emergency or crisis). Although an organization will have many policies and procedures, there will be key ones that you will need to be aware of early in your placement. For example, if your placement is in a women's shelter, you will need to quickly learn policies regarding confidentiality to ensure you can maintain the safety of the clients being served. You must also learn early on about policies on safety and emergency procedures (e.g., COVID-19 protocols). Be sure to ask your field instructor about essential policies and procedures that you need to know.

Lastly, many social workers are guided by specific legislation in their work. For example, students working with children and families or in a child welfare placement will become familiar with relevant child welfare legislation. Students working with older adults will learn about legislation regarding vulnerable adults, and students in health care placement will learn about health care consent and capacity legislation. Ask your field instructor for specific legislation related to the work in your practicum site.

Set Up Your Learning Contract

Deciding what you should learn in your practicum is a crucial step to completing a successful placement. The learning contract is a negotiated document with your field instructor, and your faculty liaison that sets out the process and content of student learning while on practicum. It can be a working document that is revised throughout the practicum. Some schools have pre-determined learning objectives for students in field, while others require students to create their own learning objectives as part of their learning plan. Although this may feel overwhelming at first, you don't have to do it alone! The learning contract is usually a balance of three main components.

Your school of social work's requirements for social work learning (usually based on the Canadian Association for Social Work Education's [CASWE] Educational Policies and Accreditation Standards which can be found here: https://caswe-acfts.ca/wp-content/uploads/2021/08/EPAS-2021-1.pdf

- Your interests and goals for your learning.
- Your placement's and field instructor's priorities for student learning.

You will need to have a dialogue with your field instructor about your interests and goals, their ideas for your learning, and the school's requirements for your learning. Once you are aware of some of the possible learning opportunities and activities available to you, you can begin developing some learning objectives (see chapter 10 of this handbook to consider how to incorporate research into your learning objectives). Most schools of social work also have faculty liaisons or integrative seminar instructors and/or field personnel who can help students with developing learning goals. Be sure to inquire about your school's supports for students in creating a learning plan for field work. The following are examples of learning activities that students might be involved in during their practicum.

- Review agency policy manuals.
- Attend training workshops.
- Read articles related to a client population.
- Shadow and observe client meetings, therapy sessions, or home visits.

- Research incidence of social issues (homelessness, incarceration, poverty, etc.) for the community that the agency serves.
- Attend interdisciplinary rounds and staff, board, or community engagement meetings.
- Review documentation and reports.
- Role play client interactions.
- Research community resources for a client.
- Participate in a committee.
- Co-lead an interview with a client.
- See clients/patients on your own.
- Document a session and have your field instructor review it.

Be sure to discuss what ways your field instructor will want you to demonstrate your learning in this placement. Sometimes field instructors evaluate learning through observation, journal entries, discussion, or field assignments.

Plan to Use Supervision Effectively

Supervision with your field instructor and meetings with colleagues in your placement are essential learning opportunities. They provide you with a space where you can ask questions, receive feedback, and engage in learning through dialogue with an experienced professional. The format for supervision can vary, such as short daily meetings or a one- to two-hour weekly meeting. Supervision can be formal meetings with an agenda and minutes or more informal discussions. The frequency and structure of your supervision meetings need to be negotiated with your field instructor. It can be helpful to consider how supervision could be structured to best meet your needs and discuss this with your field instructor. Ideally, supervision will be a time to receive specific, targeted feedback and suggestions for improvement to challenge your learning. At the same time, supervisory meetings should be a place to grow your confidence as you learn about areas of strength in your practice. If you and your field instructor have developed a trusting relationship, supervision is also a useful time to reflect inwardly and discuss your own thoughts, emotions, and reactions as they relate to your practice experiences. In your first meeting with your field instructor, be sure to discuss when to schedule regular supervision sessions, and what structure will work best for the two of you. You can then review the supervision format in a few weeks to consider if it is working or if there needs to be adjustments.

To get the most out of your supervision time, it is useful to be proactive and to plan for each supervision meeting. Here are a few suggestions on how to prepare for meetings.

- Prepare a summary of your learning for the week.
- Identify and prioritize questions and topics you would like to discuss in the meeting.
- Identify areas of your practice that are challenging for you or where you feel "stuck."

- Plan to discuss how what you see in your placement aligns or doesn't align with your classroom learning.

- Discuss social work concepts that you have learned about and that you see examples of in real world contexts.

- Explore how social work theories help you to understand a practice situation.

- Before meeting with a client, a group, or a family, consider how a particular theory can inform your practice.

- Include time each week for self-reflection. Consider your social location, thoughts, and emotions that have come up for you in various practice situations and how they may have impacted the practice situation.

Problem-Solve Challenges

"I never lose. I either win or learn." Nelson Mandela

Students sometimes encounter challenges in their practicum placement for various reasons (e.g., communication breakdown with your field instructor or other team members, difficulty managing home life and practicum placement responsibilities, assignments that feel beyond your capability, feeling triggered by practice situations, etc.). Challenges can be great learning opportunities because lots of our learning as social workers happens as we address problems in day-to-day situations. This process is central to being a social worker. Addressing problems will help you gain knowledge, expertise, and confidence in your work, as well as the ability to manage challenges in your practice and in relationships. Challenges may initially seem overwhelming; however, the sooner you identify and address issues, the more likely it is that the placement will continue successfully. Conversely, if problems or challenges are ignored, they can often be further exacerbated. Your field instructor may be the first to initiate a dialogue about an issue or concern, however if you are aware of a problem, we recommend addressing it as soon as possible.

Direct, respectful communication is usually the most beneficial approach when addressing concerns, however personal and psychological safety does need to be considered. Consult with your faculty liaison or field team if safety issues are present. Here are a few valuable steps to address challenges directly and effectively.

1. Take the time to properly understand the situation, and make sure you have enough information. This often involves initiating conversations with others and then listening to their perspective. This can involve conversations with your field instructor, faculty liaison, team members, or clients. Consultations can be helpful, but discussing the issue directly with those involved in the concern is often a crucial step.

2. Analyze the situation and identify what the main problem is. It is useful to try and develop a shared understanding of the concerns with your field instructor or whoever else is involved.

3. Determine a realistic goal: work with those involved to decide upon a preferred outcome to the problem.

4. Brainstorm possible solutions to resolve the problem and choose the most viable option.

5. Create an action plan to address the issue and implement the steps.

6. Evaluate, with the others involved, whether or not the issue has been addressed.

Staying Strong and Practicing Self-Care in Field

In your social work practice, your primary tool is yourself. It is, therefore, essential to practice good self-care. This will help you gain a deeper understanding of yourself, stay healthy in your work, and help you deal with difficult situations. Your field placement is an excellent opportunity to begin to explore and implement self-care strategies and practices. As you begin your placement, think of how you could set the right conditions for maintaining reasonable physical, mental, emotional, and spiritual wellbeing. In your first weeks, observe how your field instructor and colleagues practice self-care within your placement. Ask questions about what self-care options are available to you and how to access them.

Having lived experience can be a significant strength as a social worker. However, it can also sometimes be a challenge to our wellbeing. Our diverse backgrounds and experiences of adversity make us who we are and give us a deeper understanding of the human experience. This can help us understand what others are experiencing when faced with difficulties and feel authentic empathy. On the other hand, when meeting with people who face similar challenges or experiences to our own, we may feel overwhelmed or triggered or become convinced what worked for us should also work for our clients. This may cause us to transfer our feelings to clients (countertransference) and affect our ability to practice ethically. As you begin your field experience, you may want to reflect on your own life experience, identify potential triggers and begin to prepare coping strategies that will help when you meet others with similar experiences. You may also want to find professional resources to help you reflect on your lived experience and support your journey.

Individual self-care involves enacting strategies and practices that help to reduce stress and support our wellbeing physically, emotionally, cognitively, and spiritually. Each of us is unique and we may have a different approach to individual self-care.

ACTIVITY: Review and analyze your current self-care strategies using this self-care tool: Butler, L. (n.d.). *Self-care assessment*. Buffalo School of Social Work. https://socialwork.buffalo.edu/content/dam/socialwork/home/self-care-kit/self-care-assessment.pdf

---

However, caring for our wellbeing in practice is not only an individual endeavor. Collective care refers to the strategies and practices that organizations and groups of people in a work environment enact to take actions to promote the collective wellbeing of all (Chamberlain, 2020; Pofitt, 2008). Collective care can be intentional ways that teams or organizations build a supportive community amongst staff, or the way organizations provide formal or informal supports such as strong leadership, supervision, and peer support. It can also involve organizational policies and practices aimed to prevent stress (e.g., overtime restrictions), the provision of psychosocial support (e.g., access to mental health professionals), and staff or opportunities for collective debriefing and reflection of particularly stressful or traumatic practice experiences (e.g., critical incident stress debriefing) (Chamberlain, 2020). In your placement, observe how collective care is practiced by your team, and where appropriate take part in fostering collective care.

Here are a few ways you can promote both self-care and collective care in your placement setting.

- During placement hours:
  - ☐ plan time in your day to take breaks and to have lunch;
  - ☐ carve out time to reflect on your practice experiences and your own thoughts and emotions related to them;
  - ☐ take a few minutes alone or with a colleague when feeling overwhelmed. If helpful, you could practice "in the moment" grounding and calming strategies such as short mindfulness meditation (e.g., a body scan meditation, Anxiety Canada, (n.d.). *Mindfulness – body scan.* https://www.anxietycanada.com/articles/mindful-body-scan/);
  - ☐ ask about ways your team or unit engages in community building and participate if possible;
  - ☐ consider personal limits or boundaries you may need in your setting and initiate a discussion with your field instructor about them; and
  - ☐ use both your formal and informal supports to debrief stressful, emotional, or traumatic practice situations. This may be debriefing with your field instructor, other members of the team or classmates and/or your faculty liaison or integrative seminar instructor.

- Between placement days:
  - ☐ get adequate sleep and proper nutrition. These basic self-care strategies are often the first to go astray when we are overwhelmed. Go back to basic self-care first.
  - ☐ use some of your previously identified self-care strategies to de-stress, recharge, or support your wellbeing.

Collective and self-care are ongoing parts of a social worker's journey. Practicums can be great opportunities to begin to explore collective and self-care strategies to determine what works best for us and what will be useful to cultivate in our future work environments. Chapters 2 and 3 in this handbook have more information about wellness and self-care in practice.

Conclusion

Field education is often one of the most memorable and influential experiences in your social work education. However, starting a practicum can be both exciting and nerve-wracking. This chapter has offered tips and suggestions for how to best prepare for your placement experience to begin in a good way. Learning a bit about your placement organization and planning and preparing for your first day will help you to ease any anxious feelings. Thinking about how you learn best and considering your own and your school's goals for your learning ahead of time allows you to co-create a meaningful learning contract that will guide your practicum experience. Finally, by contemplating how to get the most out of supervision and how to take care of your well-being during your practicum experience, you will be taking steps to maximize your practicum experience and get the most out of your social work field education.

REFERENCES

Canadian Association for Social Work Education. (2021). *Educational policies and accreditation standards for Canadian social work education.* https://caswe-acfts.ca/wp-content/uploads/2021/08/EPAS-2021-1.pdf

Chamberlain, L. (2020). From self-care to collective care. *Sur International Journal on Human Rights, 30,* 1–6. https://sur.conectas.org/en/from-self-care-to-collective-care.

Kolb, D. A. (1984). *Experiential learning: Experience as the source of learning and development.* Prentice-Hall.

Profitt, N. J. (2008). Who cares for us? Opening paths to a critical, collective notion of self-are. *Canadian Social Work Review/Revue canadienne de service social, 25*(2), 147–168. https://www.jstor.org/stable/41669891.

Shulman, L. S. (2005). Signature pedagogies in the professions. *Daedalus, 134*(3), 52–59. https://www.jstor.org/stable/20027998.

NOTES:

NOTES:

NOTES:

Making Space for Wellness in Field Education

Sherri Tanchak, Patricia Samson, and Julie L. Drolet

The Concept of Wellness and Its Importance for Social Work

Perhaps now more than ever, attention to personal and professional well-being is important. In a climate that has seen dramatic increases in isolation, job loss, and stress amidst a global pandemic, increased focus on wellness and self-care is gaining prominence in the human services sector (Downing et al., 2021; Miller & Cassar, 2021). Social work is a profession built on a mandate to challenge oppression and promote social justice in support of individuals, families, and communities. According to Grise-Owens and Miller (2021), the social work practice environment has become more complex and has resulted in a "crisis of increasing burnout of practitioners" (p. 1). To support well-being, self-care has been identified as an essential ingredient in reducing some of the adverse outcomes arising from stress (Grise-Owens et al., 2018). Dalphon (2019) echoes the importance of self-care in supporting both well-being and a sense of *ethical* social work practice, noting that there is a connection between self-care and stress. This chapter presents self-care and wellness in the context of social work field education, with readings, activities, and exercises for practicum students. We encourage students to develop a wellness plan for their practicum as a learning objective with related tasks and activities that can be included in their learning agreement.

There is no singular definition or conception of well-being; therefore, there are multiple ways of viewing this construct and bringing it to life in one's personal and professional spheres of existence. A brief overview of how this concept is imagined from a variety of perspectives will serve as a starting point for students to begin to examine their own reflections and actions surrounding this notion of well-being.

Researchers from the University at Buffalo in New York have highlighted six dimensions of self-care for practitioners in the human services field (see Butler et al., 2019). In line with the work of Dalphon (2019), Butler et al. (2019) have linked key life domains to a sense of positive well-being, including "physical, professional, relational, emotional, psychological, and spiritual" (p. 107) domains. These authors suggest that all these areas intersect with each other depending on the context, and they influence practitioners' personal and professional lives. In understanding this construct of self-care, Butler et al. (2019) detail a key objective of self-care as being the action one takes to minimize "negative outcomes of stress and improve one's own health" (p. 107). Lee and Miller (2013) further describe self-care as a "process or purposeful engagement in practice that promotes holistic health and wellbeing of the self" (p. 98). Professional self-care has been defined as a "process of engagement in practices that promote effective and appropriate use of self in the professional role" (Lee & Miller, 2013, p. 98). Scheyett (2021) highlights self-care as a critical component to being an effective social worker.

A review of the literature related to self-care and its connection to well-being in social work highlights the emergence of a holistic view in terms of personal and professional realms for social work students and practitioners. There is a call to incorporate professional self-care into both social work practice and education (Bent-Goodley, 2017; Grise-Owens & Miller, 2021; Lewis & King, 2019; Newell & Nelson-Gardell, 2014). Self-care among helping professionals is now being referred to as an "ethical imperative," where practitioners have a duty to engage in self-care via personal and professional spheres of well-being (Barnett et al., 2005; Miller & Grise-Owens, 2020; Mitchell & Binkley, 2021). Lewis and King (2019) make an explicit connection between practitioner self-care and their ability to provide "quality services" (p. 97) to those they serve. Lee and Miller (2013) describe self-care as something that is "critical to social work practice . . . [and] enables practitioners to proactively and intentionally negotiate their overall health, wellbeing and resilience" (p. 96). There is a push for social work education to be responsible for increasing attention to the concept of well-being by integrating self-care into the curriculum (Grise-Owens & Miller, 2021; Lewis & King, 2019; Newell & Nelson-Gardell, 2014), and we feel this is critical in social work field education.

In a profession that trains students to become practitioners that work to support and promote well-being in others, so too must the lens be turned inward for social workers to address their own sense of health and wellness (Grise-Owens & Miller, 2021). According to Lewis and King (2019), the field education environment is a key location where self-care skills and plans for students become vitally important, as does the intersection between the shifting contexts of the educational milieu to the organizational influences on practice. Students are exposed to organizational pressure and stressors in the field context (Newell & Nelson-Gardell, 2014). As such, self-care strategies are essential for both students and practitioners in the neoliberal environments they find themselves working in, within organizational settings.

Grise-Owens and Miller (2021) describe social worker well-being and organizational wellness as being complementary and support integrating self-care assignments across the social work education curriculum to better prepare students as emerging practitioners and to promote a culture of wellness among those in the professional practice world. Organizational wellness has a direct impact on the field supervision process; thus, there is support for the contention that organizational wellness is also an important component to the overall health and well-being of social work students and practitioners (Samson et al., 2019). Drolet et al. (2017) call for the integration of wellness as a priority in both the education and practice milieus. The next section will focus on wellness approaches and understandings from diverse perspectives.

Understanding Wellness

Mosaic Approach

There has been some work incorporating a *mosaic approach* to understanding and integrating self-care and wellness into the education and practice context. A mosaic approach emerged as an approach to conducting research with children — a way to bring forward the voice of children in the research process (Clark & Moss, 2011). From a theoretical perspective, the underlying belief in utilizing this approach is that it can "make visible the voices of the least powerful . . . members of communities, as a catalyst for change . . . local people are presumed to have a unique body of knowledge about living in their community . . . techniques developed include visual and verbal tools" (Clark & Moss, 2011, p. 12). Including diverse perspectives in conceptualizing health and wellness helps foster innovative ways to allow multiple voices to be heard, valued, and respected (Greenfield, 2011). Employing a variety of methods, tools, and ways to acknowledge diversity in conceptualizing and operationalizing concepts of self-care, health and wellness is valuable, and can support holistic ways of bringing wellness to life in ways that are culturally relevant.

Western and Non-Western Approaches

Wellness efforts grounded in cultural relevance are important. For example, in some Indigenous cultures well-being represents "diverse and interconnected dimensions" that go well beyond standard or traditional conceptions of health measures (Fleming & Manning, 2019, p. 1). It is noteworthy to acknowledge that there are multiple indigenous perspectives that are applied to conceptions of wellness. According to Salloum and Warburton (2019), some Indigenous health frameworks are based on a holistic approach to wellness that are embedded in teachings of the Medicine Wheel, which integrates physical, mental, spiritual, and emotional well-being. Incorporating holistic, culturally sensitive models of health and well-being are essential given that health outcomes for Indigenous Peoples fall below what is expected for the average person living in Canada (Indigenous and Northern Affairs Canada, 2017; Statistics Canada, 2016). We encourage students to consider multiple understandings of wellness and well-being in the development of their wellness plan for practicum.

There is a contrast between Western knowledge that is viewed as being grounded in science versus more traditional ways of knowing based on a view of life as a framework of "life-sustaining . . . relationships between all components of a sentient world" (Dods, 2004, p. 549). Salloum and Warburton (2019) note that the concept of holistic health is based on community inclusion and the Medicine Wheel — promoting a sense of inner balance in the world that surrounds us. Thus, supporting people to maintain connections with their home community, in ways that honour and respect culture can promote and support spiritual connections and overall well-being (Dapice, 2006; Salloum & Warburton, 2019).

In detailing an understanding of the holistic concepts embedded in many Indigenous ways of knowing, one example can be drawn from the Cree Medicine Wheel, as described by Mawhiney and Nabigon (2017), noting that there are multiple understandings of this concept. This depiction shows a circle split into four sections: the person is in the centre (core), surrounded by the four directions (north, east, south, and west); the inner circle is representative of light (positive), while the outside represents the dark (negative) (Mawhiney & Nabigon, 2017; Wenger-Nabigon, 2010). The Medicine Wheel is meant to provide a *pathway* for living a *balanced* life — "promoting health, growth and positive development, and minimizing risk factors that impede balance" (Wenger-Nabogon, 2010, p. 144). Additional information about the Cree Medicine Wheel, based on the work of Mawhiney and Nabigon (2017) can be found at:

> Mawhiney, A. M., & Nabigon, H. (2017). Aboriginal theory: A Cree medicine wheel guide for healing First Nations. In F. J. Turner (Ed.). *Social work treatment: Interlocking theoretical approaches* (pp. 15–29). Oxford University Press.

In our complex world, multiple ways of knowing influence our conceptualization of health and wellness. Perhaps the way forward in supporting holistic models of well-being lies in what Dods (2004) suggests — a "synthesis of western theories and traditional knowledge and, forms of inquiry [can] only add to our story" (p. 554). This synthesis of diverse ways of knowing can strengthen efforts to promote wellness in the context of social work education for students, field instructors, and the academy more broadly. As suggested by Kitson and Bowes (2010), building on the relationship and connection with the land and community supports a sense of identity and power; education plays a role in teaching this interrelatedness between people, communities, and the environment.

In examining well-being on an international scale, Fleming and Manning (2019) note that conceptions of wellness undergird societal views of morality, politics, economics, and our very institutions. There are a plethora of theories, models, and measurements aimed at detailing well-being, which can be bound to the context within which they are viewed. Rather than itemizing all the different criteria, measurements, definitions, etc., to rigidly define well-being, let us be open to viewing this construct in holistic and multidimensional ways that are fluid and flexible to individual worldviews. As social work educators, let us provide some examples and resources that students, field instructors, agency supervisors, and faculty members can leverage as they embark on a reflexive journey to establish their own wellness and self-care plans that can be works-in-progress as they navigate their professional and educational paths throughout their careers.

Opportunities to Explore, Reflect, and Practice Well-Being in Practicum — Suggested Learning Activities

Creating space for well-being in practicum invites you as social work students to imagine how you might think about and hold space for well-being throughout practicum. Holding space for personal well-being encourages you, as social work students, to reflect on what well-being means to you and what kinds of things help you to feel nurtured and nourished in your bodies, minds, and relationships. Some of the dimensions of well-being students may explore include emotional, environmental, financial, intellectual, occupational, physical, social, spiritual, and other dimensions. It is important to note that there is not a universal way to conceptualize, experience, or practice well-being. A person's lived experiences and social identity are key influences in how they conceptualize, experience, and practice well-being. To support students with exploring and developing well-being during practicum, schools and faculties of social work, practicum instructors, and field supervisors are highly encouraged to recognize and prioritize well-being as a learning goal that is critical to a student's readiness for practice and longevity in social work.

There are opportunities in all stages of practicum for social work students to explore, reflect, and practice well-being using exercises in this chapter. Opportunities for exploring well-being encourage you to review well-being resources, such as readings, webinars, presentations, websites, and self-inventories. After completing a review of well-being resources, students are encouraged to reflect and respond to a question that is based on their lived experiences and understanding of well-being. The final stage presents opportunities for students to integrate their reflections and awareness as a foundation for developing and practicing well-being, and ultimately inform your wellness and self-care plan.

Pre-Practicum Exercises

One of the key areas for students to prepare themselves for their social work practicum involves checking in with themselves around their well-being. By having a foundational understanding and attending to personal well-being, you have opportunities to enhance your self-awareness, which can help prepare you for navigating challenges and stressors in practicum. Prior to the start of practicum, you are invited to complete two exercises that focus on personal well-being and self-care practices. Exercise 1: Well-Being Check-in, asks students to review resources, self-identify their own description of well-being, and share their current self-care practices. You are also invited to select two self-care practices that you would like to try during practicum. Exercise 2: Dimensions of Well-Being, introduces students to the eight dimensions of well-being, their key characteristics, and self-care practices that support each dimension (see Swarbrick & Yudof, 2015). After reviewing the resources, you are invited to identify self-care practices that address your unique definition of well-being.

Exercise 1: Well-Being Check-In

STEP 1: EXPLORE THE LIBRARY

> **Instructions:** Select at least one resource from each section of the library and explore the concepts of wellness and well-being.

READINGS	INVENTORIES AND ASSESSMENTS
Drolet, J., & McLennan, C. (2016). Wellness and relational self-care in social work field education. *International Journal of Health, Wellness and Society 6*(4), 9–21. https://doi.org/10.18848/2156-8960/CGP/v06i04/9-21	Robertson, R., & Microys, G. (2002). *Life balance assessment and action plan.* https://settingup. weebly.com/uploads/4/2/6/6/42663717/balance_wheel.pdf
Lin, E. (2020). Well-being, part 2: Theories of well-being. *Philosophy Compass 17*(2), e12813. https://doi.org/10.1111/phc3.12813	Institute for Functional Medicine (2016). *Self-care questionnaire.* https://shayahealth.com/resources/Self-Care%2BQuestionnaire.pdf
Substance Abuse and Mental Health Services Administration [SAMHSA]. (2016). *Creating a healthier life: A step-by-step guide to wellness.* https://store.samhsa.gov/sites/default/files/sma16-4958.pdf	

VIDEOS	WEBSITES
Graham, K. (2019, September 13). *What is wellness?* [Video]. YouTube. https://youtu.be/XufC0rMCQYA?si=9uggcvS8lsu1LxfW	Foundry BC. (n.d.). *From cedar to sweetgrass: Let's talk about wellness.* https://foundrybc.ca/stories/from-cedar-to-sweetgrass-lets-talk-about-wellness/
University of Toronto. (n.d.). *Understanding holistic wellness through the Medicine Wheel.* https://q.utoronto.ca/courses/189286/pages/understanding-holistic-wellness-through-the-medicine-wheel	Davis, T. (n.d.). Self-reflection: Definition and how to do it. Berkley Well-being Institute. https://www.berkeleywellbeing.com/what-is-self-reflection.html

STEP 2: REFLECT ON PERSONAL DEFINITION OF WELL-BEING AND EXISTING ROUTINES

Instructions: Reflect on the resources you reviewed in the previous section and your lived experiences with well-being. With these reflections, write a description of what well-being means to you and what you currently do in support of your well-being.

What does well-being mean to me?

What kinds of activities do I currently do to support my well-being?

STEP 3: PRACTICE

Instructions: Think about all of the well-being practices that you've tried so far. Which practices helped to strengthen your health and which ones were interesting but didn't make a difference to your health? From the well-being practices that made a positive impact on your mind, body, or relationships, identify and describe two self-care practices that you would like to try out during practicum. What is the practice? How many days per week will you practice?

Well-being Practice 1

Details of Practice:

Well-being Practice 2

Details of Practice:

Exercise 2: Dimensions of Well-Being

STEP 1: EXPLORE THE LIBRARY

> **Instructions:** Select at least one resource from each section of the library to explore the dimensions of well-being. Consider how each dimension offers information about how we think about well-being and helps evaluate the strengths and challenges in our existing self-care practices.

READINGS	SELF-ASSESSMENTS
Swarbrick, P., & Yudof, J. (2015). *Wellness in eight dimensions.* Collaborative Support Programs of NJ, Inc. https://www.center4healthandsdc.org/uploads/7/1/1/4/71142589/wellness_in_8_dimensions_booklet_with_daily_plan.pdf	Therapist Aid LLC. (2018). *Self-care assessment worksheet.* https://www.therapistaid.com/worksheets/self-care-assessment
Butler, L., Mercer, K., Mcclain-Meeder, K., Horne, D., & Dudley, M. (2019). Six domains of self-care: Attending to the whole person. *Journal of Human Behavior in the Social Environment 29*(1), 107–124. https://doi.org/10.1080/10911359.2018.1482483	University of Colorado Health and Wellness Services. (n.d.). *Personal wellness assessment.* https://www.colorado.edu/health/sites/default/files/attached-files/personal_assessment_-_8_dimensions_of_wellness.pdf
Miller, G., & Foster, L. (2010). A brief summary of holistic wellness literature. *Journal of Holistic Healthcare 7*(1), 4–8. https://bhma.org/wp-content/uploads/2017/07/JHH7.1_article1_.pdf	
VIDEOS	**WEBSITES**
Patterson, P. (2017, April 27). *The eight dimensions of wellness* [Video]. YouTube. https://www.youtube.com/watch?v=2NR4_5dt7JA	Thunderbird Partnership Foundation. (n.d.). *Native wellness assessment.* https://thunderbirdpf.org/native-wellness-assessment/
Somerset County New Jersey Government. (2021, May 10). *8 dimensions of wellness: Wellness Wednesdays* [Video]. YouTube. https://www.youtube.com/watch?v=mBwzu71oHzc	Collaborative Support Programs of New Jersey [CSPNJ]. (n.d.). *Wellness institute.* https://cspnj.org/wellness-institute/

STEP 2: PRACTICE, DEVELOPING SELF-CARE PRACTICES

Instructions: Review each dimension of well-being and identify one self-care practice for each dimension that you would like to try out to strengthen your overall health. With each self-care practice, identify any supports you need, and how you can access these resources. From this list select two self-care practices that you are willing to try out for two weeks. After the 14 days, provide a reflection on how these practices impacted your body, mind and relationships.

Emotional Well-being →

Physical Well-being →

Nutritional Well-being →

Spiritual Well-being →

Environmental Well-being →

Occupational Well-being →

Financial Well-being →

Social Well-being →

Practicum Exercises

In preparing for social work practice, you are invited to use your practicum as a platform for professional and personal growth. When considering what types of knowledge and skills you may want to develop and practice during practicum, learning goals tend to focus on theory, practice approaches, research, policy, diversity and oppression, and ethics. What if we were to take a step back and ask what else helps social work students be successful in their practicum and on-going practice? What if students were encouraged and supported to engage in regular well-being practices that they self-identify as meaningful and beneficial to their wellness? Without having consistent and regular opportunities for well-being, it is likely that competing demands on social workers will result in well-being routines being sacrificed for attending to professional demands. By integrating a well-being related learning goal in the practicum agreement/contract and developing a personal well-being plan we can protect time and space for well-being.

Within the first two weeks of starting practicum, students are invited to complete Exercise 3: Practicum Learning Goals on Well-Being, which offers students an opportunity to review resources and ideas for including well-being in practicum and how to document well-being ideas as a learning goal. One suggested learning activity that may help to protect time and space for well-being in practicum is for students to create a personal well-being plan. In Exercise 4: Personal Well-Being Plan, you are guided through a process of creating a blueprint that outlines how you will protect your well-being during practicum. Each step in this exercise presents you with questions about your thoughts, preferences, resources, and barriers to practicing self-care. By completing all the steps, you develop a personalized plan for regular and emergency self-care to follow during practicum.

Exercise 3: Practicum Learning Goals Specific to Well-Being

STEP 1: EXPLORE THE LIBRARY

Instructions: Select at least one resource from each section of the library for resources and ideas about developing well-being-related learning goals and personal well-being plans..

READINGS	SELF-ASSESSMENTS
Baird, B., & Mollen, D. (2019). *Stress and self-care. Internship, practicum, and field placement handbook. A guide for the helping professions* (8th ed.). Routledge.	Goldberg, S. (2017). *Self-care tool kit.* https://socialworkmanager.org/wp-content/uploads/2017/10/Selfcare-toolkit.pdf
Dalphon, H. (2019). Self-care techniques for social workers: Achieving an ethical harmony between work and well-being. *Journal of Human Behavior in the Social Environment 29*(1), 85–95. https://doi.org/10.1080/10911359.2018.1481802	King's University School of Social Work. (n.d.). *Self-care assessment.* https://socialwork.kings.uwo.ca/socialWork/assets/File/field/self-care/Self-Care-Assessment.pdf
Owens-King, A. P. (2019). Secondary traumatic stress and self-care inextricably linked. *Journal of Human Behavior in the Social Environment 29*(1), 37–47. https://doi.org/10.1080/10911359.2018.1472703	
VIDEOS	**WEBSITES**
National Association for Social Workers Michigan [NASW Michigan]. (2022, February 9). *Self-care 101* [Video]. YouTube. https://www.youtube.com/watch?v=BY8S4ZlOJhA	University of Buffalo School of Social Work. (n.d.). *Introduction to self-care.* https://socialwork.buffalo.edu/resources/self-care-starter-kit/introduction-to-self-care.html
National Association for Social Workers [NASW]. (n.d.). *Self-care for social workers.* https://www.socialworkers.org/Practice/Infectious-Diseases/Coronavirus/Self-Care-for-Social-Workers	King's University School of Social Work. (n.d.). *Wellness and self-care.* https://socialwork.kings.uwo.ca/field-education/wellness-and-self-care/
The Social Workers. (2017, December 7). *The a-to-z self-care handbook for social workers and other helping professionals* [Video]. YouTube. https://www.youtube.com/watch?v=HOF7F2B67Xw	

STEP 2: REFLECTION OF EXPERIENCES WITH WELL-BEING PLAN

Instructions: It's time to journal. Prior to starting this journal, take a moment to think further about the resources you reviewed in step 1 of this exercise and your existing self-care practices. Take 15 minutes and journal about how you would like to include wellbeing in your practicum.

JOURNAL PROMPT: How do I want to include well-being in my practicum? What are 2 ideas for well-being-specific learning goals?

STEP 3: PRACTICE — LEARNING GOALS FOR THE PRACTICUM LEARNING AGREEMENT

> **Instructions:** Consider the two ideas that you identified in part two of this exercise. For each idea, develop a learning goal, two to three learning activities, and a plan that will help you measure the outcome of each learning activity. Review the provided example and develop your own well-being goals.

Example of Learning Goal, Learning Activities and Evaluation.

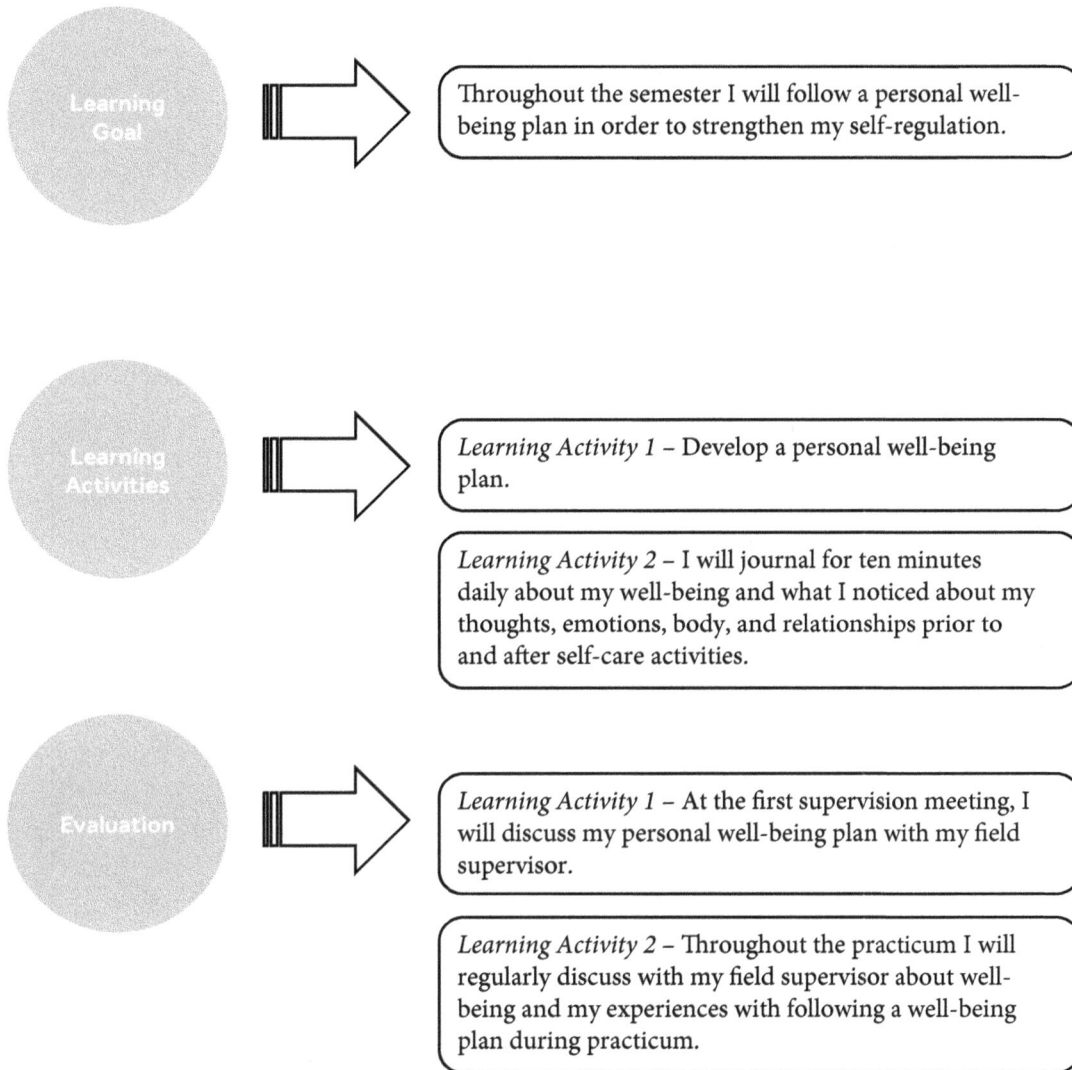

Learning Goal → Throughout the semester I will follow a personal well-being plan in order to strengthen my self-regulation.

Learning Activities →

Learning Activity 1 – Develop a personal well-being plan.

Learning Activity 2 – I will journal for ten minutes daily about my well-being and what I noticed about my thoughts, emotions, body, and relationships prior to and after self-care activities.

Evaluation →

Learning Activity 1 – At the first supervision meeting, I will discuss my personal well-being plan with my field supervisor.

Learning Activity 2 – Throughout the practicum I will regularly discuss with my field supervisor about well-being and my experiences with following a well-being plan during practicum.

IDEAS NOTED IN PREVIOUS EXERCISE (PART 2)	LEARNING GOAL *What do I want to learn about well-being and practice during practicum?*	LEARNING ACTIVITIES *What can I do that will help me learn and practice well-being?*	EVALUATION *How can I demonstrate my learning?*
IDEA 1:			
IDEA 2:			

Exercise 4: Developing a Personal Well-Being Plan

STEP 1: EXPLORE THE LIBRARY: WELL-BEING PLANS AND SELF-CARE PRACTICES

Instructions: Review at least one resource from each section of the library for information on occupational hazards in social work, personal well-being plans, and various ideas for self-care practices students can adopt to support their wellness during practicum.

READINGS	SELF-ASSESSMENTS
El-Osta, A., Webber, D., Gnani, S., Banarsee, R., Mummery, D., Majeed, A., & Smith, P. (2019). The self-care matrix: A unifying framework for self-care. *Self-Care 10*(2), 38–56. https://selfcarejournal.com/article/the-self-care-matrix-a-unifying-framework-for-self-care/	King's University School of Social Work. (n.d.). *Self-care assessment.* https://socialwork.kings.uwo.ca/socialWork/assets/File/field/self-care/Self-Care-Assessment.pdf
Miller, J. L. (2016). Seven self-care strategies. *Reflections: Narratives of Professional Helping 21*(1), 52–58. https://reflectionsnarrativesofprofessionalhelping.org/index.php/Reflections/article/view/747	Burns, K., O'Mahoney, C., & O'Callaghan, E. (2018). *SPARK: A self-care tool for professionals.* https://www.ucc.ie/en/media/academic/nswpti/spark_tool1_1b.pdf
Skovholt, T. M., & Trotter-Mathison, M. (2016). *The resilient practitioner: Burnout and compassion fatigue prevention* and self-care strategies for the helping professions. Routledge.	
VIDEOS	**WEBSITES**
Florida State University College of Social Work. (2022, October 21). *Social work stress — 8 tips for self-care* [Video]. YouTube. https://www.youtube.com/watch?v=G9h5DhKkoI8	Tan, E. (2019, July 24). *Managing self-care through self-reflective journal writing.* https://uwaterloo.ca/writing-and-communication-centre/blog/managing-self-care-through-self-reflective-journal-writing

STEP 2: REFLECTIONS ON SELF-CARE AND WELL-BEING

Instructions: Take some time to reflect on the information you reviewed on self-care and well-being in step 1 of this exercise and consider how this information may help you clarify what you need for well-being and what types of self-care practices appeal to you. Pour yourself a glass of water or herbal tea, sit down in your favorite chair, set a timer for 15 minutes and journal about what you need to feel well in your body, thoughts, emotions, and relationships.

JOURNAL PROMPT: How do I want to include well-being in my practicum? What are 2 ideas for well-being-specific learning goals?

STEP 3: HOW CAN I SUPPORT MY WELL-BEING WITH SELF-CARE

AREAS OF WELL-BEING	Circle four areas of well-being that you would like to commit to during practicum. Identify a self-care activity for each well-being area that you will adopt into your personal well-being plan and follow during practicum.
EMOTIONAL	
ENVIRONMENTAL	
FINANCIAL	
INTELLECTUAL	
OCCUPATIONAL	
PHYSICAL	
SOCIAL	
SPIRITUAL	
OTHER	

Emergency self-care

Emergency self-care is used after we have experienced a negative event that dysregulates our thoughts, emotions, and body. An emergency self-care plan supplements your regular well-being plan and includes three components: actions, thoughts, and avoidance. To create this plan, think about experiences where you felt overwhelmed, angry, hurt, or upset and determine actions you can take to help regulate and ground yourself. What thoughts are helpful affirmations of your strengths? What and who might you need to avoid?

STEP 4: PERSONAL WELL-BEING FOR PRACTICUM

Reflect on your responses in previous sections you are invited to create your personal well-being plan for your practicum. It is recommended that you print a copy of your wellness plan and post at home.

Post-Practicum Exercise

Congratulations on completing your practicum! It is time for you to take a moment and celebrate your personal and professional growth. As you transition from your education program there is a final opportunity for you to integrate your learning and experiences and bring them forward as key competencies that will continue to provide you with resources to navigate the multiple demands and challenges of social work practice.

Exercise 5: Post-Practicum Well-Being Plan, offers students a chance to reflect on their experiences with their practicum well-being plan. What self-care practices went well and resulted in positive outcomes for your well-being? What self-care practices were eliminated because you created more stress than support? After completing practicum, you are asked to develop a new plan that considers changes in your personal and professional life.

Exercise 5: Developing a Post-Practicum Personal Well-Being Plan

STEP 1: EXPLORE THE LIBRARY

Instructions: Select at least one resource from each section of the library to explore some of the issues that support and challenge social workers with responding to occupational hazards and to maintain a consistent practice of well-being.

READINGS	SELF-ASSESSMENTS
Jaskela, S., Guichon, J., Page, S. A., & Mitchell, I. (2018). Social workers' experience of moral distress. *Canadian Social Work Review / Revue Canadienne de Service Social 35*(1), 91–107. https://doi.org/10.7202/1051104ar	Professional Quality of Life. (n.d.). *ProQOL measure.* https://proqol.org/proqol-1
Kreitzer, L., Brintnell, S. E., & Austin, W. (2019). Institutional barriers to healthy workplace environments: From the voices of Canadian social workers experiencing compassion fatigue. *The British Journal of Social Work 50*(7), 1942–1960. https://doi.org/10.1093/bjsw/bcz147	Nortje, A. (2022, April 3). *Warning signs of burnout: 11 reliable tests and questionnaires.* Positive Psychology. https://positivepsychology.com/burnout-tests-signs/
Xu, Y., Darrow C. H., & Frey, J. J. (2019). Rethinking professional quality of life for social workers: Inclusion of ecological self-care barriers. *Journal of Human Behavior in the Social Environment 29*(1), 11–25. https://doi.org/10.1080/10911359.2018.1452814	MindTools (2020). *Burnout self-test: Checking yourself for burnout.* https://www.mindtools.com/auhx7b3/burnout-self-test
VIDEOS	**WEBSITES**
Canadian Association of Social Workers. (26 January 2022). *Vicarious trauma, wellness, and resilience in the field of child welfare webinar* [Video]. YouTube. https://www.youtube.com/watch?v=wBlN7m7btN8	Neff, K. (n.d.). *Self-compassion.* https://self-compassion.org/
Canadian Association of Social Workers [CASW]. (2022, March 21). *Part 1: Triggers of moral distress during COVID-19: Experiences of health care social workers* [Video]. https://www.youtube.com/watch?v=B6G3xeYmwug	Professional Quality of Life. (n.d.). *Core concepts — Handouts.* https://proqol.org/self-care-tools-1
Canadian Association of Social Workers [CASW]. (2022, March 29). Part 2: *What now? Multi-level interventions to reduce moral distress and heighted self-care* [Video]. YouTube. https://www.youtube.com/watch?v=GBtXDvj5GMY	University of Buffalo School of Social Work. (n.d.). *Checklists and measures.* https://socialwork.buffalo.edu/resources/self-care-starter-kit/self-care-assessments-exercises/checklists-and-measures.html

STEP 2: POST-PRACTICUM REFLECTION

Instructions: Reflect on your experiences with using your well-being plan during practicum and how it impacted your social work practice, what did you notice? What well-being practices were supportive of your well-being? Take fifteen minutes and journal about your experiences and what you'd like to focus on in your post-practicum well-being plan.

JOURNAL PROMPT: Moving forward from your practicum, what are some areas of well-being and self-care practices that you would like to focus on?

Conclusion

Amidst the complexity of our post-COVID world, the need for self-care and well-being for social work students, educators, and practitioners seems to be even more pronounced. This chapter has detailed the context and value of professional self-care and well-being to foster resilience in our profession, specifically for students as emerging social workers. There are diverse ways of knowing and being that you can embrace and integrate within your own work in developing fluid, flexible plans that promote self-care through the many transitions you will encounter as students who will evolve from student-to-professional social work practitioner. Exercises in this chapter are provided for your consideration as you navigate your programs of study and embark on your field placement experiences. Having a plan for self-care and wellness is critical to support transformative social work field education. An essential foundation for effective social work practice is engagement in an ongoing process of critical reflection. This can be a valuable process as you work on integrating a fulsome approach to personal and professional well-being as an integral component to your emerging social work identity and practice framework moving forward.

REFERENCES

Baird, B., & Mollen, D. (2019). *Stress and self-care. Internship, practicum, and field placement handbook. A guide for the helping professions* (8th ed.). Routledge.

Barnett, J. E., Johnston, L. C., & Hillard, D. (2005). Psychotherapist wellness as an ethical imperative. In L. VandeCreek and J. B. Allen (Eds.), *Innovations in clinical practice: Focus on health and wellness* (pp. 257–271). Professional Resource Press/Professional Resource Exchange.

Bent-Goodley, T. B. (2017). Being intentional about self-care for social workers. *National Association of Social Workers, 63*(1), 5–6. https://doi.org/10.1093/sw/swx058

Burns, K., O'Mahoney, C., & O'Callaghan, E. (2018). *SPARK: A self-care tool for professionals.* https://www.ucc.ie/en/media/academic/nswpti/spark_tool1_1b.pdf

Butler, L., Mercer, K., McClain-Meeder, K., Horne, D., & Dudley, M. (2019). Six domains of self-care: Attending to the whole person. *Journal of Human Behaviour in the Social Environment, 29*(1), 107–124. https://doi.org/10.1080/10911359.2018.1482483

Canadian Association of Social Workers [CASW]. (2022, March 21). *Part 1: Triggers of moral distress during COVID-19: Experiences of health care social workers* [Video]. https://www.youtube.com/watch?v=B6G3xeYmwug

Canadian Association of Social Workers. (26 January 2022). *Vicarious trauma, wellness, and resilience in the field of child welfare webinar* [Video]. YouTube. https://www.youtube.com/watch?v=wBlN7m7btN8

Canadian Association of Social Workers [CASW]. (2022, March 29). *Part 2: What now? Multi-level interventions to reduce moral distress and heighted self-care* [Video]. YouTube. https://www.youtube.com/watch?v=GBtXDvj5GMY

Collaborative Support Programs of New Jersey [CSPNJ]. (n.d.). *Wellness institute.* https://cspnj.org/wellness-institute/

Clark, A., & Moss, P. (2011). *Listening to young children: The mosaic approach.* Jessica Kingsley Publishers.

Dalphon, H. (2019). Self-care techniques for social workers: Achieving an ethical harmony between work and well-being. *Journal of Human Behaviour in the Social Environment, 29*(1), 85–95. https://doi.org/10.1080/10911359.2018.1481802

Dapice, A. N. (2006). The Medicine Wheel. *Journal of Transcultural Nursing, 17*(3), 251–260. https://doi.org/10.1177/1043659606288383

Davis, T. (n.d.). *Self-reflection: Definition and how to do it.* Berkley Well-being Institute. https://www.berkeleywellbeing.com/what-is-self-reflection.html

Dods, R. R. (2004). Knowing ways/ways of knowing: Reconciling science and tradition. *World Archeology 36*(4), 547–557. https://doi.org/10.1080/0043824042000303719

Downing, K., Brackett, M., & Riddick, D. (2021). Self-care management 101: Strategies for social workers and other frontline responders during the COVID-19 pandemic in rural communities. *Journal of Human Behavior in the Social Environment, 31*(1–4) 353–361. https://doi.org/10.1080/10911359.2020.1825265

Drolet, J., & McLennan, C. (2016). Wellness and relational self-care in social work field education. *International Journal of Health, Wellness and Society, 6*(4), 9–21. https://doi.org/10.18848/2156-8960/CGP/v06i04/9-21

Drolet, J., Samson, P., Tanchak, S., Kreitzer, L., & Hilsen, L. (2017). Self-care and well-being in social work education: Creating new spaces for learning. *Journal of Educational Thought, 50*(2/3), 200–215. https://www.jstor.org/stable/26372404

El-Osta, A., Webber, D., Gnani, S., Banarsee, R., Mummery, D., Majeed, A., & Smith, P. (2019). The self-care matrix: A unifying framework for self-care. *Self-Care, 10*(2), 38–56. https://selfcarejournal.com/article/the-self-care-matrix-a-unifying-framework-for-self-care/

Fleming, C., & Manning, M. (2019). *Routledge handbook of Indigenous wellbeing.* Routledge.

Florida State University College of Social Work. (2022, October 21). *Social work stress — 8 tips for self-care* [Video]. YouTube. https://www.youtube.com/watch?v=G9h5DhKkoI8

Foundry BC. (n.d.). From cedar to sweetgrass: Let's talk about wellness. https://foundrybc.ca/stories/from-cedar-to-sweetgrass-lets-talk-about-wellness/

Goldberg, S. (2017). *Self-care tool kit.* https://socialworkmanager.org/wp-content/uploads/2017/10/Selfcare-toolkit.pdf

Graham, K. (2019, September 13). *What is wellness?* [Video]. YouTube. https://youtu.be/XufC0rMCQYA?si=9uggcvS8lsu1LxfW

Greenfield, C. (2011). Personal reflection on research process and tools: Effectiveness, highlights and challenges in using the Mosaic approach. *Australasian Journal of Early Childhood, 36*(3), 109–116. https://doi.org/10.1177/183693911103600314

Grise-Owens, E., Miller, J. J., Escobar-Ratcliff, L., & George, N. (2018). Teaching note—Teaching self-care and wellness as a professional practice skill: A curricular example. *Journal of Social Work Education, 54*(1), 180–186. https://doi.org/10.1080/10437797.2017.1308778

Grise-Owens, E., & Miller, J. J. (2021). The role and responsibility of social work education in promoting practitioner self-care. *Journal of Social Work Education, 57*(4), 636–648. https://doi.org/10.1080/10437797.2021.1951414

Indigenous and Northern Affairs Canada. (2017). *First Nation profiles.* https://fnp-ppn.aadnc-aandc.gc.ca/fnp/Main/Index.aspx?lang=eng

Institute for Functional Medicine (2016). *Self-care questionnaire.* https://shayahealth.com/resources/Self-Care%2BQuestionnaire.pdf

Jaskela, S., Guichon, J., Page, S. A., & Mitchell, I. (2018). Social workers' experience of moral distress. *Canadian Social Work Review / Revue Canadienne de Service Social, 35*(1), 91–107. https://doi.org/10.7202/1051104ar

King's University School of Social Work. (n.d.). *Wellness and self-care.* https://socialwork.kings.uwo.ca/field-education/wellness-and-self-care/

King's University School of Social Work. (n.d.). *Self-care assessment.* https://socialwork.kings.uwo.ca/socialWork/assets/File/field/self-care/Self-Care-Assessment.pdf

Kitson, R., & Bowes, J. (2010). Incorporating Indigenous ways of knowing in early education for Indigenous children. *Australian Journal of Early Childhood, 35*(4), 81–89. https://doi.org/10.1177/183693911003500410

Kreitzer, L., Brintnell, S. E., & Austin, W. (2019). Institutional barriers to healthy workplace environments: From the voices of Canadian social workers experiencing compassion fatigue. *The British Journal of Social Work, 50*(7), 1942–1960. https://doi.org/10.1093/bjsw/bcz147

Lee, J. L., & Miller, S. E. (2013). A self-care framework for social workers: Building a strong foundation for practice. *Families in Society, 94*(2), 96–103. https://doi.org/10.1606/1044-3894.4289

Lewis, M., & King, D. (2019). Teaching self-care: The utilization of self-care in social work practicum to prevent compassion fatigue, burnout, and vicarious trauma. *Journal of Human Behaviour in the Social Environment, 29*(1), 96–106. https://doi.org/10.1080/10911359.2018.1482482

Lin, E. (2020). Well-being, part 2: Theories of well-being. *Philosophy Compass, 17*(2), e12813. https://doi.org/10.1111/phc3.12813

Mawhiney, A. M., & Nabigon, H. (2017). Aboriginal theory: A Cree medicine wheel guide for healing First Nations. In F. Turner (Ed.), *Social work treatment: Interlocking theoretical approaches* (pp. 15–29). Oxford University Press.

Miller, G., & Foster, L. (2010). A brief summary of holistic wellness literature. *Journal of Holistic Healthcare 7*(1), 4–8. https://bhma.org/wp-content/uploads/2017/07/JHH7.1_article1_.pdf

Miller, J. L. (2016). Seven self-care strategies. *Reflections: Narratives of Professional Helping, 21*(1), 52–58. https://reflectionsnarrativesofprofessionalhelping.org/index.php/Reflections/article/view/747

Miller, J. J., & Grise-Owens, E. (2020). Self-care: An imperative. *Social Work, 65*(1), 5–9. https://doi.org/10.1093/sw/swz049

Miller, J. J., & Cassar, J. R. (2021). Self-care among healthcare social workers: The impact of COVID-19. *Social work in health care, 60*(1), 30–48. https://doi.org/10.1080/00981389.2021.1885560

MindTools (2020). *Burnout self-test: Checking yourself for burnout.* https://www.mindtools.com/auhx7b3/burnout-self-test

Mitchell, M., & Binkley, E. (2021). Self-care: An ethical imperative for anti-racist counselor training. *Teaching and Supervision in Counseling, 3*(2), 5. https://doi.org/10.7290/tsc030205

National Association for Social Workers Michigan [NASW Michigan]. (2022, February 9). *Self-care 101* [Video]. YouTube. https://www.youtube.com/watch?v=BY8S4ZlOJhA

National Association for Social Workers [NASW]. (n.d.). *Self-care for social workers.* https://www.socialworkers.org/Practice/Infectious-Diseases/Coronavirus/Self-Care-for-Social-Workers

Neff, K. (n.d.). *Self-compassion.* https://self-compassion.org/

Newell, J., & Nelson-Gardell, D. (2014). A competency-based approach to teaching professional self-care: An ethical consideration for social work educators. *Journal of Social Work Education 50*, 427–439. https://doi.org/10.1080/10437797.2014.917928

Nortje, A. (2022, April 3). *Warning signs of burnout: 11 reliable tests and questionnaires.* Positive Psychology. https://positivepsychology.com/burnout-tests-signs/

Owens-King, A. P. (2019). Secondary traumatic stress and self-care inextricably linked. *Journal of Human Behavior in the Social Environment, 29*(1), 37–47. https://doi.org/10.1080/10911359.2018.1472703

Patterson, P. (2017, April 27). *The eight dimensions of wellness* [Video]. YouTube. https://www.youtube.com/watch?v=2NR4_5dt7JA

Professional Quality of Life. (n.d.). *Core concepts — Handouts.* https://proqol.org/self-care-tools-1

Professional Quality of Life. (n.d.). *ProQOL measure.* https://proqol.org/proqol-1

Robertson, R., & Microys, G. (2002). *Life balance assessment and action plan.* https://settingup.weebly.com/uploads/4/2/6/6/42663717/balance_wheel.pdf

Salloum, M., & Warburton, D. (2019). Importance of spiritual wellbeing in community-based health interventions in Indigenous Peoples in BC. *Health & Fitness Journal, 12*(1), 117–123. https://doi.org/10.14288/hfjc.v12i1.264

Samson, P., Tanchak, S., Drolet, J., Kreitzer, A., & Fulton, A. (2019). The contribution of supervision to wellness in the workplace: Implications for social work field education. *Field Educator, 9*(1), 1–24. https://www.proquest.com/openview/a76e8467988e8108c2a0ee18f226c858/1/advanced

Scheyett, A. (2021). The responsibility of self-care in social work. *National Association of Social Workers, 66*(4), 281–283. https://doi.org/10.1093/sw/swab041

Skovholt, T. M., & Trotter-Mathison, M. (2016). The resilient practitioner: Burnout and compassion fatigue prevention and self-care strategies for the helping professions. Routledge.

Somerset County New Jersey Government. (2021, May 10). *8 dimensions of wellness: Wellness Wednesdays* [Video]. YouTube. https://www.youtube.com/watch?v=mBwzu71oHzc

Statistics Canada. (2016). *Aboriginal population profile, 2016 census.* https://www12.statcan.gc.ca/census-recensement/2016/dp-pd/abpopprof/index.cfm?Lang=E

Substance Abuse and Mental Health Services Administration [SAMHSA]. (2016). *Creating a healthier life: A step-by-step guide to wellness.* https://store.samhsa.gov/sites/default/files/sma16-4958.pdf

Swarbrick, P., & Yudof, J. (2015). *Wellness in eight dimensions.* Collaborative Support Programs of NJ, Inc. https://www.center4healthandsdc.org/uploads/7/1/1/4/71142589/wellness_in_8_dimensions_booklet_with_daily_plan.pdf

Tan, E. (2019, July 24). *Managing self-care through self-reflective journal writing.* https://uwaterloo.ca/writing-and-communication-centre/blog/managing-self-care-through-self-reflective-journal-writing

The Social Workers. (2017, December 7). *The a-to-z self-care handbook for social workers and other helping professionals* [Video]. YouTube. https://www.youtube.com/watch?v=HOF7F2B67Xw

Therapist Aid LLC. (2018). *Self-care assessment worksheet.* https://www.therapistaid.com/worksheets/self-care-assessment

Thunderbird Partnership Foundation. (n.d.). *Native wellness assessment.* https://thunderbirdpf.org/native-wellness-assessment/

University of Buffalo School of Social Work. (n.d.). *Checklists and measures.* https://socialwork.buffalo.edu/resources/self-care-starter-kit/self-care-assessments-exercises/checklists-and-measures.html

University of Buffalo School of Social Work. (n.d.). *Introduction to self-care.* https://socialwork.buffalo.edu/resources/self-care-starter-kit/introduction-to-self-care.html

University of Colorado Health and Wellness Services. (n.d.). *Personal wellness assessment.* https://www.colorado.edu/health/sites/default/files/attached-files/personal_assessment_-_8_dimensions_of_wellness.pdf

University of Toronto. (n.d.). *Understanding holistic wellness through the medicine wheel.* https://q.utoronto.ca/courses/189286/pages/understanding-holistic-wellness-through-the-medicine-wheel

Wenger-Nabigon, A. (2010). The Cree medicine wheel as an organizing paradigm of theories of human development. *Native Social Work Journal, 7*, 139-161. https://zone.biblio.laurentian.ca/bitstream/10219/387/1/NSWJ-V7-art6-p139-161.pdf

Xu, Y., Darrow C. H., & Frey, J. J. (2019). Rethinking professional quality of life for social workers: Inclusion of ecological self-care barriers. *Journal of Human Behavior in the Social Environment, 29*(1), 11–25. https://doi.org/10.1080/10911359.2018.1452814

NOTES:

NOTES:

Trauma- and Resilience-Informed Practice for Self-Care Among Social Work Students

Evalyna Bogdan and Elaine Miller-Karas

Field education is an exciting stage in the social work academic program as students have the opportunity to see how theory and practice meet in the real-world and to interact with the populations with whom they want to work. The field experience also provides insight into what being a social worker will be like on a day-to-day basis and in the long-term. Although social work is a fulfilling profession with a focus on helping others, social workers have a high rate of burnout and therefore need self-care practices and peer support.

Social workers often work with people who have experienced stressful or traumatic events, or chronic overwhelming stress, and lack the resources, skills, or supports to deal with these events. Social workers may have, or may in the future, experience similar levels or types of stressful or traumatic events. Or they may experience secondary or vicarious trauma caused by second-hand exposure to traumatic events such as hearing stories shared by clients. There are many definitions of trauma but in the Community Resiliency Model (CRM), the simple definition used is that it is an event or situation that is "too little or too much for too long" (Trauma Resource Institute [TRI], 2021b, p. 31), which can dysregulate the nervous system. Individual perception is an important element because an event or situation that may be perceived by one person as highly stressful or traumatic may not be perceived as that severe when experienced by another person. The individual perception of threat is shaped by biological, social, and other factors including the ability to deal with the stressor. Trauma can also be differentiated into "large-T" Trauma which are major events such as natural disasters, war, assault, or "small-t" trauma which are minor events such as an interpersonal conflict, financial worries, or routine medical procedure (see Barbash, 2017). There is also what the Trauma Resource Institute (TRI, 2021a) identifies as cumulative trauma or "C-trauma" such as the impact of colonialism, genocide, racism, etc. The key point is whether a person's nervous system becomes dysregulated and stuck in fight, flight, or freeze response which can then result in symptoms of stress and trauma, as described further below.

Resilience is the most common reaction of those who experience trauma, observed Bonanno (2009) and the Trauma Resource Institute. There are multiple definitions of resiliency[1], including "bouncing back" from challenges. The definition used in this chapter is the Community Resiliency Model definition developed by TRI: "Resiliency is an individual's and community's ability to identify and use individual and collective strengths in living fully in the present moment, and to thrive while managing the activities of daily living" (Miller-Karas, 2019, as cited in TRI, 2021b, p. 10). In CRM, there are many components of resiliency identified. Resiliency includes "cultivating our well-being, embracing our individual and collective assets and strengths, being solution-focused about life's challenges, being compassionate, optimistic, and acknowledging individual and collective suffering with kindness. Accomplishing all of this as we live our lives" (TRI, 2021a, p. 10). Resilience strengthens our ability to overcome adversity, manage stress, and heal trauma. Helping clients and communities build resilience is a key role of social workers (Johnson, 2017). To help build the resilience of others, social workers first need to practice and demonstrate resilience skills themselves.

Resiliency is like a muscle that can be strengthened with practicing CRM. This chapter introduces three of the six CRM wellness skills with brief descriptions and accompanying activities which can be practiced by anyone at any time. Learning and practicing the CRM wellness skills as a student can help with stress management during the academic social work program and when transitioning into one's career dedicated to improving individual and collective wellbeing.

Background on the Community Resiliency Model

The CRM approach strengthens individual and community resilience by teaching biology/body-based wellness skills to bring the nervous system back into regulation after stressful and traumatic events (Miller-Karas, 2015). CRM's goal is to create trauma-informed and resiliency-informed communities that share a common understanding of the impact of trauma and stress on the nervous system and how resiliency can be restored or increased (Miller-Karas, 2021). CRM's approach differs from cognitive-based approaches such as cognitive behavioural therapy (CBT), a type of talking therapy, which helps people change their thinking and subsequently their troublesome emotions and behaviours (see Miller-Karas, 2019). In CRM, the focus is on the body and sensations in the body.

CRM is research informed. CRM workshops and trainings have been implemented in more than 100 countries for nurses (Grabbe et al., 2020a) and led by nurses during COVID-19 (Duva et al., 2022); frontline workers including providers of social services, health care, and public safety (Grabbe et al., 2021); genocide survivors in Rwanda (Habimana et al., 2021); women who struggle with addiction (Grabbe et al., 2020b); and high need/low resourced traumatized community of Latino, African-American, LGBTQ, Asian Pacific Islander, and veteran participants initiated through the California Mental Health Services Act (Freeman et al., 2021). These studies, some of which were randomized control trials, report statistically significant results in reduction of distress indicators, and symptoms from first- and second-hand posttraumatic stress disorder (PTSD), anxiety, depression, burnout, as well as increase in wellness indicators and daily functioning, among others.

To begin, individuals are educated about how their nervous system functions using accessible concepts and are taught six easy-to-learn wellness skills for self-regulation/stabilization, and self-care. For example, one skill is tracking sensations to distinguish between those of distress (such as tense muscles or shallow and rapid breaths) versus wellness (such as relaxed muscles or deep and slow breaths). Once these skills are learned, individuals are encouraged to practice these skills in caring for others and to share this knowledge within their wider social network to practice together, hence the term "community" in the Community Resiliency Model.

The Nervous System as a Guardian

Why is understanding the nervous system important to wellbeing and resilience? Tracking the nervous system provides insights into our current mental, emotional, and physical states through sensations in the body. Being aware of these states can then inform what actions to take to shift away from situations that reduce our well-being towards situations that enhance our wellbeing. The term used in CRM for wellbeing is the "Resilient Zone."

The Resilient Zone is state of wellbeing in mind, body, and spirit (figure 3.1). When in the Resilient Zone, you are able to handle the stresses of life. When you are in your Resilient Zone or "OK Zone" you are OK excited, OK worried, OK relaxed, OK calm, OK sad, or OK happy. In this Resilient Zone or OK Zone, you are your best self in a range of emotions. Being able to recognize when you are in your own Resilient Zone and when you are bumped out is one of the major concepts in CRM. Notice that the Resilient Zone is like a wave as there can be times in your day when you have more stress and other times during your day when you are calmer. There is ebb and flow, and you can manage the challenges that you face during your day by being your best self in mind, body, and spirit.

The depth of our Resilient Zone can change depending on life experiences. Also, some people are born with a wider Resilient Zone and others have a narrow Resilient Zone. The good news is that the depth of our Resilient Zone can be expanded. Once we are able to discern between sensations of distress and sensations of wellbeing, we can focus on the sensations of wellbeing associated with resiliency to reduce responses associated with threat and fear (Miller-Karas, 2019). For example, when someone disappoints us or hurts our feelings, we no longer lie awake all night or eat an entire chocolate bar. The more we learn and practice the wellness skills and the more the skills are integrated into our lives, the more we can work to widen our Resilient Zone. The goal of CRM is to widen your Resilient Zone which can be done through the wellness skills described below. But first, we return to the description of the nervous system.

The Resilient Zone - "OK" Zone
Zone of Well-Being

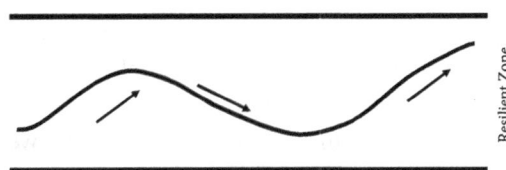

Figure 3.1: The Resilient Zone (TRI, 2021a)

The nervous system is made up of the brain, spinal cord, and nerves and helps all parts of the body to communicate with one another. It is one of the most ancient primitive systems in the body of all organisms in the animal kingdom. Every human has a nervous system – that is one thing we all have in common and brings us together as shared humanity. One of the nervous system's functions is to keep us alive by sensing and moving away from danger and towards safety. In essence, our nervous system is our guardian.

Our nervous system consists of two parts: the Central Nervous System (CNS) and the Peripheral Nervous System (PNS). The CNS is in the centre of our bodies and consists of the brain and spinal cord which have the function of processing information and motor output (facilitating movement), among other functions. The PNS is the system that contains all the nerves that our outside or the periphery of the CNS such as the nerves in our skin, limbs, and organs. The primary role of the PNS is to connect the CNS (brain and spinal cord) to other parts of our bodies (figure 3.2).

The PNS is divided into three branches. First, the PNS consists of the Somatic Nervous System (SNS) which connects the CNS with muscles and skin. The PNS includes skeletal muscles and voluntary muscles such as arm and communicates with sense organs. Second, the PNS consists of the Autonomic Nervous System (ANS) which regulates involuntary physiologic processes that are independent of our thinking and control and are unconscious, hence the name autonomic. These include heart rate, blood pressure, respiration, digestion, and sexual arousal. Think of the ANS as the accelerator and the brake of the nervous system (TRI, 2021a). The ANS communicates with internal organs and glands. Third, the PNS also branches off into the visceral nervous system which consists of nerves and other sensors that relay information from the visceral organs (heart, digestive tract, etc.) to the CNS and monitors the internal environment. The ANS contains three anatomically distinct divisions: sympathetic, parasympathetic, and enteric, which is the digestive tract which is out of scope for this chapter but just as important for wellbeing as the brain (Enders, 2015). To learn more about the complex and fascinating gastrointestinal system, also referred to as the second brain, read the informative and entertaining book *Gut: The Inside Story of Our Body's Most Underrated Organ* by Enders (2015).

The sympathetic division helps us prepare for action of fight or flight to respond to actual danger (e.g., a bully) or perceived danger (e.g., public speaking), by raising breathing and heart rate and blood pressure to get as much oxygen carrying blood to muscles. It does so by diverting blood away from the digestive and reproductive system (see figure 3.3). An easy way to remember is that sometimes when we are stressed, we feel like there is a knot in our stomach and our mouth is dry and we feel like we can't eat anything. In contrast, the parasympathetic division helps us prepare to recover from fight/flight by resting and digesting, and it does so by decreasing breathing and heart rate and blood pressure. One way to remember that the PNS prepared us for rest is how pleasant it feels to be having a relaxing dinner with family or friends.

Life experiences and circumstances, such as stressful or traumatic events (symbolized as the red lightning bolt in figure 3.4 below) can bump us out of our Resilient Zone. In the case of chronic stress or unresolved trauma, the sympathetic nervous system can get stuck in an overactivated state either in the high zone (hyper-arousal) resulting in anxiety and panic, angry

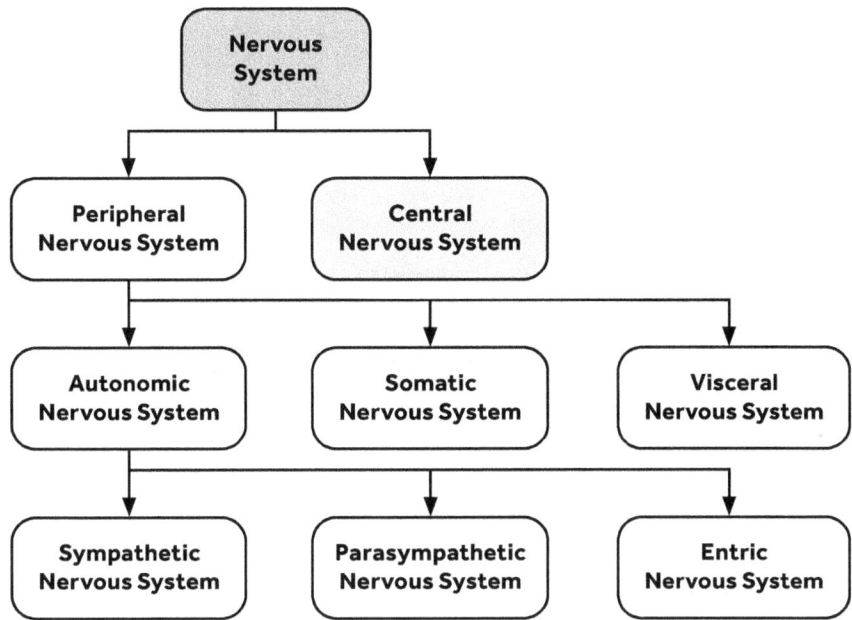

Figure 3.2: The divisions of the nervous system (Rachel, 2020)

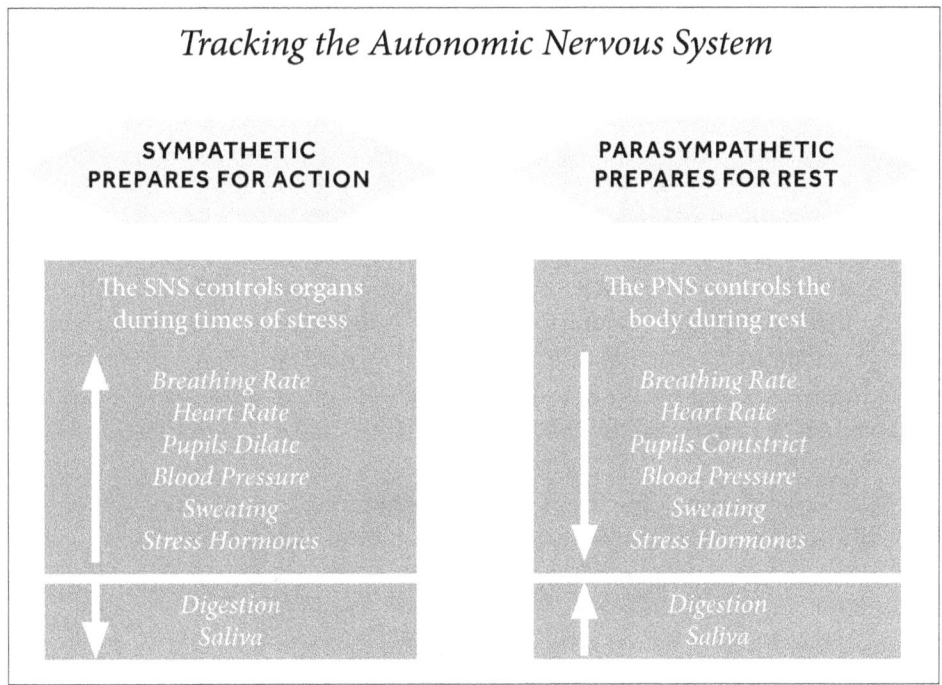

Figure 3.3: Tracking the autonomic nervous system (TRI, 2021a)

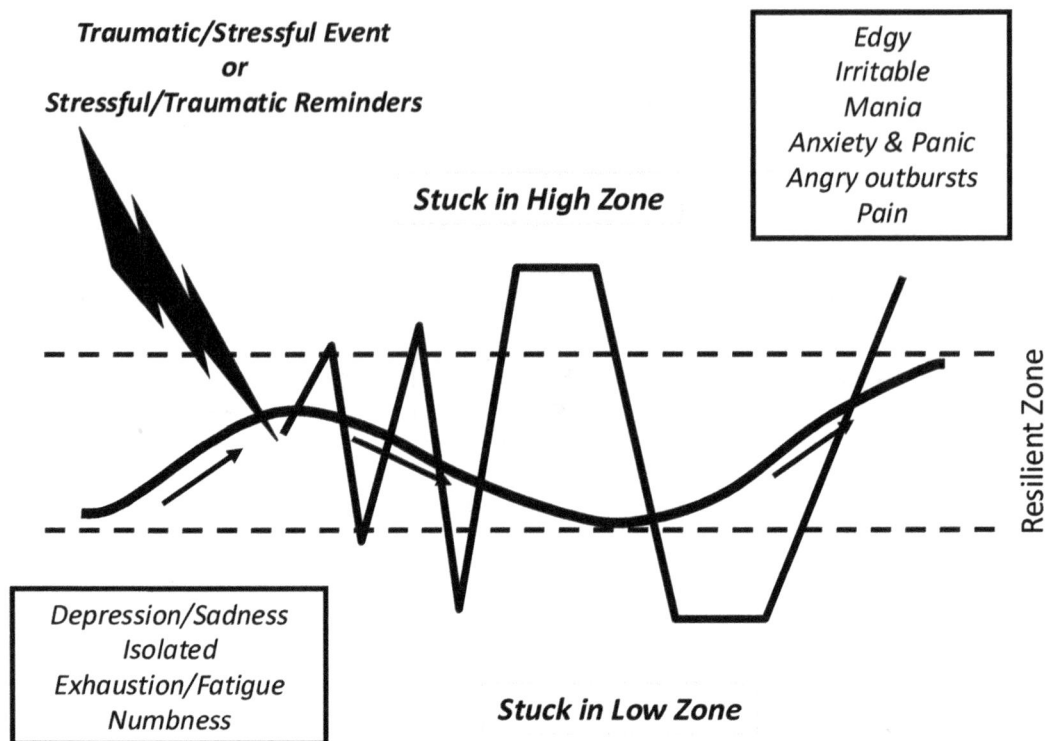

Figure 3.4: Nervous system stuck in the high zone or low zone (TRI, 2021a)

outbursts, pain, irritability, and other states, or in the low zone (hypo-arousal) resulting in depression, isolation, exhaustion, fatigue and other states (figure 3.4).

In extreme situations in which fight or flight does not seem like an option when responding to a threat, the nervous system enters a state of freeze[2]. This can feel like numbness and look like tonic immobilization (an involuntary, reflexive reaction characterized by a rigid, unmoving state) to prepare for the possibility of death. An example would be a client speaking about abuse and then suddenly they stop speaking and instead sits motionless with the "1000-yard stare" – their eyes looking "through" you, their breathing becomes rapid and shallow, and their jaw is clenched.

One of the most important teachings in CRM is the biology of the stress response in order to enhance the understanding that biology is not human weakness (TRI, 2021a). Feeling anxious, depressed, exhausted, or numb happens because of biological responses of our bodies to a situation rather than because we are weak and not strong enough. Understanding these biological responses helps us to be more non-judgemental towards ourselves and others who are struggling with stress and trauma.

Optimal functioning can be achieved when the nervous system is able to return to the Resilient Zone. There are several exercises and activities that are described below that can help you return to your Resilient Zone. Research on the brain has revealed that the brain has neuroplasticity, meaning that the brain changes and rewires itself in response to stimulation from learning and experiences[3]). Also, the brain undergoes neurogenesis or creates new neurons (nerve cells in the brain) and connections between neurons throughout a lifetime (Altman, 1962, as cited in Wnuk, 2016). You may have heard of the saying coined by Carla Schatz: "What fires together, wires together" (Keysers & Gazzola, 2014)[4]. This means that when brain cells fire together (or stimulate each other), strong neuronal pathways form, which increase the speed of communication between neurons. Think of these pathways as a super high-speed highway. The takeaway is that there is hope in the ability of our brain and our responses to change. By practicing the CRM wellness skills, we can enhance our resiliency responses.

Below are activities section divided into three parts. First, activities for defining and assessing wellness. Second, CRM wellness skills. Third, CRM care plans. Feel free to write, draw, doodle, and express yourself creatively in these activity sections to make this chapter your own. If at any time an activity is too uncomfortable, you are invited to stop and shift your attention to something comfortable or pleasant. It's important to recognize that we are living in a world with specific systems and structures in place (capitalist, patriarchal, hierarchical, consumerist, etc.) which contribute to nervous system dysregulation, and make it challenging to embody the wellness skills all the time. Being non-judgemental and kind to ourselves are attitudes that can help us regulate our individual nervous system and collective, societal nervous system responses and hence strengthen individual and collective resilience.

Part 1: What is Wellness and Wellness Check-In

ACTIVITY 1

For Activity 1, there are four components: Activity 1a to define wellness and/or resilience, Activity 1b to describe what wellness/resilience feel like, Activity 1c to understand what the lack of, or shortage of, wellness/resilience feels like, and Activity 1d to assess your current level of resiliency.

Activity 1a: Defining Wellness/Resiliency. What does wellness/resiliency mean to you? What are similarities or differences between individual and community wellness/resiliency?

Activity 1b: What Does Wellness/Resilience Feel Like? How does it feel when you are in your Resilient Zone mentally, emotionally, physically, and/or spiritually?

The following is a list of some common reactions to stressful or traumatic events:

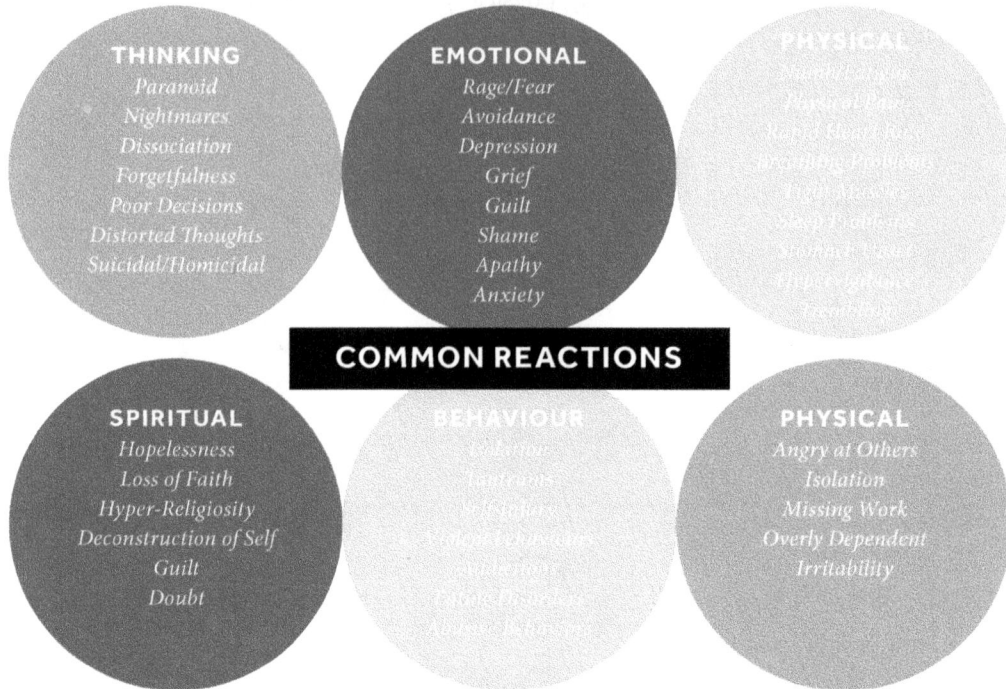

THINKING
Paranoid
Nightmares
Dissociation
Forgetfulness
Poor Decisions
Distorted Thoughts
Suicidal/Homicidal

EMOTIONAL
Rage/Fear
Avoidance
Depression
Grief
Guilt
Shame
Apathy
Anxiety

PHYSICAL

COMMON REACTIONS

SPIRITUAL
Hopelessness
Loss of Faith
Hyper-Religiosity
Deconstruction of Self
Guilt
Doubt

BEHAVIOUR

PHYSICAL
Angry at Others
Isolation
Missing Work
Overly Dependent
Irritability

Figure 3.5: Common reactions to stressful or traumatic events (TRI, 2021a)

Activity 1c: What Does a Lack of Wellness/Resiliency Feel Like? Beyond the signs that were mentioned above in Figures 3.4 and 3.5, there may be other signs or behaviours that are specific to you signalling that you are in the low zone (e.g., sleeping more than 9-10 hours/day) or high zone (e.g., chewing nails or overeating when nervous). Note some of the signs and behaviours:

LOW ZONE	HIGH ZONE

Activity 1d: Current Level of Resiliency. The next activity is to check in on your current level of resiliency. There are different ways to do so using the CRM approach:

1. Use the iChill app.

2. Identify where you are on the Resilient Zone scale on the iChill app (figure 3.6).

3. Or combine the Resilient Zone scale and the iChill app (as in figure 3.7, see Activity 2).

The free iChill app[5] (figure 3.6) explains CRM 6 wellness skills, allows you to track where you are on the Resilient Zone before and after practicing wellness skills, and has Resilient Zone images such as the graph from Figure 3.8. If you do not have a smart phone, the skills of CRM can be learned by going to iChillapp.com with translations in English, Spanish and Ukrainian.

The iChill app can also be used together with the Resilient Zone graph as shown below in figure 3.7 in which the numerical values (ranging from 1 low zone to 10 high zone) have been placed on the graph.

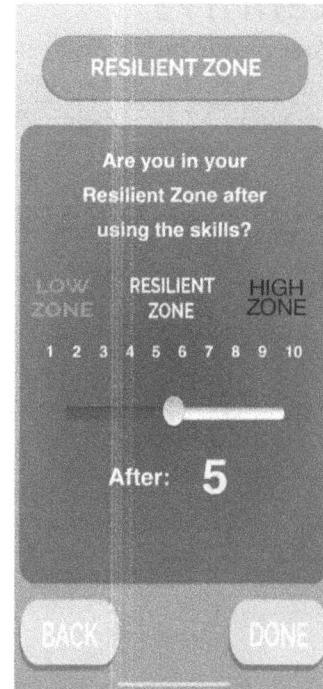

Figure 3.6: Image of the Resilient Zone scale in the iChill app (TRI, 2021a)

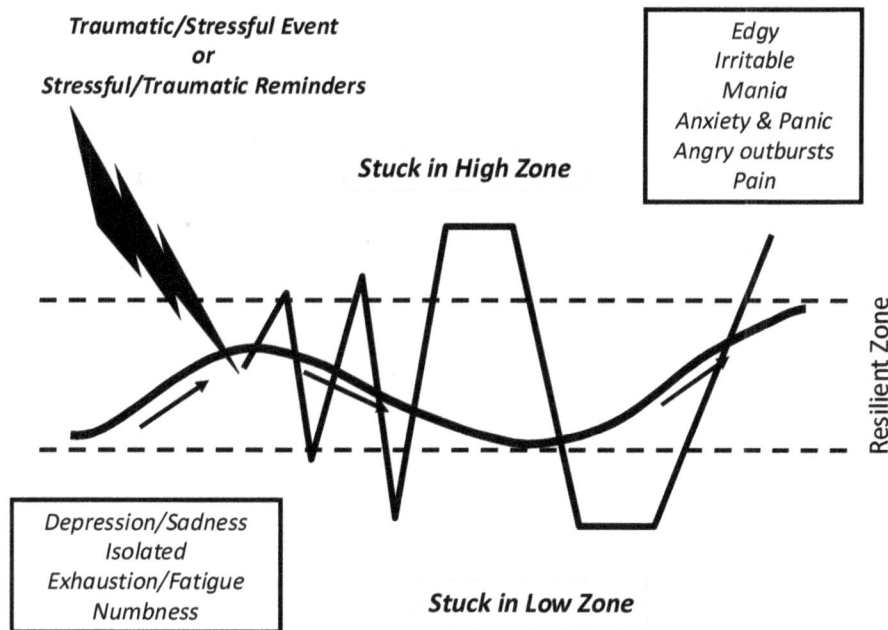

Figure 3.7: Using the iChill app together with the Resilient Zone graph (TRI, 2021a)

Assess your current resiliency level by indicating where you are on the Resilient Zone graph in figure 3.8 (TRI, 2021a) and applying your iChill app score (your score from Activity 1d step 3 – see figure 3.7 as an example):

SIX Skills are in the Palms of your Hands

Figure 3.8: The six CRM wellness skills (TRI, 2020a)

Note that where you indicate you are on the Resilient Zone graph can change throughout the day. Regardless of where you are on the Resilient Zone graph, the CRM wellness skills described in Part 2 can help to bring the nervous system back into the Resilient zone.

Part 2: CRM Wellness Skills

There are six CRM wellness skills:

1. Tracking (reading sensations)
2. Resourcing
3. Grounding
4. Help Now!
5. Gesturing
6. Shift and stay

This chapter introduces the first four of the six wellness skills depicted in figure 3.8. You can learn about the remaining two skills on the iChill app.

TRACKING

Tracking is most important for self-care; hence it is the first wellness skill. Tracking is essential when practicing each of the other five skills. Tracking is the foundation for helping to stabilize the nervous system and involves noticing or paying attention to sensations in the body from moment to moment. Examples of sensations include temperature, pain, tingling or itching. There are several metaphors for tracking:

- "Tracking is like the GPS of the body: if I know where I am I can't get lost."
- "It's like having a conversation with the body. It's already talking to you, but Tracking gives you the ability to talk back and converse."

Sensations can be categorized as pleasant, unpleasant, or neutral. Sensations originate from billions of receptors throughout the body. Every thought, emotion, and experience have corresponding body sensations. Therefore, paying attention to sensations can give a person greater awareness of their emotions and thoughts.

The insula is the part of the brain involved with interoception, or the ability to observe body sensations in response to thoughts, feelings, and movement. The insula helps the mind and the body to communicate with one another and helps to initiate actions to keep the body in a state of internal balance. For example, if you feel too cold, you think to put on a sweater. Body awareness can bring about emotional regulation and clearer thinking (Paulus et al., 2010). Sensory awareness skills that focus on pleasant or neutral sensations may establish new neural networks and result in positive neural pathways that compete with or replace existing negative neural pathways (Grabbe et al., 2020a). There are many types of sensations, some are listed in figure 3.10.

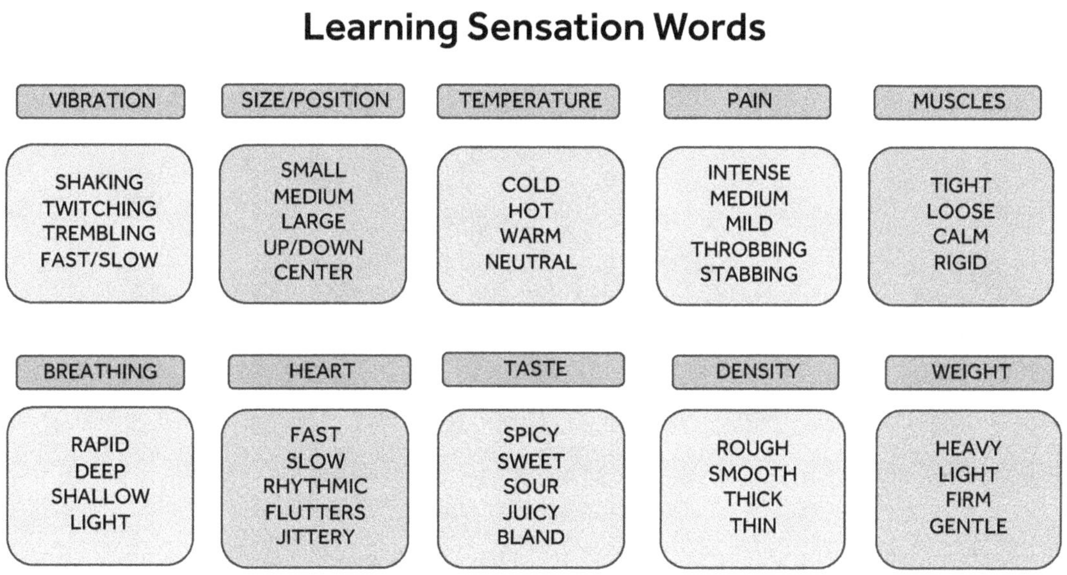

Learning Sensation Words

VIBRATION	SIZE/POSITION	TEMPERATURE	PAIN	MUSCLES
SHAKING TWITCHING TREMBLING FAST/SLOW	SMALL MEDIUM LARGE UP/DOWN CENTER	COLD HOT WARM NEUTRAL	INTENSE MEDIUM MILD THROBBING STABBING	TIGHT LOOSE CALM RIGID

BREATHING	HEART	TASTE	DENSITY	WEIGHT
RAPID DEEP SHALLOW LIGHT	FAST SLOW RHYTHMIC FLUTTERS JITTERY	SPICY SWEET SOUR JUICY BLAND	ROUGH SMOOTH THICK THIN	HEAVY LIGHT FIRM GENTLE

Figure 3.9: Sensation words (TRI, 2021a)

Sensations can also include yawning, stomach gurgling, burping, and other gastrointestinal signs as the nervous system shifts from sympathetic nervous system response of fight/flight to parasympathetic nervous system response of rest and digest. Sensations can be tracked from head to toe, focusing on just one part of the body such as the hands, or checking in on other or all parts of the body one-by-one. To practice the tracking skill, try out Activity 3a and 3b.

ACTIVITY 3A

Rub your hands together really fast and identify the sensations while you are rubbing them and then when you stop. Note the sensations:

RUBBING HANDS	STOPPING RUBBING HANDS

ACTIVITY 3B

Ask yourself: "What sensations am I aware of on the inside when I think about or experience something (pleasant, unpleasant, or neutral)?" For the unpleasant thoughts or experiences, do not choose a topic that is too triggering or traumatic. If you would like to address very unpleasant issues, do so in conjunction with assistance from a mental health care practitioner.

Tracking also involves paying attention to others we interact with. It is good to try this with people we know as we are likely to be more attuned to people that we know well and care about. What do you notice about a person who is talking about a pleasant experience? Do they smile and do their muscles look relaxed? Do you then find yourself also smiling and feeling relaxed? Conversely, what if they are talking about an unpleasant experience? Are they frowning and does their voice break or shake? Are you frowning and feeling sad?

PLEASANT	UNPLEASANT	NEUTRAL

RESOURCING

Identifying resources and tracking sensations connected to the resource develops internal resiliency and a renewed sense of one's own abilities and capacity to stabilize the nervous system. Individuals are often surprised about how many resources that they have in their life.

However, if a person cannot identify a resource, the hope of creating one can also bring about changes within the nervous system. As the person begins to sense pleasant, neutral, or less distressing sensations in the body connected to the identified resource, they can begin to feel hope and possibility. Resourcing is a strength-building skill. Resources can be expanded by including pleasant smells, sights, touch, taste, sounds, places, people, and traditions. Note that what might be a resource for one person may not be a resource for someone else, in fact the same resource can cause an unpleasant memory or sensation for someone else. For example, for some people, a dog might be a resource but for someone who was bitten by a dog it may not be a resource.

ACTIVITY 4A

Answer one or some of these questions to identify your resources, feel free to write, draw, or identify your resources according to your preference:

- What or who uplifts you?

- What or who gives you strength?

- What or who helps you get through hard times?

ACTIVITY 4B

Activity 4b is resource intensification which strengthens the "felt sense" of the resource and overrides attention that automatically goes to unpleasant sensations arising from other thoughts, emotions, or experiences. Either close your eyes or keep them open, whatever feels comfortable for you, and think about one resource and track sensations that arise. Spend a few minutes exploring the following questions for resource intensification and then write or draw your observations if you wish.

- What does your resource look like?
- What are the colours?
- What are the smells?
- What does it feel like?
- Where do you experience those sensations?
- Is there a temperature associated with it such as cool or warm?
- Are there sounds?
- Do the sensations change?

GROUNDING

Grounding is the direct contact of the body with a surface or with something that provides support to the body. When we are grounded, we are aware of our body in the present moment which can help reduce worries about the past or the future.

There are different ways to ground the body. For those who have experienced an earthquake, using the ground may trigger unpleasant sensations and memories. There are other ways to ground such as by using our hands to push against the wall or another solid object. Below is a grounding exercise that you can read line by line or record yourself (such as on your phone) reading it out loud and then playing it back to yourself. Feel free to write your observations from exercise A or B into the space provided below, or both and compare similarities and differences.

ACTIVITY 5: TRY OUT THE GROUNDING EXERCISE

1. Find a comfortable position, sitting, lying down or standing, take your time. Open or close your eyes, whichever you prefer. Notice how your body is making contact with a surface.

2. If sitting, bring attention to your seat making contact with the sofa, chair, etc....now notice your legs...and then your feet making contact with a solid surface.

3. Notice the sensations that are more pleasant to you or neutral within your body... take your time...notice your breathing...heart rate...muscle relaxation.

4. If you become aware of uncomfortable sensations, bring your attention to places that feel neutral or more comfortable/pleasant.

5. As you bring your attention to neutral or comfortable/pleasant sensations, notice any change.

6. Spend some moments noticing sensations that are pleasant and/or neutral.

7. As you get ready to end, slowly scan your body and bring your attention to all sensations that are pleasant or neutral.

Write down any observations you would like to note and remember.

> *Evalyna's Corner*
>
> *I ground daily while I am walking my dog or waiting at the bus stop. I focus on how my feet feel on the ground as my heel first touches the ground and then my toes.*

HELP NOW/RESET NOW!

Help Now! is a list of ten strategies that can reset the nervous system when a person is bumped into the High or Low Zones. Help Now! Strategies can be used in crisis situations and can help you return to your Resilient Zone.

ACTIVITY 6: TRY OUT THE HELP NOW! STRATEGIES

1. Drink a glass of water, a cup of tea, or a cup of juice.
2. Look around the room or wherever you are, noticing anything that catches your attention.
3. Name six colors you see in the room (or outside).
4. Open your eyes and soften your gaze (if eyes are tightly closed).
5. Count backwards from 10 as you walk around the room.
6. If you're inside or outside, touch a surface. Is it hard, soft, cool, warm?
7. Notice the temperature in the room.
8. Notice the sounds within and outside the room.
9. Walk and pay attention to the movement in your arms and legs and how your feet are making contact with the ground.
10. Push your hands against the wall or door slowly and notice your muscles pushing; or stand against a wall, facing forward and gently push your back into the wall.

Write down your favourite three Help Now! strategies.

Evalyna's Corner

The most frequent Help Now! Strategy that I use is drinking water or hot chocolate/tea. Another strategy that I use daily is to notice sounds within and outside the room as it helps me to instantly be in the present moment.

Part 3: CRM Care Plans

Now to apply the concepts (The Resilient Zone), and the skills learned (Tracking, Resourcing, Grounding, Help Now!) to your self-care plan and then to your community care plan. It can be helpful to share your self-care and community-care plans with others.

CRM SELF-CARE PLAN

Before we care for others, it is important that we care for ourselves. This is similar to the instructions on a plane to put one's own oxygen mask on first before helping others put their mask on.

ACTIVITY 6A

Answer one or some of the following questions:

1. What are you already doing in your life to widen your Resilient Zone?

2. If you found the skills helpful, how could you weave the skills into your daily routine? Which skills would be the most helpful?

3. What specifically do you need to do differently to embark on a better self-care plan if you think yours needs improvement?

4. Write a statement of encouragement to yourself that could strengthen your resolve to improve your self-care plan and stay with it.

ACTIVITY 6B

1. Read your statement of encouragement to yourself.

2. As you read the statement of encouragement to yourself, pay attention to the sensations inside your body.

3. Draw your attention to the neutral or pleasant sensations.

4. New beliefs, feeling or meanings may come up. As something new and positive comes up, pay attention to sensations that are pleasant or neutral.

Write down any observations you would like to note and remember.

CRM COMMUNITY CARE PLAN

Sharing CRM with family members, friends, peers, colleagues, neighbours, organizations, and community members (they can all be referred to as community for the purpose of Activity 6c) can create a culture of understanding about how the nervous system functions to encourage a resiliency-focused approach and enhance support when we or others are experiencing stressful or traumatic events.

ACTIVITY 6C

Answer one or some of the following questions:

1. How could you use CRM Skills in your community?

2. What steps would you need to take to begin using CRM Skills in your community?

3. What strengths does your community have that would support bringing CRM Skills to more people?

4. What challenges would you expect?

5. When can you start and with whom?

Summary

We all experience difficult times at different times in our lives. However, we can reduce our suffering by shifting from our low or high zone to our Resilient Zone and we can also help others by assisting them in returning to their Resilient Zone. Figure 3.11 below brings together some of the concepts, skills, and activities.

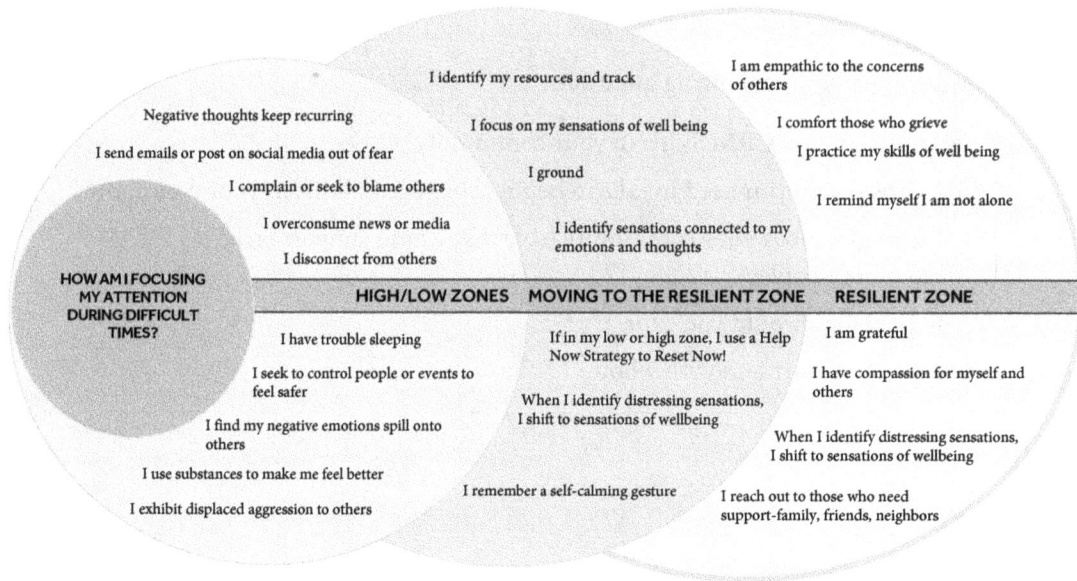

Figure 3.10: Shifting from the low or high zone to the Resilient Zone (TRI, 2021a)

As noted earlier, all human beings share the same type of nervous system, and it is a quality we all have in common and brings us together: our shared humanity. The CRM model was designed to be easily accessible, transportable, affordable, and adaptable. Feel free to use CRM to enhance your resilience and to share with others to enhance their resilience. An easy way to share about CRM is through the iChill app which is free and available in several languages. You can also learn more about CRM and CRM training by visiting https://www.traumaresourceinstitute.com/.

Evalyna's Acknowledgements

I am thankful for Elaine Miller-Karas, LCSW, who is the key developer of the CRM wellness skills. Thank you, Elaine, for your innovative spirit and your commitment, as well as that of the Trauma Resource Institute team, to ensuring that CRM is accessible to everyone anywhere in the world to strengthen their resiliency. Thank you to the Trauma Resource Institute for providing me with a scholarship to become a certified CRM teacher. In return, I am committed to sharing CRM in Canada and internationally. I am also grateful to Dr. Julie Drolet, my postdoctoral supervisor, who suggested that Elaine and I facilitate a CRM workshop for the Social Work and Disaster (SWAD) Network and introduce it to professionals, volunteers, and students who are working in, or studying, emergencies and disasters. For more information about CRM and the Trauma Resource Institute, visit: https://www.traumaresourceinstitute.com/

NOTES

1   Resilience and resiliency are used interchangeably in this chapter.

2   The term freeze has been interpreted differently and can include orienting freeze, tonic immobility, or death feigning. For more information visit https://www.nicabm.com/topic/freeze/.

3   William James first mentioned plasticity in regards to the nervous system in 1890. However, the term 'neuroplasticity' is credited to Jerzy Konorski in 1948 and then within 1 year was popularized by Donald Hebb (Puderbaugh & Emmady, 2022).

4   The mnemonic created by Carla Schatz, which is not entirely accurate, is based on psychologist Donald Hebb's research on neurophysiological account of learning and memory and is referred to as Hebbian learning (Keysers & Gazzola, 2014).

5   The iChill app can be downloaded for free from iChillapp.com and has both visual and audio components.

REFERENCES

Barbash, E. (2017, March 13). Different types of trauma: Small 't' versus large 'T'. *Psychology Today.* https://www.psychologytoday.com/us/blog/trauma-and-hope/201703/different-types-trauma-small-t-versus-large-t

Bonanno, G. (2009). The Other side of sadness: *What the new science of bereavement tells us about life after loss.* Basic Book: New York, NY.

Duva, I. M., Murphy, J. R., & Grabbe, L. (2022). A nurse-led, well-being promotion using the Community Resiliency Model, Atlanta, 2020–2021. *American Journal of Public Health, 112,* S271_S274, https://doi.org/10.2105/AJPH.2022.306821

Fair, J. (2018). Components of the nervous system are outlined in the graph. https://commons.wikimedia.org/wiki/Category:Nervous_system_components#/media/File:Components_of_the_Nervous_System.png

Freeman, K., Baek, K., Ngo, M., Kelley, V., Karas, E., Citron, S., & Montgomery, S. (2021). Exploring the usability of a community resiliency model approach in a high need/low resourced traumatized community. *Community Mental Health Journal,* 1–10. https://doi.org/10.1007/s10597-021-00872-z

Grabbe, L., Higgins, M. K., Baird, M., Craven, P. A., & San Fratello, S. (2020a). The Community Resiliency Model® to promote nurse well-being. *Nursing Outlook, 68*(3), 324–336. https://doi.org/10.1016/j.outlook.2019.11.002

Grabbe, L., Higgins, M., Jordan, D., Noxsel, L., Gibson, B., & Murphy, J. (2020b). The Community Resiliency Model®: A pilot of an interoception intervention to increase the emotional self-regulation of women in addiction treatment. *International Journal of Mental Health and Addiction, 19,* 793-808. https://doi.org/10.1007/s11469-019-00189-9

Grabbe, L., Higgins, M. K., Baird, M., & Pfeiffer, K. M. (2021). Impact of a resiliency training to support the mental well-being of front-line workers: Brief report of a quasi-experimental study of the Community Resiliency Model. *Medical Care, 59*(7), 616–621. https://doi.org/10.1097/mlr.0000000000001535

Habimana, S., Biracyaza, E., Habumugisha, E., Museka, E., Mutabaruka, J., & Montgomery, S. (2021). Role of Community Resiliency Model skills trainings in trauma healing among 1994 Tutsi genocide survivors in Rwanda. *Psychology Research and Behavior Management, 2021*(14), 1139–1148. https://doi.org/10.2147/PRBM.S319057

Johnson, K. (2017). Behavioral health brief: Advancing trauma-informed approaches and resilience. *Social Work Today, 17*(6), p. 32.

Keysers, C., & Gazzola, V. (2014). Hebbian learning and predictive mirror neurons for actions, sensations and emotions. *Philosophical transactions of the Royal Society of London. Series B, Biological Sciences, 369*(1644), 20130175. https://doi.org/10.1098/rstb.2013.0175

Miller-Karas, E. (2015). *Building resilience to trauma: The trauma and community resiliency models.* Routledge.

Miller-Karas, E. (2019). *Position paper using the Community Resiliency Model*. Trauma Resource Institute.

Miller-Karas, E. (2021). *Trauma Resource Institute organization overview: The community and trauma resiliency models.* Trauma Resource Institute. https://www.traumaresourceinstitute.com/s/TRI-Overview_20210528.pdf

Paulus, M. P, & Stein, M. B. (2010). Interoception in anxiety and depression. *Brain Structure & Function, 214*(5-6), 451-463. 10.1007/s00429-010-0258-9

Puderbaugh, M., & Emmady, P. D. (2022). *Neuroplasticity.* StatPearls Publishing.

Trauma Resource Institute [TRI]. (2021, September 20a). *Community Resiliency Model (CRM)® teacher training* [PowerPoint Slides].

Trauma Resource Institute [TRI]. (2021, September 20b). *Community Resiliency Model (CRM)® teacher training PowerPoint slide guide* [PDF file].

Wnuk, A. (2016, July 21). *Neurogenesis: An overview.* BrainFacts.org. https://www.brainfacts.org/Thinking-Sensing-and-Behaving/Brain-Development/2016/Neurogenesis-An-Overview-072116

NOTES:

NOTES:

NOTES:

Remote Field Instruction and Supervision

Eileen McKee, Jenna Nieves, Kelly Allison, Cyndi Hall, and Shella Zagada

The COVID-19 global pandemic resulted in a shift in how social workers deliver services. Technology has been key in facilitating a continuity and exchange of information. E-counselling, e-therapy, and videoconferencing are becoming as familiar as emails, texts, and telephone calls for engaging with clients, colleagues, and stakeholders.

Because of this move toward remote service delivery, field education, considered the signature pedagogy for social work education (CSWE, 2008), has also changed. Since 2020, many social work students have experienced practicum placements that involve remote or hybrid models of field learning and/or service delivery.

In recognition of the critical role that technology now has in the education of social work students, students and field instructors will find in this chapter, resources to support e-learning and supervision such as:

- Descriptions of e-methods in remote field instruction,

- The elements of an effective field instructor–student relationship in the context of remote field instruction,

- Examples of important ethical considerations in remote field instruction,

- Strategies and approaches in remote field instruction to enhance the education of social work students, and

- Considerations for equity and diversity in remote field education.

ACTIVITY 1: WATCH AND REFLECT

As an introduction to remote field instruction and remote practicums, student and field instructor can together review and reflect on Video 4.1. In their debrief, they may consider challenges in a remote practicum.

In the video, a field instructor and student discuss their experiences of a social work practicum that was interrupted by the pandemic and the resulting need for social distancing. Their experience is applicable to beginning a full practicum as well.

Video 4.1: Factor-Inwentash Faculty of Social Work. (2020, May 26). *MSW E supervision: A student and her field instructor share their experience* [Video]. YouTube. https://youtu.be/X0MLftRrqx0

Developing Digital Literacy in Remote Field Education

Methods of Remote Field Education

There are several options for communicating remotely in field education. The choice of method is dependent on available technology as well as personal preferences. The most commonly used modalities include:

Teleconferencing. This term refers to a telephone meeting between two or more people in different locations through a telecommunication system. Terms like telephone conferencing, phone conferencing, and audio conferencing also describe this modality. The advantage of teleconferencing is that it requires very little technology in comparison to videoconferencing.

Emailing and Texting. These terms include one-way written communication via a computer, tablet, or smartphone. Email and text messages can be useful to communicate small pieces of information or brief questions between student and field instructor. However, tone and subtext of the communication may be difficult to read, which may result in misunderstandings and misinterpretations; therefore, emails and texts should be brief and to the point and both parties should ask if clarification is required.

Videoconferencing. This term refers to a meeting between two or more people in different locations by means of a computer network to transmit both video and audio concurrently. Videoconferencing (using Skype, Zoom, Microsoft Teams, etc.) allows all parties to both see and hear each other. Body language and other nonverbal cues are important for effective communication (Bambaeeroo & Shokrpour, 2017; Segal et al., 2015; Foley & Gentile, 2010; Mast, 2007), which is a major advantage of this modality. However, technology problems (audio or video) and poor network connections or bandwidth can present challenges in using videoconferencing. When using videoconferencing for field instruction, it is important that both the field instructor and student are familiar with the chosen platform. There are many useful guides, including those found in Image 4.1 and Video 4.2.

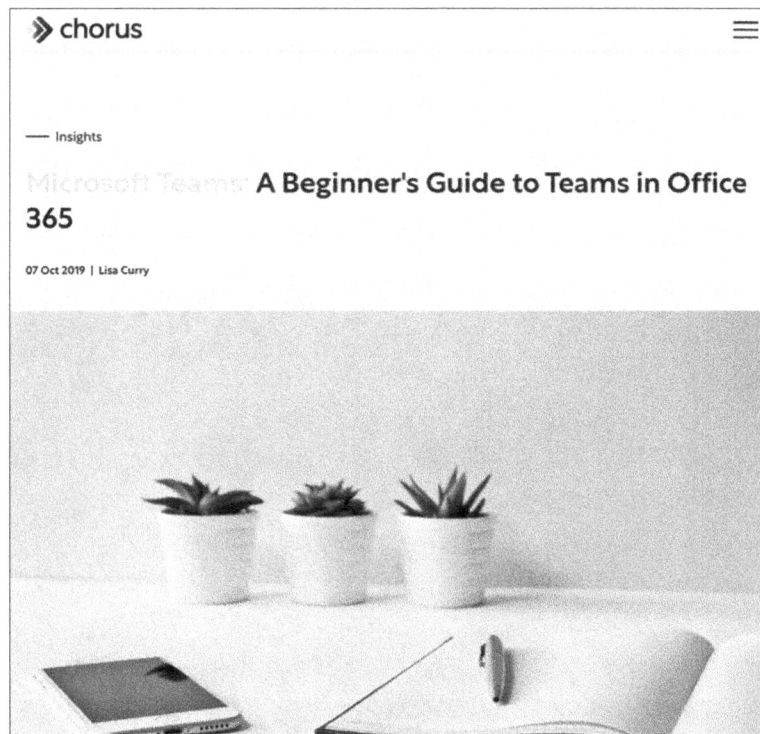

Figure 4.1: Curry, L. (2019, October 7). Microsoft Teams: A beginner's guide to Teams in Office 365. Chorus. https://www.chorus.co/resources/news/microsoft-teams-a-beginners-guide-to-teams-in-office-365

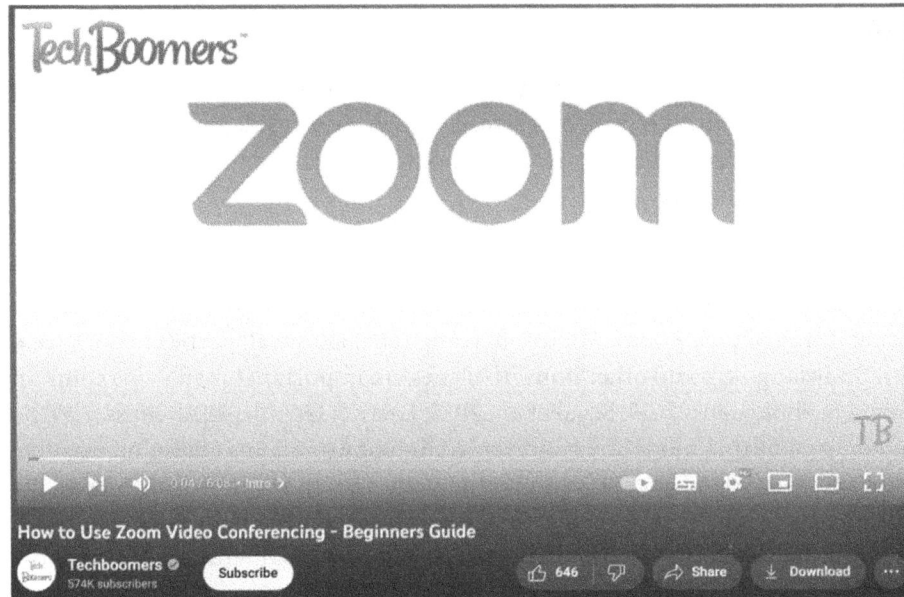

Video 4.2: Dawson, J. (2020, April 2). *How to Use Zoom Video Conferencing—Beginners Guide—Techboomers.* [Video]. YouTube. https://www.youtube.com/watch?v=POyXj9NR7FY

ACTIVITY 2: WATCH AND REFLECT

Lighting, audio, camera height, and background affect the quality of video conferencing. In this activity, the student reviews and reflects on Video 4.3 and how they might use this information to improve skills in communicating remotely.

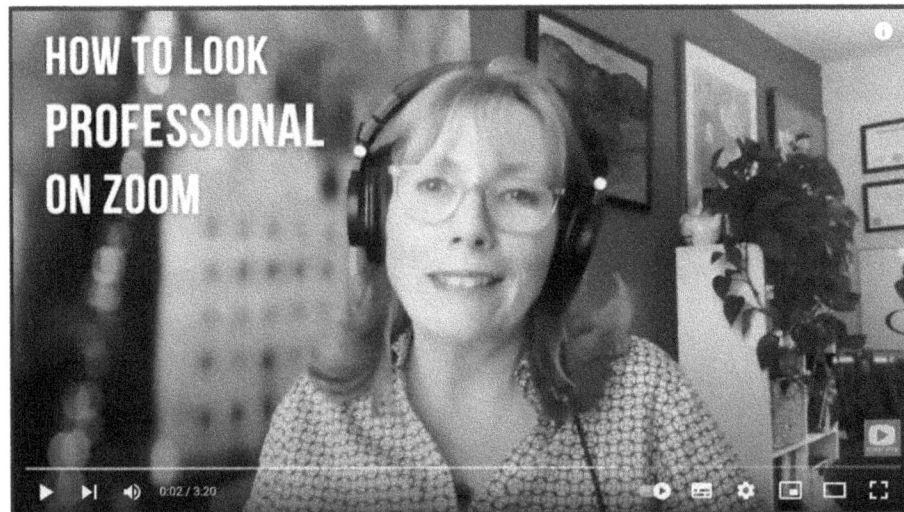

Video 4.3: Video 4.3. Crappy Childhood Fairy. (2020, March 25). *How to look professional on Zoom* [Video]. YouTube. https://www.youtube.com/watch?v=m5AxcjUHBEE

ACTIVITY 3: COMPARE PROS AND CONS

It is ultimately the field instructor and their agency that determines the format of service and education delivery. There are multiple issues that affect the decision, including whether the student will have direct contact with clients; whether the student will be engaging in indirect activities working on behalf of clients; whether the learning environment itself is conducive to remote work; access and accessibility considerations for the students, field instructor and clients, etc.

With the above context as well as with knowledge and experience, the student uses the table below to develop a list of advantages and disadvantages of remote field education, then compares this with field education that may be completely in-person. When listing "potential disadvantages," the student should consider how to mitigate the disadvantages with forethought, research, and communication.

Table 4.1: Comparing remote versus in-person field education.

MODALITY	(POTENTIAL) ADVANTAGES	(POTENTIAL) DISADVANTAGES
REMOTE		
IN-PERSON		

ACTIVITY 4: EXPERIMENTING WITH METHODS

In this activity, the students discuss with their field instructor the possibility of engaging with service users using different methods (phone contact, zoom call, etc.). After using several different methods, the student reflects on the strengths and limitations of each, then compares their experience with their list above.

Ethics in Remote Service Delivery and Education

Ethical challenges are common in social work practice as we work within and outside both formal and informal systems to assist marginalized individuals and communities. During field placements, students are exposed to various situations that demonstrate how our Canadian Association of Social Work (CASW) Code of Ethics (CASW, 2005) and Standards of Practice (CASW, 1995) guide decision-making in complex situations. Field instructors are able to support this learning with real world examples in practice. The onset of the pandemic crisis has fundamentally shifted thinking about ethics and standards in this unprecedented era. In an international study, Banks et al. (2020) highlight how the pandemic has exposed flaws and gaps in the social safety nets and discusses the ethical challenges social workers face because of the prolonged crisis.

The global pandemic has compelled social work as well as the learning environments to shift quickly to remote platforms and virtual spaces, and the use and quality of digital technology has been consistently on the rise nationally and globally. Nearly all Canadians access the internet daily, although inequities in digital access exist among low income and rural and remote populations (Weinberg, 2020). Digital technology is rapidly changing the way we communicate and relate to the world in which we live and the people around us. It is likely that some forms of remote work will remain an aspect of social work practice post pandemic and this will impact placements.

In managing this new context, all involved in social work and social work education must continue to refer to our Code of Ethics (CASW, 2005) and other practice resources, such as national or provincial standards for social work and technology and articles focused on the ethics of virtual service (NASW et al., 2017; Reamer, 2013; Van Sickle, 2014), to guide our approaches to integrating digital technology. Banks et al. (2020) suggest that social workers can "[r]aise with employers, professional associations and policymakers the serious harm and inequity experienced by people during the pandemic, the difficulties in delivering social work services and make proposals for improvements" (p. 22).

Technical/Professional Competence

It is important for students to understand the systems (e.g., access, storage, communication) used to manage electronic communication and applications used by their organization to ensure that the confidentiality and integrity of records are protected. Students need to familiarize themselves with practice guidelines and relevant legislation (e.g., professional regulations or local, provincial, and national legislation) involving the use of communication technology, as applicable in their geographic locations and service delivery contexts with clients, families, and communities.

Students must possess adequate technical knowledge to work remotely and to ensure compliance with the security requirements of their organization. As such, discussions between students and field instructors may include the potential benefits and risks of professional practice using technology (McInroy, 2019; National Association of Social Workers [NASW] et al., 2017; Van Sickle, 2014). In the context of ethical practice, ensuring confidentiality in a virtual world has its challenges and opportunities, and learning how to work with the technology is part of ethical practice. Students should reach out for assistance and discuss the various aspects of remote working during the interview at their potential placement sites. Assistance may be available through schools and university help desks if that is required.

Professional Boundaries

Students need to be provided with clear boundaries regarding expected response time to communications, permissible means of communication (e.g., email, video, texting, social media), and preventing conflicts of interest and dual relationships (e.g., connecting with clients on social media). Field instructors can clearly outline for students their expectations regarding the use of personal devices in field instruction, including accessing confidential student records and carrying out practicum learning activities. Professional communication using technology should be modelled by field instructors (e.g., not using casual or cryptic texting language when communicating professionally). Full compliance with technical security of data is critical to practice. A breach of data can lead to lack of trust by clients. In addition, the student, field instructor and learning environment will likely undergo an investigation by relevant privacy officers to determine the extent of the breach and mitigate further risks. It is important to review these expectations prior to beginning the placement to minimize risk.

Given the increased use of social media and other digital platforms, it is not unusual for people to encounter each other randomly and unexpectedly in online settings or when participating in online events (Reamer, 2013). Proactively discussing and setting expectations around potential online chance encounters outside of professional activities with field instructors, colleagues, and clients will help to clarify professional boundaries. Universities and schools of social work have well-developed policies including the use of social media in the context of placements. These policies must be adhered to as part of ethical practice in the age of technology. The following section deals specifically with the importance of privacy and confidentiality in the digital world.

Privacy and Confidentiality

Social workers have the responsibility to adhere to the CASW Code of Ethics (2024) and applicable regulations and legislation, including Canada's Privacy Act and Personal Information Protection and Electronic Documents Act (PIPEDA; Office of the Privacy Commissioner of Canada, 2019). Students need to recognize that all personnel (student, field instructor and the field setting) are responsible for the protection and security of their data and that all people within the field setting are required to follow the rules (Canadian Counselling and Psychotherapy Association [CCPA], 2019). Field instructors need to discuss and clarify with students the field setting's policies and procedures regarding the collection, use, and disclosure of personal information as well as the access, storage, and overall management of private and confidential information.

The ease of access to digital technology makes it convenient to transfer information. However, to avoid confidentiality breaches, it is important for students to know it is not ethical to discuss or post client or colleague information in social media, websites, or blogs. Googling clients and colleagues, particularly for non-crisis information, is also unethical. Furthermore, it is important for students to be aware of their surroundings and prevent accidental disclosure of personal information through their audio or video conferencing background.

Use of Social Media and Digital Networks

Most social work education programs and many field settings have social media policies and/or guidelines. Students should discuss with their field instructors any further social media guidelines regarding personal and professional relationships, including their interactions with

Tip: Consider using virtual backgrounds during videoconferencing to limit access to your personal information. Many platforms offer a virtual background of your choice. For example, the following video describes how to change your background in Zoom.

Video 4.4: Howfinity. (2020, March 22). *How to change your background in Zoom – Zoom virtual background* [Video]. YouTube. https://www.youtube.com/watch?v=d0ZIE5Ynuxc

clients. The field setting policies and procedures regarding social media should be provided to and discussed with students. If they are not, then students should be proactive and ask for the guidelines.

Placement sites may choose to use one platform for personal use and another for professional use. They also may establish boundaries regarding online exchanges with students and reiterate privacy and confidentiality in handling personal and organizational information while in their field practicum. It is important to promote professional online behaviour, including respectful communication, confidentiality, academic integrity, and social work ethical standards (CCPA, 2019; NASW et al., 2017; Van Sickle, 2014).

Understanding that online posts may be permanent may compel users to be thoughtful and intentional in their communication. Students must be made aware of and comply with policies and procedures regarding their use of unfounded, derogatory statements or misrepresentation of organizational principles and operating standards (Renison, 2013). Examples provided of unacceptable use of social media include: sharing confidential information about the School of Social Work, the practicum setting and/or clients and colleagues; name calling or behavior that will reflect negatively on the School of Social Work or a practicum's reputation; taking and sharing photographs without consent.

Learning and Supervision in Remote Placements

Remote Agency Practicum Orientation

As a student entering a field practicum, you can expect to have an orientation or onboarding process facilitated by your field instructor. As you learn more about your field practicum setting and the work that you will be doing, think about using the time with your field instructor to ask any questions about your role and opportunities for growth and learning, as well as make sure to discuss expectations, learning goals, and forms of support that will be helpful to you. The next sections highlight topics that you may want to discuss with your field instructor as you begin your practicum.

Defining Roles, Expectations, and Learning Goals

It is important that at the beginning of the working relationship, field instructors and students have a conversation about roles and expectations for both parties. It is essential to explore learning goals and how best to fulfil them. Getting clarification regarding your role, the field instructor's role, and the practicum setting's expectations of students will allow you to be more productive and confident in your new role. These discussions may evolve over time as expectations and learning goals change and develop.

Students and field instructors are expected to set a mutually agreed upon time and timeframe for remote field instruction. Guidelines for the structure of these meetings, such as a systematic review of learning activities, the integration of theory and practice, student questions, etc., and clear expectations regarding preparation for field instruction need to be discussed in your first onboarding meeting. Access to the field instructor during an emergency or on an ad hoc basis needs to be negotiated. It is important to review the remote field instruction plan on a regular basis so that adjustments can be made to enhance the remote field instruction experience for both you and the field instructor.

Discussing Learning Preferences, Providing Support, and Demonstrating Professionalism

Effective relationship-building requires both the student and the field instructor to observe, actively listen, and be open to the needs of each other. As there will be ongoing remote conversations, students should consider and be prepared to discuss their learning preferences, as well as how they can be supported in their professional and personal development. Although students do not need to discuss specifics regarding disabilities with their field instructors, field instructors should be made aware of any accommodations needed to best support the student's learning in the field. Students should also be prepared to participate in self-evaluation and self-reflection, in addition to hearing the feedback provided by the field instructor. It is essential that interactions are based on mutual respect and trust. It is important for students to consider and discuss with their field instructor how they can be best supported in their learning.

Building an Online Working Relationship

The working alliance is an integral component to developing competency in social work practice. Building a relationship requires a concentrated effort, even more so when developing a working relationship remotely and online. It is important to be mindful that, depending on the technology used, nonverbal communication may or may not be visible. This may require a discussion with your field instructor to set aside time for engaging in social chats and building rapport before discussing practicum tasks or your learning plan. It is also important for students to discuss concerns in the practicum and how best to develop a strong field instructor-student relationship.

> **Tip:** Students may consider using these meetings as a preparation for future meetings with their employers. Evanish (n.d.), in his online Lighthouse blog, provides suggestions for developing a strong working relationship for professionals and their managers such as developing an agenda for supervision meetings. For one-on-one field instruction meetings, students may include agenda items such as learning goals, challenges experienced, or advice on how to handle a situation or task.

Communications and Feedback

In order to build an effective relationship remotely, ongoing and open communication between the field instructor and the student is essential. There needs to be opportunities for dialogue wherein the field instructor can provide meaningful and constructive feedback for the student in reference to their learning, their performance, and their personal development (Cicco, 2014). Building a positive relationship based on open and respectful communication, including considerations for critical cultural consciousness, allows ease with debriefing and discussing concerns about the student's development and obtaining support when the student is faced with challenges in the practicum experience. With remote field instruction, communication is an even more vital aspect of the practicum experience and the field instructor-student relationship.

Student and field instructor may discuss what works for them in terms of feedback as well as to learn and grow professionally and personally.

ACTIVITY 5: REVIEW AND REFLECT

Students can review and consider implementing these suggestions for remote internships from Princeton University Career Development Office.

https://careerdevelopment.princeton.edu/sites/g/files/toruqf1041/files/media/how_to_make_the_most_of_a_virtual_internship_students_2.pdf

Learning Activities for Remote Field Practicums

Direct Practice Learning Opportunities in Remote Field Practicums

The learning objectives and activities for each individual field practicum will vary, depending on the placement's mandate and their provision of services. Each student and field instructor will need to consider remote learning activities relevant to the practicum requirements and the opportunities available in the field setting. Listed below are examples of possible learning activities that may be completed remotely:

- Orientation to placement: students can explore the agency website to become familiar with the mission, mandate, programs, policies, and structure. Students may participate in teleconferencing or videoconferencing to meet team members.

- Complete literature reviews on best practices for particular client groups or social issues.

- Network within the community and develop resources. For example, students may contact other service providers in local communities to create a resource of agency names, contacts, and a description of the services offered.

- Review ethical decision-making tools used in the field setting or write ethical guidelines for online engagements with clients, colleagues, and other service providers.

- Engage in online direct practice with individuals, families, and/or groups, based on agency guidelines, best practices, and relevant legislation.

- Participate in policy formulation or advocacy. For example, students may review laws, policies, and procedures impacting the population served by the agency. The student may be required to write a summary of the review, a policy brief, or draft guidelines for new policy.

- Engage in research activities. Examples include: needs assessment; program evaluation; literature reviews; development of research tools; data collection; data analysis; report writing.

- Provide remote case management and family support for child welfare and family resource centres (liaising with social workers to support clients virtually).

Field liaisons and field education coordinators can assist students and field instructors with further ideas for remote learning activities.

All remote learning is shaped by the particular agency context in a manner that assists students in situating that agency and population within the larger formal and informal social service and health care systems. The field instructor and their colleagues can identify viable learning activities and projects that are both significant for the agency and can provide important learning opportunities for students.

Clinical Practice Learning Opportunities in Remote Field Practicums

In recognition of the growth in remote mental health service delivery, the Mental Health Commission of Canada developed a toolkit: Mental Health Commission of Canada. (2018, September 18). *Toolkit for e-mental health implementation.*

Equity, Diversity and Inclusion in Remote Social Work Service Delivery and Learning

During COVID-19, we have become familiar with the expression "we may be in the same storm, but we are not in the same boat." This statement is a reflection on the deep social, economic, political, cultural, and health inequities experienced by many Canadians across cultures and societies that already existed but were highlighted by the pandemic (Gips, 2020).

When the Canadian Association for Social Work Education (CASWE), social work's accreditation body, made the historic decision to shift to remote placements and allowed for reduced practicum hours in the beginning of COVID-19 pandemic, field education staff rapidly implemented the directive and responded to the ensuing administrative and pedagogical implications (CASWE, 2020). While adjustments were made in the modalities and practice tools, there were also renewed calls for responsiveness to social inequities and racial injustices, particularly anti-Black, anti-Indigenous, and anti-Asian racism, which were further exposed during the pandemic.

In recognition of the significance of social justice, equity, and anti-racist approaches within the profession, CASWE's changes in its recent Educational Policies and Accreditation Standards (EPAS; 2021) added and strengthened these principles and related competencies as core learning objectives for social work education. EPAS 2021 defines equity as "the fair treatment, access, opportunity, and advancement for all people while at the same time striving to identify and eliminate barriers that have prevented the full participation of some groups" (CASWE, 2021, p. 19). Equity is achieved when barriers, biases, and obstacles that prevent equal access and opportunity to participate in society are eliminated.

Social workers are ethically bound to pursue social justice, act in the service of humanity, and respect human dignity (CASW, 2005). In thinking about service delivery and learning whether in remote or in-person environments, social workers need to consider how to prioritize equity, support diversity and embrace inclusion to impact future social work practice.

Case Study

Racial biases and microaggressions may be intentional or unintentional, delivered by individuals or embedded within systems, including in the systems in which social workers and the larger society operate. As a result, they can be difficult for field instructor and student to identify, express, and discuss. Below is a case that presents several opportunities for field instructor and student to identify microaggressions and biases and discuss strategies to address them in their relationship and practice.

War forced Leila and her family to flee her country of origin; they settled in Canada several years ago. Leila worked for a United Nations agency as a counsellor in a refugee camp prior to coming to Canada. She was advised that she needed to obtain the appropriate credentials to be able to work in a similar capacity in her new country. She decided to pursue a Master of Social Work degree and was in the process of looking for a field placement when the pandemic hit, requiring her to explore a remote practicum. Leila speaks English fluently, however, the language teacher at the settlement services told her that she had a "thick" accent. She found it difficult to find a placement and she began to question whether her name or the way she communicated affected the process. She and the field education staff at her university reached out to more than twenty agencies. Leila was called for an interview twice, but they did not result in a placement offers. Feedback received from the agencies indicated they decided to go with more "suitable" placement students. Leila realized it was difficult to find an agency and field instructor to supervise her practicum within a large urban area. Heavy social work caseloads and inadequate technological resources further limited some of the agencies' ability to support a remote practicum.

After a few months, Leila found a racialized field instructor, Melanie, who expressed a willingness to supervise her practicum within a social services agency that caters to children and families. They agreed to plan for a hybrid placement, starting remotely and transitioning to in-person when public health regulations allowed. The agency was in the process of setting up their online operations to serve clients. Melanie told Leila that her own manager, Trevor, expressed reservations about Melanie's ability to supervise Leila. Without directly expressing it, Melanie seemed to allude to racial microaggressions within the agency. The student and field instructor included learning objectives on critically examining the placement context and practice considerations from an equity and social justice lens.

Remote placements create concerns about students', field instructors', and clients' sense of safety and wellbeing, particularly in sharing experiences of racism and discrimination. Establishing caring and compassionate relationships is key to social work practice, but this can become challenging in remote environments where empathic engagement is diminished and non-verbal clues may be difficult to detect (Blakemore & Agllias, 2020). Field instructors may not be able to fully witness the learning process and may miss out on nonverbal communication (Sawrikar et al., 2015). While working relationships can be established online or in-person, the lack of non-verbal cues that express warmth, care, and empathy may impede relational practice (van Luitgarden & van der Tier, 2016). Safety can be enhanced by intentionally and deliberately taking time to establish good relationships between students, field instructors, and staff.

It can be important for racialized students to have access to online spaces to talk about equity, diversity and inclusion issues, race, and racism, to provide counternarratives and to offer and find resources (Eschmann, 2021). Eternity Martis, award-winning journalist and author of *They Said This Would Be Fun: Race, Campus Life and Growing Up* (2020) indicated that she was supported by her friends and on-campus peers and services when she experienced racism and sexual assault on campus many years ago. In the context of COVID-19 and remote learning, Martis (2020) acknowledges the importance of community, having a social experience, and being connected with a support system. Students are burned out due to COVID-19, remote learning, and social activism. Having allies and people who will listen and understand the impacts of internalized and external oppressions will make a difference (Martis, 2022).

Creating Equitable and Inclusive Virtual Spaces

Creating equitable and inclusive virtual spaces requires critical reflection on the foundational philosophies and theoretical frameworks that social workers and social service agencies adopt for service delivery or use in training social work students. Mullaly and West (2018) contend that many social work theories that underpin current social work interventions focus on maintaining the dominant culture or social order. This means that many social practice theories and intervention mechanisms may have produced and continue to sustain the systemic oppressions experienced by marginalized individuals and communities.

As face-to-face social work practices and interventions are increasingly shifting to remote spaces, the dominant worldviews and cultural expectations that discriminate or subjugate those who are in the minority can be reproduced in virtual forms and transferred to remote platforms. Students, with the support of their field instructor, need to consider the theoretical frameworks they are using in both face-to-face and remote service delivery to critically reflect on the ways they and the system they work within may continue to unknowingly oppress clients.

Technology, software, and platforms are designed, written, and tested primarily among people from dominant cultures and groups. It is important for students and field instructors to be mindful of not reproducing discrimination, marginalization, and oppression in virtual spaces (McInroy, 2019). Online microaggressions can and do occur frequently. Both field instructors and students are challenged to facilitate inclusive and decolonizing learning and service delivery, including engaging with racialized and marginalized colleagues in ways that respect their ways of being and knowing. Biased decision-making processes that could be both conscious and unconscious can lead to further inequities and disempowerment.

Azzopardi and McNeil (2016) describe the development of a critical cultural consciousness as an important aspect of working across differences and supporting equity and inclusion. Having evidence-based knowledge of colonization, discrimination, intersectionality, and neoliberal ideology, as well as choosing critical approaches grounded in ecological systems and strength-based orientation are important aspects of this critical cultural consciousness. They suggest that cultural empathy combined with linking personal experiences to larger social structures are important aspects of interventions. Finally, critical self-awareness is essential for the development of a critical cultural consciousness (Azzopardi & McNeill, 2016). Critical cultural consciousness requires individuals to consider how their own social identity and positionality, values, and biases impact their work and relationships and employing it can be beneficial for both students and field instructors.

As it relates to remote field learning, students and field instructors may consider and discuss with each other the following to develop a critical cultural consciousness and an equity mindset (adapted from Beasley et al., 2021).

- Are remote field activities, experiences, and reflections assisting students with active self-awareness opportunities?

- Has the implementation of online anti-racist field assignments and projects been considered? If so, what are the plans for implementation?

- How are concepts such as cultural humility, critical reflexivity, self-awareness, and self- regulation defined and operationalized within remote field practice and supervision?

- Does remote field education allow space to discuss the harms racialized social work students may experience in their field education experience and the profession? Does it allow space to discuss self-care practices related to this harm?

- Other than field evaluations, are there subsequent measures in place in remotely accessing the skill sets of diverse students?

Remote Field Education: Challenges and Future Considerations

The pandemic has fundamentally shifted social service delivery. The need for "social distancing" required agencies to quickly adapt to offering social work services via phone, email, and videoconferencing to a much larger degree than before the onset of COVID-19. Social service agencies have adapted to this new reality, albeit not without challenges and limitations. The shift to remote service delivery, while offering increased access to service for some, also has some disadvantages. Creating and maintaining trusting, empathic relationships with clients via phone or Zoom can be challenging (Banks et al., 2020). Some agencies have not been able to maintain the full spectrum of their service delivery, and some may be challenged to maintain both remote and in-person service delivery. As discussed above, ethical breaches are an ongoing risk due to the potential for failure of technology and the vulnerability of digital systems.

Social work education has also pivoted in this new reality. The national field education network harnessed their combined experiences, skills, and collaborative spirit to share resources and ideas to support the development of remote or hybrid practicums for social work students across Canada. Students who completed their field education in these types of practicums developed enhanced skills for remote service delivery as well as specific skills around overcoming adversity, adapting to rapid changes regarding technology, accessibility, instruction and service delivery format, and coping in a crisis. Many students appreciated the flexibility of remote placements, the opportunity to connect with agencies outside of their geographic location, and the increased opportunities to be involved in learning activities that fell outside of their regular practicum days (Allison, 2021; Mantulak, 2021).

However, remote practicums also create some challenges. Informal relationship-building opportunities with field instructors and other agency staff are more limited. Going for coffee and the casual discussions before a meeting or eating lunch with staff are examples of the informal experiences that a remote practicum does not offer. These relationship- and community-building activities in a traditional practicum setting contribute to a student's sense of belonging in the organizations they are placed in.

Delayed communication and lower productivity have also been identified as challenges in remote practicums (Allison, 2021). Where a student in a traditional placement might be able to pop by their field instructor's office to ask a question, remote practicum students need to wait for an email reply. Learning can sometimes be hindered because of this lag time. Screen fatigue from being in a full day Zoom meeting or long hours in front of a computer were also cited as barriers to productivity in learning (Allison, 2021).

Some students also expressed concerns about having the necessary skills and competencies for face-to-face social work practice when restrictions lifted after not completing an in-person practicum (Allison, 2021). Even in a clinical setting where students worked with clients remotely, students worried about the transferability of skills to a face-to-face environment (Allison, 2021). Although "being prepared for practice" is a common concern for many students upon graduation, this seemed to be exacerbated by remote practicums (Allison, 2021).

The Future of Remote Service Delivery and Practicums

Despite the challenges outlined above, remote service delivery, and thus remote social work learning and field practicums, will likely remain with us to some degree. Aligned with social work's ethic of "meeting people where they are at," remote service delivery and practicums allow for flexibility and accessibility for both clients and students. As agencies and schools of social work grapple with defining a "new normal" for work and education, they will need to consider the best ways to move forward. Schools of social work will need further research regarding best practices for remote learning and teaching. Further, there is a need to develop more effective evaluation methods for these types of practicums that maintain the competencies and standards expected of social work graduates. Additionally, relationships are at the heart of social work practice. Therefore, students and field instructors involved in remote learning and service delivery will need to deliberately and intentionally put time and effort into developing and sustaining caring relationships remotely. Actively making time for "connecting" with field instructors, other agency staff, and clients is crucial for success in this type of practicum.

Clarity of communication is more critical than ever when working and learning remotely. Ensuring that students have a clear plan for how to communicate with their field instructor and other agency staff and have discussed what methods of communicating are appropriate and ethical for various tasks is essential.

Equity, inclusion and diversity practices need to continue to be priorities for social workers and students in remote environments. Students as well as field instructors should be mindful of and discuss the ways in which their own diversity can be supported in their remote field experience. They also need to be aware of the ways in which remote service delivery can inadvertently reproduce discrimination and the subjugation of minorities. Student and graduate social workers must consciously use technology, methods and frameworks, some discussed here, that actively resist this. An example is selective use of remote meetings when an in-person meeting is a barrier or hardship. In other situations, an in-person meeting may be selected when it is the service-user's choice to facilitate communication or impact.

Although a return to more traditional in-person practicums is welcomed and preferred by many students, faculty, and agency partners, remote practicums will likely continue to be offered. While remote field learning has benefits, students and field instructors need to be critically aware of challenges and disadvantages. Students will need to have a good understanding of the technical competencies for remote learning and supervision, intentionally build effective relationships with their field instructor and service users, and strive to create safe, equitable, and ethical learning and practice environments. By doing so, social work students can effectively use remote field practicum opportunities to learn to effectively respond to the needs of individuals, families, groups, and communities and to advance social justice.

ACTIVITY 6: RECAP

As a helpful recap of the content of this chapter, the following has been provided to students and field instructors to consider and discuss before proceeding to the next chapter.

1. Name three skills and techniques important for building a relationship between student and field instructor when supervision is online.

2. Consider this scenario: A student was accepted for a placement in a rural-based agency. The agency is located within a geographic area where services to vulnerable populations are limited. However, the qualified social work supervisor is located in another rural site of the agency. A remote placement is considered. The field instructor, who has extensive practice experience, is not familiar with the use of technology in field instruction yet feels obligated to mentor the student and support the local community. How should the student approach this remote placement? What ethical dilemmas does this situation present? What steps needed to be taken in order to proceed?

3. What ethical issues need to be addressed in field instruction when a social worker and a student consider including a Google search of a client to gather information to complete their assessment?

4. List three projects or learning activities that can be remotely completed in a field practicum in your agency.

5. Dependent upon provincial Code of Ethics and Standards of Practice, student and field instructor can discuss strategies in a remote placement setting to ensure compliance with codes and standards.

6. Potential disadvantages of remote field education were discussed in this chapter. Student and field instructor might consider mitigating these disadvantages with forethought, research, and communication strategies.

REFERENCES

Allison, K. (2021). Remote field placements: Lessons learned at the UBC School of Social Work. *Perspectives: Newsmagazine of the BC Association of Social Workers, 43*(3), 14–15.

Azzopardi, C., & McNeill, T. (2016). From cultural competence to cultural consciousness: Transitioning to a critical approach to working across differences in social work. *Journal of Ethnic & Cultural Diversity in Social Work, 25*(4), 282–299. https://doi.org/10.1080/15313204.2016.1206494

Bambaeeroo, F., & Shokrpour, N. (2017). The impact of the teachers' non-verbal communication on success in teaching. *Journal of Advances in Medical Education and Professionalism, 5*(2), 51–59. https://pubmed.ncbi.nlm.nih.gov/28367460

Banks, S., Cai, T., de Jonge, E., Shears, J., Shum, M., Sobočan, A. M., Strom, K., Truell, R. Úriz, M. J., & Weinberg, M. (2020). *Ethical challenges for social workers during COVID-19: A global perspective.* International Federation of Social Work. https://www.ifsw.org/wp-content/uploads/2020/07/2020-06-30-Ethical-Challenges-Covid19-FINAL.pdf

Beasley, C. C., Singh, M. I., & Drechsler, K. (2021). Anti-racism and equity-mindedness in social work field education: A systematic review. *Journal of Ethnic & Cultural Diversity in Social Work, 31*(3-5), 1–13. https://doi.org/10.1080/15313204.2021.1991868

Blakemore, T., & Agllias, K. (2020). Social media, empathy and interpersonal skills: Social work students' reflections in the digital era. *Social Work Education, 39*(2), 200–213. https://doi.org/10.1080/02615479.2019.1619683

Canadian Association for Social Work Education (n.d.). *EPAS 2021 approved.* https://caswe-acfts.ca/epas-2021-approved/

Canadian Association of Social Workers (2024).). *CASW code of ethics, values and guiding principles 2024.* https://www.casw-acts.ca/en/casw-code-ethics-2024

———. *Standards of Practice.* https://www.casw-acts.ca/en/tags/standards-practice

———. (2011, May 6). *What is social work?* https://www.casw-acts.ca/en/what-social-work

———. (2020, March 18). *COVID-19 communication—Field education placements.* https://caswe-acfts.ca/covid-19-communication-field-education-placements/

Canadian Counselling and Psychotherapy Association. (2019). *Guidelines for uses of technology in counselling and psychotherapy.* https://www.ccpa-accp.ca/wp-content/uploads/2019/04/TISCGuidelines_Mar2019_EN.pdf

Cicco, G. (2014). Building effective supervisory relationships in the online counseling course: Faculty and student responsibilities. *I-manager's Journal on School Educational Technology, 10*(2), 1–8. https://files.eric.ed.gov/fulltext/EJ1097715.pdf

Council on Social Work Education. (2008). *Educational policy and accreditation standards.* Alexandria, VA: Author.

Eschmann, R. (2021). Digital Resistance: How online communication facilitates responses to racial microaggressions. *Sociology of Race and Ethnicity, 7*(2), 264–277. https://doi.org/10.1177/2332649220933307

Evanish, Jason. (n.d.) Lighthouse Blog. *7 essential tips for effective 1-on-1 meetings with your manager.* https://getlighthouse.com/blog/effective-1-on-1-meetings/.

Foley, G. N., & Gentile, J. P. (2010). Nonverbal communication in psychotherapy. *Psychiatry, (Edgmont), 7*(6), 38. https://pubmed.ncbi.nlm.nih.gov/20622944

Gips, D. (2020, October 29). The color of Covid-19: Disparate impacts, inequitable responses. Virtual town hall presented by the Skoll Foundation. https://skoll.org/session/the-color-of-covid-19/

Mantulak, A. P., Arundel, M. K., & Csiernik, R. (2021). A creative solution to the social work practicum amid a pandemic: The remote learning Plan. *Journal of Teaching in Social Work, 41*(5), 535–549.

Martis, E. (2020). *They said this would be fun: Race, campus life, and growing up.* McClelland & Stewart.

———. (2022, April 27). *Riding the wave of change.* Keynote address. 2022 Advisor Conference, University of Waterloo, ON, Canada.

Mast, M. (2007). On the importance of nonverbal communication in the physician-patient interaction. *Patient Education and Counseling, 67*(3), 315–318. https://doi.org/10.1016/j.pec.2007.03.005

McInroy, L. (3 May 2019). *Social work practice in a digital world: professional identities, ethics, and opportunities.* Guest Speaker Presentation. Annual General Meeting, Ontario Association of Social Workers, Toronto, ON.

Mullaly, R. P., & West, J. (2018). *Challenging oppression and confronting privilege: A critical approach to anti-oppressive and anti-privilege theory and practice* (3rd ed.). Oxford University Press.

National Association of Social Workers, Association of Social Work Boards, Council on Social Work Education, and Clinical Social Work Association. (2017). "NASW, ASWB, CSWE, and CSWA standards for technology in social work practice." https://www.socialworkers.org/includes/newIncludes/homepage/PRA-BRO-33617.TechStandards_FINAL_POSTING.pdf

Office of the Privacy Commissioner of Canada. (2019). PIPEDA in brief. https://www.priv.gc.ca/en/privacy-topics/privacy-laws-in-canada/the-personal-information-protection-and-electronic-documents-act-pipeda/pipeda_brief/

Reamer, F. G. (2013). *Social work practice in a digital ethical and risk-management challenges. CASW-ACTS.* https://www.casw-acts.ca/files/attachements/reamer-ethical_issues_-_electronic_digital-webcast_2013.pdf

Renison University College School of Social Work. (2013). *Social media policy.* https://uwaterloo.ca/school-of-social-work/social-media-policy

Sawrikar, P., Lenette, C., McDonald, D., & Fowler, J. (2015). Don't silence 'the dinosaurs': Keeping caution alive with regard to social work distance education. *Journal of Teaching in Social Work, 35*(4), 343–364. https://doi.org/10.1080/08841233.2015.1068262

Segal, J., Smith, M., Boose, G., & Jaffe, J. (2015). *Nonverbal communication and body language.* HelpGuide.org. https://www.helpguide.org/articles/relationships-communication/nonverbal-communication.htm

van de Luitgaarden, G., & van der Tier, M. (2018). Establishing working relationships in online social work. *Journal of Social Work, 18*(3), 307–325. https://doi.org/10.1177/1468017316654347

Van Sickle, C. (2014). *Practice notes: Professional and ethical: Communication technology practices and policies for a digital world.* https://www.ocswssw.org/wp-content/uploads/PN-Communication_Technology_Practices_Policies_for_Digital_World.pdf

Weinberg, M. (2020). Exacerbation of inequities during COVID-19: Ethical implications for social workers. *Canadian Social Work Review, 37*(2), 9–15. https://doi.org/10.7202/1075117ar

Weinberg, M., & Fine, M. (2020). Racisms and microaggressions in social work: The experience of racialized practitioners in Canada. *Journal of Ethnic & Cultural Diversity in Social Work, 31*(2), 96–107. https://doi.org/10.1080/15313204.2020.1839614

NOTES:

NOTES:

NOTES:

Integrating Research into Social Work Field Education – Beginning with your Learning Contract

Sheri M. McConnell and Melissa Noble

This chapter explores how social work students and field educators can include research and research activities in field practicums. We lay the foundation by exploring the importance of integrating research into field education, what we mean by research, student and social worker attitudes toward research, the integration of research into field practicums, and the inclusion of research in learning contracts. Next, we provide concrete examples of research-focused learning objectives and activities that can be integrated into Bachelor of Social Work (BSW) and Master of Social Work (MSW) learning contracts and evaluation forms, and links to learning contracts for research-based practicums and social work research internships. We conclude the chapter with a series of recommendations for integrating research and research activities into social work undergraduate and graduate field education, a list of resources, and discussion questions.

Our hope is that this chapter generates discussion about and new ideas for integrating research into field education. We want to open the door for students to add their own research-based learning objectives and activities to their field practicum learning contracts. We also want to encourage field educators to expand their conceptualization of field education to include research and, in doing so, to integrate research and research activities into social work field manuals, learning contracts, and evaluations.

The Importance of Integrating Research into Social Work Field Practicums

Recognition of the importance of engaging in and understanding research has increased among social workers, particularly those who actively engage in evidence-informed practice. Possessing the knowledge and ability to understand and practice research is a fundamental expectation of professional social workers. The Canadian Association of Social Workers - l'Association canadienne des travailleuses et travailleurs sociaux (CASW-ACTS) (2005) Guidelines for Ethical Practice outlines the ethical responsibilities of social workers engaged in research, including the necessity to "observe the conventions of ethical scholarly inquiry when engaged in study and research" (section 6.1.2) and to "educate themselves, their students, and their colleagues about responsible research practices" (section 6.1.1). For example, practicing social workers may engage in research to evaluate practices, programs, or policies; conduct individual or community needs assessments; and identify evidence-informed practices reported in academic literature.

Yet it can be challenging through course work alone to develop applied research skills and to nurture a meaningful relationship between research and practice. "Advocates of experiential learning posit that hands-on activities are the most effective way of helping students not only master content and skills but also navigate the socialization process" (Svoboda et al., 2013, p. 663). As such, it is essential that classroom learning is paired with experiential learning, wherein students can develop, enhance, and integrate research skills into their practice (Cameron & Este, 2008; Chakradhar, 2018; Chilvers et al., 2012; Holbrook & Chen, 2017; Maidment et al., 2011; Rubin et al., 2010; Svoboda et al., 2013; Whipple et al., 2015; Wulf-Andersen et al., 2013). Given that field education is the cornerstone of social work education, wherein social work values, knowledge, and skills are integrated into real work situations through applied learning, practice, and supervision and mentoring, BSW and MSW field practicums provide a perfect fit for research activities and/or projects. In a systematic review of research placements for students in a variety of professional degrees, Zuchowski et al. (2020) advocated that "research placements could become an integral and valued part of the field education experience for all students" (p. 60).

Both social work students and practitioners (including field instructors) may be reluctant to engage in research projects and activities (Cameron & Este, 2008; Chakradhar, 2018; Chilvers et al., 2012; Holbrook & Chen, 2017; Maidment et al., 2011; Neden et al., 2018; Zuchowski et al., 2020). As such, it is essential that students and field educators are encouraged and supported to integrate practice research and learning in a manner that nurtures the development and application of research values, knowledge, and skills throughout BSW and MSW field practicums. Doing so necessitates exploring and using consistent and clear language around practice research, paired with a shared understanding of what constitutes research (including research projects, activities, and skills), and how research can be integrated into practice opportunities in social work field education. This integration can be achieved in a variety of ways, and range of research activities can be included in direct practice and community field practicums, or students can engage in research-focused placements.

What Do We Mean By "Research"?

"Research is the ultimate telling of a story; the goal of all research is to shed light on that which previously remained in the dark" (Phillips et al., 2012, p. 785).

In reviewing field education materials on the websites of CASWE-ACFTS accredited social work education programs, it quickly becomes apparent that there is a lack of clarity as to what constitutes "research" and "research activities." Research components, skills, or activities, including literature reviews, assessments, and focus groups were not always identified as "research." As such, it is important to define and describe "research," as understood in the context of this chapter.

The Tri-Council Policy Statement: Ethical Conduct for Research Involving Humans (Secretariat on Responsible Conduct of Research, 2018) provides a clear and succinct definition of research.

> The scope of research is vast . . . Research involving humans ranges widely, including attempts to understand the broad sweep of history, the workings of the human body and the body politic, the nature of human interactions and the impact of nature on humans… Research is defined as an undertaking intended to extend knowledge through a disciplined inquiry or systematic investigation (Chapter 1).

In contrast, Chapter 6 of this book, Sally St. George and Daniel Wulff define "Research As Daily Practice" as involving social work practice itself as a research process. Therefore, "doing practice is doing research." They explain that the steps involved in doing research coincide with the steps of doing practice, which places social workers and other practitioners at the center of studying their own work within their practice skill sets. This alternative to learning discrete research skills or activities fundamentally alters social workers' approach to research and provides another way of integrating research into field education.

Within the context of this chapter, the term "research" describes independent or supervised research projects and research-focused field practicums. "Research skills" and "research activities" refer to elements of research that are undertaken either as components of a larger research project or outside of the scope of a formal research project, and include activities related to research planning, implementation, and reporting. As such, a wide range of research activities and skills can be included in direct practice or community field practicums, including, but not limited to:

- research planning: designing research projects, writing research proposals, writing ethics proposals and reviews, designing research forms and data collection tools, creating databases, gathering resources, conducting literature reviews, conducting jurisdictional scans, and reviewing policies;
- research implementation: collecting data (e.g., through surveys, interviews, focus groups, community meetings), transcribing interviews, analyzing documents, entering data, analyzing data; and
- research reporting: preparing and presenting reports, articles, presentations, workshops, trainings, and other means of knowledge exchange and dissemination.

Practice research may involve needs assessments, community consultations, policy reviews, program evaluations, and more. Research and research activities may involve qualitative, quantitative, mixed methods, or action methods, and can be grounded in a multitude of theoretical orientations.

Student and Social Worker Attitudes Toward Research

What social work students believe and how they feel about research fundamentally impact their experience as learners and their development as active researchers. Social work student attitudes towards research are dominated by ambivalence, anxiety, discomfort, and disinterest (Adam et al., 2004; Cameron & Este, 2008; Chakradhar, 2018; Chilvers et al., 2012; Holbrook & Chen, 2017; MacIntyre & Paul, 2013; Neden et al., 2018; Vallet, 2019; Zuchowski et al., 2020). "Research is the curricular content area that evokes the greatest amount of anxiety and the least sense of confidence among social work students" (Adam et al., 2004, p. 2). Given the range of negative feelings and attitudes experienced by students, it is no surprise that "making the step from education and practice into research is the key challenge for many students" (Phillips et al., 2012, p. 788).

This uneasy relationship between social work students and their engagement in research is fueled by a professional climate in which the importance of research and evidence-informed practice is emphasized, yet most social workers feel uncomfortable and inadequately prepared to understand or engage in research (Cameron & Este, 2008; Chakradhar, 2018; Chaudet, 2011; Chilvers et al., 2012; Holbrook & Chen, 2017; Maidment et al., 2011; Neden et al., 2018). "Despite emphasis from professional organizations and available empirical tools to facilitate research use, social work students and practitioners remain reluctant to embrace research in practice; they seem to approach research with trepidation at best and absolute aversion at worst" (Adam et al., 2004, p. 4).

Student aversion to engaging in research carries into the profession where social work practitioners often lack the skills and motivation to incorporate research into their practice (Adam et al., 2004; Cameron & Este, 2008; Chilvers et al., 2012; Maidment et al., 2011; MacIntyre & Paul, 2013; Zuchowski et al., 2020). Negative attitudes and perceptions about research, coupled with the difficulty of comprehending the connection between research and practice (Cameron & Este, 2008; Neden et al., 2018) result in students and practitioners who are less likely to integrate research into practice.

Practicing social workers, in their roles as field instructors and mentors, may be reticent to help students integrate research activities and projects into field education learning opportunities (Chilvers et al., 2012; Maidment et al., 2011; Zuchowski et al., 2020), and may feel unprepared to engage in applied research, even when urged to do so by their professional associations and regulators (Chaudet, 2011). When social workers are uncomfortable integrating research into their practice, the pool of potential mentors and educators able to engage student learners is limited. This lack of research mentorship perpetuates the disconnection between research and practice. This disconnection necessitates the exploration of alternative methods of engaging students in research, and in providing tools and resources to alleviate the professional discomfort experienced by some social workers in integrating research into their practice and in mentoring students in research activities and projects.

Integrating Research into Field Practicums

Research is an essential component in social work because it furthers our understanding of the context in which we work, and a means to foster the development of the professional body of knowledge for social work and the provision of optimal care and service to clients (Cameron & Este, 2008, p. 404). Further, "the hands-on experience of researching practice issues 'brings research alive' for students" (MacIntyre & Paul, 2013, p. 694). As such, it is essential to provide students with a wide range of opportunities to engage in practice research, including through integrating research into field practicums and other experiential learning (Baralonga, 2018; Cameron & Este, 2008; Chakradhar, 2018; Chilvers et al., 2012; Fraga-Levivier & Tourrilhes, 2012; Hewson et al., 2010; Holbrook & Chen, 2017; Maidment et al., 2011; Rubin et al., 2010; Svoboda et al., 2013; Tourrilhes, 2018; Vallet, 2019; Walsh et al., 2019; Whipple et al., 2015; Wulf-Andersen et al., 2013; Zuchowski et al., 2020).

Rubin et al. (2010) explain that "there is an expectation that students bring some knowledge from their undergraduate study that they can build on through their graduate study" (p. 52). As such, if BSW students are not exposed to and engaged in applied practice research, they are not likely to possess the foundational knowledge and skills to engage in research as graduate students. This lack of foundational knowledge and skills will inhibit them as social workers, particularly in their role as field instructors, from engaging with and mentoring students in practice research in field practicums.

Effective engagement in research and research activities in field practicums requires "the engagement of host agencies, field educators, students, and academic staff in a collaborative process focused on developing research knowledge and skills" (Chilvers et al., 2012, p. 36). Student success is facilitated by:

- adequate preparation (e.g., tutorials for students and field instructors),
- availability of community-based or university-based research projects,
- goodness of fit between the practicum and the research project (e.g., clear research questions, achievable tasks, realistic timelines),
- material support for students (e.g., computers, software, research tools),
- professional support for students (e.g., peer, field instructor, academic),
- collaborative knowledge production, and
- regular and timely supervision and evaluation

    (Cameron & Este, 2008; Chilvers et al., 2012; Flanagan & Wilson, 2018; Hewson et al., 2010; Maidment et al., 2011; Neden et al., 2018; Walsh et al., 2019; Whipple et al., 2015; Wulf-Andersen et al., 2013; Zuchowski et al., 2020).

The integration of research into field education can be achieved in a variety of ways, including integrating research activities into traditional direct practice or community-based field practicums, or providing research-focused placements. Hewson et al. (2010) and Walsh et al. (2019)

describe research-based field practicums, wherein the primary objectives are to provide opportunities to:

- develop a range of research knowledge and skills,
- integrate cognitive, affective, relational, and experiential learning,
- challenge negative stereotypes about research,
- generate passion and excitement for practice research,
- integrate research theory and methods with social work practice,
- experience community-based research, and
- prepare students to integrate research into their future practice as social workers.

In addition to fulfilling, in various degrees, the above-noted objectives, students who participated in these research-focused placements noted improvement in their skills in writing, interviewing, data collection and analysis, project management, and preparing and delivering presentations (Hewson et al., 2010; Walsh et al., 2019). They also described building stronger resumes, improving their access to graduate education, and developing marketable skills for their future careers (Hewson et al., 2010; Walsh et al., 2019).

Whether integrating research into field practicums or engaging in research-focused placements, students are presented opportunities to develop confidence and competence in research skills, and draw links between research and practice (Baralonga, 2018; Chilvers et al., 2012; Fraga-Levivier & Tourrilhes, 2012; Hewson et al., 2010; Holbrook & Chen, 2017; Maidment et al., 2011; Neden et al., 2018; Vallet, 2019; Walsh et al., 2019; Zuchowski et al., 2020). Application of research concepts to the field practicum setting can strengthen students' comprehension of course content as well as deepen their understanding of the field agency context. "Ultimately, these approaches have the potential to enhance the connection between research and practice" (Holbrook & Chen, 2017, p. 72). In bridging this gap between practice and research, students identified a wide range of learning emerging from the integration of research activity into clinical practice, including learning how evidence can be influential as a conduit for introducing change to an organisation and how organisational culture can limit that potential (Neden et al., 2018, p. 10).

Integrating research into field practicums (and other forms of experiential learning) positively improves students' relationship with research and encourages future engagement in research (Chakradhar, 2018; Chilvers et al., 2012; Hewson et al., 2010; Holbrook & Chen, 2017; Maidment et al., 2012; Neden et al., 2018; Walsh et al., 2019; Whipple et al., 2015; Zuchowski et al., 2020). In their examination of an initiative to teach social work research through student-community partnerships, Chakradhar (2018) reports that "the shift from fear and bewilderment to relief and excitement in the learning and skill-building accomplished by the students, as well as a sense of empowerment in being able to empower agencies, was evident" (p. 438). Students participating in field practicums that include research and research activities report positive learning experiences and deepened engagement through experiential learning about research.

This results in students who are capable of dynamic social work practice (Baralonga, 2018; Fraga-Levivier & Tourrilhes, 2012; Hewson et al., 2010; Walsh et al., 2019). Further, students who engage in research activities in their practicums are more likely to be engaged in research as social workers (Chilvers et al., 2012; Svoboda et al., 2013) and to apply critical thinking skills in their practice (Tourrilhes, 2018).

Integrating Research into Field Education Learning Contracts

"In general, the learning contract has been used to specify student activities in the field, record relevant learning objectives, and serve as a basis for evaluation" (Boitel & Fromm, 2014, p. 614). The construction of learning contracts is a collaborative process between students, field instructors, agency mentors (where there is no social worker on site), and field liaisons (the connection between the social work education program and the field agency) (Molina et al., 2018). In Canada, service users generally are not involved in the development of learning contracts. The content of learning contracts and the process of developing them varies significantly, according to the social work program, the field practicums learning goals and objectives, the field agency, the field instructor, and student learning goals (Boitel & Fromm, 2014). The structure of learning contracts exists along a continuum, ranging from free form to very prescriptive (Bone, 2014).

Succinctly, "a learning contract is about learning through action" (Bone, 2014, p. 115). Learning contracts have proven to be one of the best ways to encourage an active approach to learning and development, and to introduce students to the research process. It is essential that students take an active role in diagnosing their learning needs and planning how to fulfil them (Bone, 2014, p. 122). However, students cannot learn that which is neither available nor visible. It is challenging for students to contemplate integrating research activities into their field practicums when research knowledge and skills are non-existent in learning objectives and activities within learning contracts. This is true whether learning contracts are entirely free form, highly prescriptive, or somewhere in between. Omitting research activities from learning contracts contributes to student perceptions of "research activities as extra work or disconnected from 'real' social work skills that would be required to demonstrate competence" (Chilvers et al., 2012, p. 35). It is essential that learning contracts and evaluation forms clearly connect research tasks to the practicum assessment process, that students and field educators understand that connection, and that the assessment process is applied seamlessly to research-focused practicums and field practicums involving research activities (Chilvers et al., 2012).

Poon et al. (2020), as part of a Transforming the Field Education Landscape project (TFEL) student research team, noted the dearth of literature addressing the integration of research into social work learning contracts. In response to this scant literature, they completed eleven guiding consultations, with eight BSW and three MSW TFEL student researchers, in order to gain a more fulsome understanding of student experiences in research-based practicums and their integration of research into field learning contracts. They found that students experienced their learning contracts as "restrictive and rigid" (p. 2) and that they struggled to integrate research into existing learning contracts. Students indicated that they could not have integrated research into their learning contracts without collaboration, group supervision, and the guidance and support of their field instructor, who had extensive experience in both research and field education. As evidenced by Poon et al. (2020), there is a need to build capacity with field instructors, field education coordinators, and faculty involved in field education to adopt a research-mindedness approach in their work with students.

How to Include Research and Research Activities in Field Practicums

The following sections provide practical, concrete examples of how to include research and research activities in field practicums by integrating research-focused learning objectives and activities into BSW and MSW learning contracts and evaluation forms, and by designing research-based field practicums. Examples of learning contracts, objectives, and activities are drawn from the websites of anglophone CASWE-ACFTS accredited social work programs. As such, they provide a "snapshot in time" of the integration of research activities and projects into field education manuals, learning contracts, and evaluation forms on social work education program websites.

How social work education programs communicate information about practice research in field education to students, including via websites and field manuals and forms, significantly impacts students' feelings about, attitudes toward, perceptions of, and willingness to engage in research. If research and research activities are not visible as learning opportunities in field education materials, students may not be aware of or encouraged to include research projects or activities among their field practicum learning opportunities. The data collected for this chapter reflects the websites of CASWE-ACFTS accredited anglophone BSW and MSW programs at a particular moment in time. Not all university websites provide comprehensive or complete information about their social work programs or about field education, including field education manuals, learning contracts, and evaluation forms.

Research Activities and Skills as Learning Objectives

Next are a variety of learning objectives from field education manuals, learning contracts, and evaluation forms available on the websites of anglophone CASWE-ACFTS accredited social work programs (sorted alphabetically by university). Field educators, field instructors, and students can incorporate these learning objectives, which focus on research skills and activities, into BSW and MSW field education learning contracts. By doing so, and with the support of the field instructor and agency, students can engage in concrete learning opportunities to develop and enhance research values, knowledge, and skills.

Examples of BSW Learning Objectives

CARLETON UNIVERSITY, BSW FIELD MANUAL

- "Demonstrates entry-level practice competence in direct intervention with individuals, families, groups, and communities and/or research, social administration, and policy" (p. 17).

- "To describe the basic principles of social work research and importance for social work practice and critically evaluate and apply research findings" (p. 17).

- "To identify the research and policy issues that affect practice" (p. 18).
- "To review professional literature and use research methods to inform practice" (p. 20).
- "To identify research questions and policy issues that emerge from practice" (p. 20).

KINGS UNIVERSITY COLLEGE, BSW FIELD MANUAL

- "Understands the role of research in Social Work practice" (p. 18).
- "Able to describe the purpose of the research and identify its potential contribution to Social Work practice, policy, or program development" (p. 18).
- "Able to describe the project methodology, identify design limitations, and be able to appropriately comment on the impact of these limitations to knowledge creation" (p. 18).
- "Able to conduct or demonstrate ability to carry out at least one particular activity related to a research project, and be able to provide a written summary of their task and its role in the research process" (p. 18).

MCMASTER UNIVERSITY, BSW FIELD MANUAL

- "Conceptual = relates to ideas, theory, knowledge, socio-political analysis, policy, research issues" (p. 6).
- "Integration of Macro Analysis/Skills = student is involved in research and/ or program evaluation – definition of research questions, research design, and methodology are thoughtfully completed" (p. 6).

ST. THOMAS UNIVERSITY, BSW FIELD MANUAL

- "The ability to understand the use of research in practice" (p. 24).

TORONTO METROPOLITAN UNIVERSITY, BSW FIELD MANUAL

- "Contribution to initiatives/strategies/research that promote social policy change and the well-being of people who experience marginalization/lack of access/ exclusion" (p. 21).
- "To demonstrate the use of research, policy, advocacy, and mobilization in strategic and transformative change" (p. 30).

UNIVERSITY OF CALGARY, BSW FIELD MANUAL

- "Use the CASW Code of Ethics and ACSW Standards of Practice to guide practice, including: to develop professional relationships and demonstrate respect for clients, research participants, colleagues, administrative personnel, and other stakeholders" (p. 40).

- "Perform generalist practice roles across settings and populations (resource developer, advocate, educator, clinician, consultant, broker, researcher, project leader, etc.)" (p. 40).

- "Articulate how various forms of knowledge (e.g., scientific, intuitive, experiential) and different kinds of research methods (e.g., qualitative, quantitative, participatory) contribute to social work knowledge and practice" (p. 40).

UNIVERSITY OF WINDSOR, BSW FIELD MANUAL

- "Complete a literature review/web search to determine social, economic and political factors affecting client system" (p. 78).

Examples of MSW Learning Objectives

CARLETON UNIVERSITY, MSW FIELD MANUAL

- "Apply findings of social work research and knowledge from other disciplines to advance professional practice, policy development, research, and service provision" (p. 16).

- "Demonstrate advanced practice knowledge and skills in specialized direct intervention with individuals, families, groups, and communities and/or research, social administration, and policy" (p. 16).

- "Identify opportunities for further inquiry stimulated by social work practice and conceptualize/develop research projects that contribute to the body of knowledge surrounding emerging and/or persistent questions in policy analysis and direct intervention" (p. 16).

- "To identify and begin to challenge the research and policy issues and structures that affect practice" (p. 19).

- "To review professional literature and use research methods to inform practice and identify avenues for new knowledge creation" (p. 21).

- "To identify research questions and policy issues that emerge from practice and contribute to new knowledge creation where possible" (p. 21).

KINGS UNIVERSITY COLLEGE, MSW FIELD MANUAL

- "To enhance research skill and increase competency in the development of practice skills which are evidenced-based" (p. 27).

MCGILL UNIVERSITY, MSW FIELD EVALUATION FORM

- "Appreciates and navigates the complexities of applying research, theory, and policy to practice and visa versa."

UNIVERSITY OF BRITISH COLUMBIA, OKANAGAN CAMPUS, MSW FIELD MANUAL

- "Value the role of scholarship and develop the capability to undertake practice related research" (p. 8).
- "Engage in research-informed practice and practice-informed research" (p. 8).

UNIVERSITY OF CALGARY, MSW FIELD MANUAL

- "Learners understand and appreciate different ways of knowing, and effectively use or apply research to guide practice. Learners will be able to:
  - ☐ Appreciate the significance of world-view on people's lives, particularly in the clinical setting.
  - ☐ Critically reflect on the role of research in developing and informing practice.
  - ☐ Identify a variety of research approaches (e.g., qualitative, quantitative, appreciative, Indigenous).
  - ☐ Evaluate research studies and apply results appropriately to clinical practice.
  - ☐ Evaluate their own practice interventions.
  - ☐ Engage in continuous practices of accountability with respect to service provision" (pp. 42-43).
- "Apply leadership theories and research skills to guide practice" (p. 44).
- "Perform complex international/community development roles that are transferable across settings and populations (e.g., facilitator, advocate, educator, consultant, resource developer, researcher)" (p. 46).
- "Incorporate research, evaluation, and community feedback into practice" (p. 47).

YORK UNIVERSITY, MSW FIELD MANUAL

- "Develops, identifies skills which are relevant and important for a successful placement at the organization, such as policy, community development, research, direct practice, advocacy, and program development" (p. 4).

Examples of Research Activities and Skills

KINGS UNIVERSITY COLLEGE, BSW FIELD MANUAL

"Practice Skills include:

- Social and Policy Development

  ☐ to conduct independent research to support a needed aspect of policy development and submit a written document that is useful to policy developers"

- Program Planning

  ☐ able to conduct independent research to support a needed aspect of program development and submit a written document that is useful to program developers (depending on the stage of program development)" (p. 17).

MEMORIAL UNIVERSITY, BSW FIELD MANUAL

"Research activities can be included as part of intervention strategies, such as:

- assessment/risk assessment
- program/event evaluation
- community analysis
- policy analysis, development, and management
- issue analysis
- financial resource development
- resource development
- needs assessment" (section 1.6).

"Field settings engaged in work with individuals, families, groups:

- students engage in at least one project (community development, policy analysis, research, program development, committee work). The project may also inform the basis of the student's verbal presentation" (section 2.6.2a/b).

UNIVERSITY OF WINDSOR, BSW FIELD MANUAL

"There are several ways that students can engage in research or research tasks:

- student driven research projects
- existing agency research projects
- program assessment or evaluation tasks that might meet the definition of research
- systematic data collected directly from individuals (internal or external) or groups that could meet the definition of research" (pp. 51-52).

WILFRID LAURIER, BSW MANUAL
"Learning goals and practice areas include:

- Implementing strategies, methods, practices:
  - ☐ apply these interventions, including the following skills: empathy, active listening, support, empowering, focusing, tuning into non-verbal communication, problem-solving, effective use of resources, referral, advocacy, negotiating, consulting, program development, policy analysis, research techniques, mediating, facilitating, motivating, networking

- Evaluating:
  - ☐ contribute to agency evaluative research projects where feasible (e.g., program evaluation)" (pp. 22-23).

Examples of Research-Focused Field Practicums and Social Work Research Internships

As demonstrated above, research can be integrated into the learning contracts of direct practice or community field practicums by incorporating research-based learning objectives and activities. Field practicums also can provide opportunities to engage more deeply in research through research-focused practicums and other research internships.

Examples of BSW Research-Focused Field Practicums

LAKEHEAD UNIVERSITY
BSW students may complete "a macro, community development, or research focused field practicum" (p. 89).

ST THOMAS UNIVERSITY (STU)
STU has designed a STU Progressive (Social Action) Field Model in which BSW students engage in research (among other field activities). Students participate in an initiative or project related to social issues (e.g., bullying, homelessness, homophobia, poverty, racism, violence against women).

THE UNIVERSITY OF VICTORIA
"Experienced students may embark on a variety of senior practicum activities, for example:

- Community development work for a new community resource.
- Teaching at a community college in a Social Service Worker program.
- Revitalizing a branch of your local Social Work professional organization
- Developing workshops and training fellow social workers.
- Working in policy and administration, planning and research" (section 2.3).

"Students in their fourth year practicum may consider a research practicum within a field agency. They should also ensure that someone in the agency will be able to continue with the research after the practicum is completed. Unless the student has a significant research background, the current UVic School of Social Work research course will be considered a pre-requisite for a research-based practicum" (section 2.3).

Examples of MSW Research-Focused Field Practicums and Research Internships

MEMORIAL UNIVERSITY

Memorial University requires that MSW students complete a field practicum plus either a Pathway Scholarship project or a thesis. As such, students in their MSW field practicum are not permitted to engage in research per se, however, they can engage in research activities. The MSW Pathway provides an opportunity to pursue a specific, concentrated, specialized, or expert area of practice, research, scholarly work, or career-related pursuits – and culminates in a tangible, innovative, and creative scholarly product.

UNIVERSITY OF TORONTO

The University of Toronto facilitates a research-focused practicum (indirect practice learning contract) and the development of research competencies as part of a practicum (mixed practice learning contract).

YORK UNIVERSITY

York University offers the choice between a research paper and a field practicum. The practicum provides experiential learning, while the practice-based research paper encourages theoretical and conceptual exploration of student areas of interest. During their practicum, students may engage in a research-focused learning experience.

Recommendations for Integrating Research into Social Work Field Education

It is crucial to develop, enhance, support, and make visible opportunities to engage in research activities and projects in both BSW and MSW field practicums. Our recommendations for integrating research and research activities into BSW and MSW field practicum learning contracts are generated from a broad review of websites of CASWE-ACFTS accredited social work education programs and relevant literature. We recommend that social work education programs and field educators do the following:

- Integrate research activities and projects into BSW and MSW field practicums;

- Incorporate research activities and skills into learning objectives in field manuals, learning contracts, and evaluation forms;

- Design research activities and projects in partnership with field agencies, at a level consistent with student learning, to develop and enhance research values, knowledge, and skills in students as well as benefit field agencies;

- Develop and use consistent and clear language to describe practice research;

- Develop and integrate a shared understanding of what constitutes research (including research projects, project components, activities, and skills);

- Clearly and consistently communicate (including via program websites, field education manuals and forms, field seminars) to BSW and MSW students the value of practice research and the availability of applied research learning opportunities in BSW and MSW field practicums;

- Encourage, support, and mentor field instructors to integrate practice research and learning into BSW and MSW field practicums in a manner that nurtures the development and application of research values, knowledge, and skills; and

- Develop, implement, and support a range of opportunities for students to integrate research into practice in BSW and MSW programs, such as incorporating research into direct practice and community field practicums, conducting research-focused field practicums, holding researching internships, implementing research projects, engaging in experiential learning, and practicing community engagement (McConnell et al., 2023).

Resources for Integrating Research and Research Activities into Field Practicums

Annotated Bibliography: *Practice Research in Social Work Field Education*. https://tfelproject.com/2021/06/16/annotated-bibliography-practice-research-in-social-work/

Annotated Bibliography: *Research-Based Practicum in Social Work Field Education*. https://tfelproject.com/2021/06/16/annotated-bibliography-research-based-practicum/

Infographic: *Integrating Practice Research into Social Work Field Education*. https://tfelproject.com/2021/08/30/infographic-integrating-practice-research-into-social-work-field-education/

Publication: *Integrating Practice Research into Social Work Field Education*. https://tfelproject.com/2021/06/19/report-integrating-practice-research-into-social-work-field-education/

Webinar: *Integrating Practice Research into Social Work Field Education*. (CASWE-ACFTS conference 2021) https://tfelproject.com/2021/06/03/webinar-integrating-practice-research-into-social-work-field-education/

Webinar: *Practice Research Module in Field Education*. https://tfelproject.com/2020/07/15/webinar-practice-research-module-in-field-education/

Workshop: *Models for Integrating Research and Practice*. (Virtual Field Summit 2020) https://tfelproject.com/2020/07/15/workshop-models-for-integrating-research-and-practice/

ACTIVITY

Students and field educators are invited to reflect upon and discuss the following questions.

These discussions could occur during field preparation seminars, in initial meetings between field instructors and students, between students as they complete their learning contracts, during field integration seminars, or during field instruction sessions. Discussions amongst field education coordinators and field instructors could occur during field instructor trainings and workshops, field instructor orientation, or other field education gatherings.

1. What are your feelings about and experience with research?

2. Why is important for social work students and practitioners to learn about research and engage in research activities?

3. Why does the goodness of fit between research and field practicums matter to research projects?

4. What concrete steps could you take to integrate research and research activities into your field practicum?

5. What kinds of research might be beneficial to your past, current, or future field agency and the people they serve?

REFERENCES

Adam, N., Zosky, D. L., & Unrau, Y. A. (2004). Improving the research climate in social work curricula: Clarifying learning expectations across BSW and MSW research courses. *Journal of Teaching in Social Work, 24*(3/4), 1–18. https://doi.org/10.1300/J067v24n03_01

Baralonga, L. (2018). Mettre en travail les représentations ethno-raciales par la recherche-intervention: le cas de la formation en travail social. *Connexions, 2*, 191–202. https://www.cairn.info/revue-connexions-2018-2-page-191.htm

Boitel, C. R., & Fromm, L. R. (2014). Defining signature pedagogy in social work education: Learning theory and the learning contract. *Journal of Social Work Education, 50*(4), 608–622. https://doi.org/10.1080/10437797.2014.947161

Bone, Z. (2014). Using a learning contract to introduce undergraduates to research projects. *Electronic Journal of Business Research Methods, 12*(2), 115–123. https://academic-publishing.org/index.php/ejbrm/article/view/1321

Cameron, P. J., & Este, D. C. (2008) Engaging students in social work research education. *Social Work Education, 27*(4), 390–406. https://doi.org/10.1080/02615470701380006

The Canadian Association of Social Workers - l'Association canadienne des travailleuses et travailleurs sociaux (CASW–ACFTS). (2005). *Guidelines for ethical practice.* Canadian Association of Social Workers. https://www.casw-acts.ca/files/documents/casw_guidelines_for_ethical_practice.pdf

Chakradhar, K. (2018). Forging and sustaining research-minded professionals: Teaching undergraduate research through student-community partnerships. *Social Work Education, 37*(4), 428–441. https://doi.org/10.1080/02615479.2017.1420769

Chaudet, V. (2011). L'instrumentation des formateurs de terrain en travail social: quelle formation aux démarches de recherche? Fonctions et enjeux des outils et dispositifs pour la formation, l'éducation et la prévention. *Fonctions et enjeux des outils et dispositifs pour la formation, l'éducation et la prevention,* 159–166. https://recherche.uco.fr/publication/ID-UCO-8917

Chilvers, D., Maidment, J., & Crichton-Hill, Y. (2012). Promoting learning and teaching about research through collaborative work integrated learning: Implications for students, agencies, and practitioners. In M. Campbell (Ed.), *Collaborative education: Investing in the future—Proceedings of the 2012 ACEN National Conference*, pp. 31–36.

Flanagan, N., & Wilson, E. (2018). What makes a good placement? Findings of a social work student-to-student research study. *Social Work Education, 37*(5), 565–580. https://doi.org/10.1080/02615479.2018.1450373

Fraga-Levivier, A. P. V., & Tourrilhes, C. (2012). La recherche-action comme cadre de formation en travail social. *Pensée Plurielle, 2*, 243–253. https://www.cairn.info/revue-pensee-plurielle-2012-2-page-243.htm

Hewson, J., Walsh, C. A., & Bradshaw, C. (2010). Enhancing social work research education through research field placements. *Contemporary Issues in Education Research, 3*(9), 7–15. https://doi.org/10.19030/cier.v3i9.230

Holbrook, A. M., & Chen, W. Y. (2017). Learning by doing: An experiential approach to program evaluation. *Social Work Education, 36*(1), 62–74. https://doi.org/10.1080/02615479.2016.1266322

Maidment, J., Chilvers, D., Crichton-Hill, Y., & Meadows-Taurua, K. (2011). Promoting research literacy during the social work practicum. *Aotearoa New Zealand Social Work Review, 23*(4), 3–13. https://search.informit.org/doi/abs/10.3316/INFORMIT.877161049909248

MacIntyre, G., & Paul, S. (2013). Teaching research in social work: Capacity and challenge. *British Journal of Social Work, 43*(1), 685–702. https://doi.org/10.1093/bjsw/bcs010

McConnell, S. M., Noble, M., Hanley, J., Finley-Roy, V., & Drolet, J. (2023). Integrating practice research into social work field education. *Journal of Teaching in Social Work, 43*(1), 1-19. https://doi.org/10.1080/08841233.2022.2147259

Molina, V., Molina-Moore, T., Smith, M. G., & Pratt, F. E. (2018). Bridging education and practice with a competency-based learning contract. *Journal of Teaching in Social Work, 38*(1), 18–27. https://doi.org/10.1080/08841233.2017.1407387

Neden, J., Boddy, J., Davies, B., Hunt, S., Young, S., & Wooler, S. (2018). Designing integrative learning on placement: A study of student experiences. *Advances in Social Work and Welfare Education, 20*(1), 157–169. https://search.informit.org/doi/abs/10.3316/informit.810918299697923

Phillips, J., MacGiollaRi, D., & Callaghan, S. (2012). Encouraging research in social work: Narrative as the thread integrating education and research in social work. *Social Work Education, 31*(6), 785–793. https://doi.org/10.1080/02615479.2012.695200

Poon, E., Holt, J., & Bosire, J. (2020). *Transforming the Field Education Landscape (TFEL) – Guiding consultation report*. [Manuscript submitted for publication].

Rubin, D., Robinson, B., & Valutis, S. (2010). Social work education and student research projects: A survey of program directors. *Journal of Social Work Education, 46*(1), 39–55. https://doi.org/10.5175/JSWE.2010.200800040

Svoboda, D., Williams, C., Jones, A., & Powell, K. (2013). Teaching social work research through practicum: What the students learned. *Journal of Social Work Education, 49*(4), 661–673. https://doi.org/10.1080/10437797.2013.812889

Secretariat on Responsible Conduct of Research. (2018). *Tri-Council Policy Statement: Ethical conduct for research involving humans – TCPS 2*. Government of Canada. https://ethics.gc.ca/eng/policy-politique_tcps2-eptc2_2018.html

Tourrilhes, C. (2018). De l'expérience à la démarche de recherche. Transmission d'une posture interrogative dans la formation en travail social. *Le Sociographe, 5*, 83–98. https://www.cairn.info/revue-le-sociographe-2018-5-page-83.htm

Vallet, P. (2019). Préalables à toute participation des personnes concernées aux formations en travail social. *Vie Sociale, 1*, 243–254. https://www.cairn.info/revue-vie-sociale-2019-1-page-243.htm

Walsh, C. A., Gulbrandsen, C., & Lorenzetti, L. (2019). Research practicum: An experiential model of social work research education. *Open Sage, 9*(1), 1–11. https://doi.org/10.1177/2158244019841922

Whipple, E. E., Hughes, A., & Bowden, S. (2015). Evaluation of a BSW research experience: Improving student research competency. *Journal of Teaching in Social Work, 35*(4), 397–409. https://doi.org/10.1080/08841233.2015.1063568

Wulf-Andersen, T., Morgensen, K., & Hjort-Madsen, P. (2013). Researching with undergraduate students: Exploring the learning potentials of undergraduate students and researchers collaborating in knowledge production. *Journal of Research Practice, 9*(2), article M9. https://eric.ed.gov/?id=EJ1043509

Zuchowski, I., Heyeres, M., & Tsey, K. (2020). Students in research placements as part of professional degrees: A systematic review. *Australian Social Work, 73*(1), 48–63. https://doi.org/10.1080/0312407X.2019.1649439

Field Education Materials from CASWE-ACFTS Accredited Social Work Education Programs

Carleton University, BSW Field Manual. https://carleton.ca/socialwork/wp-content/uploads/BSW-Practicum-Manual-February-2018-AE.pdf

Carleton University, MSW Field Manual. https://carleton.ca/socialwork/wp-content/uploads/MSW-Manual-December-2019.pdf

Kings University College, BSW Field Manual. https://socialwork.kings.uwo.ca/socialWork/assets/File/field/BSW_3_FE_Manual.pdf

Kings University College, MSW Field Manual. https://socialwork.kings.uwo.ca/socialWork/assets/File/field/msw_as_manual.pdf

Lakehead University, HBSW Field Education Manual. https://www.lakeheadu.ca/sites/default/files/uploads/103/HBSW%20Field%20Manual%202019%202020%20Revised%20Jan%2010%202020.pdf

McGill University, MSW Field Evaluation Form. https://www.mcgill.ca/socialwork/files/socialwork/msw_field_evaulation_feb_2020.pdf

McMaster University, BSW Field Manual. https://socialwork.mcmaster.ca/resources/field-placements/puzzled_about_placement_2013-2014.pdf

Memorial University, BSW Field Manual. https://www.mun.ca/socialwork/field/BSW_Field_Education_Manual.pdf

Memorial University, MSW Pathway Manual. https://www.mun.ca/socialwork/programs/graduate/curriculum/pathwaymanual.php

St. Thomas University, BSW Field Manual. https://www.stu.ca/media/stu/site-content/academics/social-work/documents/BSW-Field-Handbook-2019-20.pdf

Toronto Metropolitan University, BSW Field Education Manual 2024/2025. https://www.torontomu.ca/content/dam/social-work/pdfs/student-resources/undergraduate/field-education/BSW_Field_Education_Manual.pdf

University of British Columbia, Okanagan Campus, MSW Field Manual. https://socialwork.ok.ubc.ca/wp-content/uploads/sites/8/2017/06/SSW-Field-Education-Manual-June-1-2017.pdf

University of Calgary, BSW Field Manual. https://socialwork.ucalgary.ca/sites/default/files/student%20ucalgary-field-education-manual-feb-2020_0.pdf

University of Calgary, MSW Field Manual. https://socialwork.ucalgary.ca/sites/default/files/student%20ucalgary-field-education-manual-feb-2020_0.pdf

University of Toronto, MSW Indirect Practice and Mixed Practice Learning Contracts. https://socialwork.utoronto.ca/practicum/for-students/forms/

University of Victoria, BSW Field Education Manual. https://www.uvic.ca/hsd/socialwork/assets/docs/Practicum/fieldmanual.bsw2017.pdf

University of Windsor, BSW Field Manual. https://www.uwindsor.ca/socialwork/sites/uwindsor.ca.socialwork/files/bsw_2020-2021-bsw_field_manual-policies_and_standards_final_updatedoct_26_2020.pdf

Wilfrid Laurier, BSW Manual. https://wlu.ca/academics/faculties/faculty-of-social-work/assets/documents/bsw-field-manual.pdf

York University, MSW Field Manual. https://socialwork.gradstudies.yorku.ca/msw-manuals/

York University, Research Placement Learning Contract. https://socialwork.gradstudies.yorku.ca/msw-manuals/

NOTES:

NOTES:

Research As Daily Practice as an Agency Asset

Sally St. George and Dan Wulff

In this chapter we present both the rationale for using Research As Daily Practice (St. George et al., 2015a) in social service agencies and how to do it. We will describe how this way of engaging in and merging research practice can be useful for agencies and their staff, students and practicum supervisors, and university social work programs. Social service agencies provide much-needed services for their communities, many times including serving as a site for social work students to get valuable practical experience. With heavy workloads and demands at agencies, inviting practicum students to join the agency for a semester or two may seem unreasonable, perhaps impossible. Our presentation in this chapter about using Research As Daily Practice as an agency practice can facilitate significant inclusion of practicum students as well as provide other tangible assets for the agency.

Because Research As Daily Practice is newly evolving, most agencies have not heard of it. This is written for social service agencies along with social work students and faculties with the hope that this sparks interest to take a closer look at how it could be beneficial. As you will soon read, many aspects of Research As Daily Practice may already be part of an agency's practice. We will demonstrate how those already existing practices are fundamentally research practices but perhaps just not thought of in that way.

Let us introduce ourselves. We are spouses and colleagues and have worked together for over 20 years within two different graduate social work faculties. We refer to ourselves as "pracademics," a word that highlights our integrative work across research, teaching, and clinical practice as well as across the fields of social work and marital and family therapy. We created Research As Daily Practice to work in those areas of intersection because pragmatically, keeping each activity separate was difficult, less effective, and time intensive. Additionally, we found that working at the edges of each activity or initiative and in those places of intersection allowed us to see situations differently and to develop new approaches and practices.

We believe that social agencies and the practitioners within these agencies benefit by consistently examining what they do and how they do it. One of the ways to do this is by responding to questions of concern arising within the daily work of the organization by understanding and using research processes that make sense within the organization's current practice and context. We advocate for an approach to research that we call Research As Daily Practice that is a unity of what has been customarily divided into separate activities called "research" and "practice" and happens *as we are practicing.* Reconceptualizing research and practice as that which happens in the daily activities of practitioners and agencies creates possibilities for greatly enhancing the work being done for clientele and communities in real time as well as for improving the climate of the workplace.

As we look back on our creation of Research As Daily Practice, we now see how the process we used in coming up with it actually *was* the process of Research As Daily Practice itself! We had an issue (too many disparate things to accomplish); we looked around for new ways to address it differently including consulting with others, conceptualizing how research and practice could be approached as the same thing, trying it out; and continually evolving it—even as we write this chapter. It has a commonsensical ring to it. Some see it as so basic as to be unremarkable. But the simplicity of it and the reasonableness of it are a couple of its chief selling points (Wulff & St. George, 2020).

This more inclusive conceptualization of research to include what we think of as practice can help social agencies become a learning organization that foregrounds an interest in improving what is done and how it is done through steady reflection. Learning and changing are understood as constant and desired. The organization regularly revisits its practices to confirm its value and/or modify its practices. Seeing research as embedded in everything the agency does is a key component in facilitating this ongoing reflective process.

We originally designed Research As Daily Practice in the clinical practice context because that is where we were working as social workers. However, we have seen the potential for using it in any practice or organizational context (e.g., social agencies, counseling centres, hospitals, shelters, businesses, schools) and in both domestic and international settings. Additionally, we see Research As Daily Practice as relevant for entire agencies or organizations, not just individuals or small groups within them.

What is Research As Daily Practice?

We have previously written about the conceptualization of Research As Daily Practice (St. George et al., 2015a, 2015b; Wulff & St. George, 2014) and offered some examples of how we have enacted it in a family therapy clinical setting (Wulff, St. George, & Tomm, 2015; Wulff, St. George, Tomm, & Doyle, 2015). In its most basic form, we used Research As Daily Practice as a process for practitioners to take time to attend to questions that arise in their daily work and connect with colleagues to figure out the best ways to systematically inquire into those questions. Using what we already do as part of our daily routines, we decide what data or information is necessary and design the best ways to examine the information to better understand what is happening and how to advance our work. For example, at the family therapy centre where we did our work, "reflecting teams" (Friedman, 1995) were a regular part of how family therapy was conducted. In two of the Research As Daily Practice projects we conducted, we used reflecting teams as a way to collect and analyze the data we were developing (Wulff, St. George, & Tomm, 2015). Using reflecting teams also was crucial in producing some alterations in the design of the projects.

As we continue to develop the strategy, we sometimes use established research methodologies and methods or their variations that are in sync with our clinical practices (e.g., situational, discourse, and narrative analyses and mixed methods), but we are not limited by established research analyses. We center on the issues we face in the field and look for methodologies to assist us in that effort and modify them as needed. Methodologies are adjusted to fit the issues we are examining—the ones that have worked best for us have been those that mirrored the processes in which we proceed in practice.

Benefits of Including *Research As Daily Practice*

We would like to list advantages or benefits that we see (and have seen) in using *Research As Daily Practice*, highlighting particularly that this process needs no extra funding, nor does it need to take extra time. Agencies are busy places and oftentimes struggle when new initiatives require more time and more money, but because Research As Daily Practice is part of what an agency is already doing, it only requires some fine tuning of established practices.

Agency Benefits

One of the first and most obvious benefits we have noticed in including Research As Daily Practice in agencies was better morale. When staff come together in common projects that are directly related to their experience at the agency, their sense of being a part of something meaningful and that utilizes their talents increases. These initiatives need to be substantive and lead to jointly-constructed plans and actions. By working together, staff can get to know each other better, particularly if it is a large agency with lots of diverse programming. Common initiatives can help re-orient feelings of competitiveness for scarce resources.

Another benefit to incorporating Research as Daily Practice into a social agency is that a learning community is created. By participating in Research As Daily Practice, all members become community collaborators and co-learners. The agency may come to be seen as a flexible and responsive organization that learns from experience and makes use of practice-based evidence. Rather than becoming rigid in its practices, this process valorizes change and newness. This can be an attractive asset for agencies when recruiting new staff.

A third advantage of Research As Daily Practice to agencies is that it helps develop relevant innovative projects. Agencies and organizations can be seen as leaders in new programming approaches for their clients and communities. Agencies can be recognized as places where innovation happens, becoming a leader in their field. Inquiring into the organizational patterns can lead to the development of new initiatives to enhance current practices and programs. These new understandings of client and worker situations can lead to agencies investigating the possibilities for pilot projects to increase service delivery options. These new plans may produce new funding streams for the agency, which could help it diversify its budget, protecting the agency from economic hard times.

A fourth benefit is that engaging in Research As Daily Practice can serve as a form of supervision because it can be used as a means of group supervision that enhances good practice and support for clinicians, administrators, and other team members. Supervision can be associated with a culture of support rather than oversight and surveillance, freeing up people to be more generative in their thinking and interacting.

Practitioner Benefits

One of the greatest benefits of Research As Daily Practice for practitioners is that we could develop new ideas to help with our "stuck" cases, those we were unsure of how to work with effectively. When common aspects or issues of practice situations are noticed and shared across caseloads, new ways of seeing are possible. When a case is thought of as a one-off situation, certain elements of the situation may not surface. But when a case is thought about in terms of its similarity to other cases, more elements of the situation may become more visible. Looking across caseloads allows each case situation to be considered within a "class" of situations that may highlight elements that may be less pronounced when looking at only one item in a class of situations.

Another benefit of looking for connections across client or practice situations is the increased likelihood that larger issues involved in client situations will come to the fore, helping practitioners develop understandings of how macro issues are implicated in micro troubles. These larger patterns may promote innovative practices (e.g., bringing clients together to discuss common problems, recognizing service delivery problems in the community). Patterns within workplace regulations and policies can also reveal the unwittingly embedded constraints or enhancements that affect work with clients.

When approaching these situations as inquirers and looking for ways to make sense, practitioners can develop more and different ideas to make their work more exciting and efficient. Beyond casework, when considering other practical elements of agency work (i.e., agency policies and procedures, intakes, paperwork, workloads, office space), collective discussions inclusive of many viewpoints and perspectives increase the alternatives from which to make plans and decisions. Collaborative conversations about common agency issues and concerns ground those issues in frontline viewpoints and increase the level of commitment to whatever ideas are used.

A benefit of regular engagement in Research As Daily Practice meetings has been increased connection with other practitioners because it brings practitioners together regularly to consider issues of common concern. With agency work becoming increasingly busy, opportunities for staff to come together in meaningful common cause validates relationships and builds camaraderie. Morale boosting can be advantageous when agencies face many stresses related to time and money.

Benefits to Agency Clientele

When practitioners come together in Research As Daily Practice, the chances for new and creative ideas increase, which can translate into alternative and new practices being made available for agency clientele or customers. With new ideas on the rise, clientele can have a sense that their agency is continually developing ideas to address their particular situation or context. Rather than feel like they are being plugged into a pre-existing program or service, they might feel like the particulars of their issues or challenges are taken into account.

With new approaches being developed and applied for agency clientele, those consumers can be consulted about their experiences with new approaches and can provide direct feedback, involving them in the development of the practices that they and others benefit from. What they say matters to the practitioners who are developing alternative ideas and approaches.

Student Benefits

As practicum students have used Research As Daily Practice, they have said they feel like they are part of things at their field agency. They are included with the staff as contributors to the Research As Daily Practice process, as colleagues. Students oftentimes lack confidence because they are new to the field or the practice, but using Research As Daily Practice allows their perspectives to be valued as highly as anyone else's; their voices are invited and heard.

Students can see and experience creativity and collaboration at work. They see and hear more experienced professionals move in collaborative and forward-thinking ways—in practice not just theory—and can provide valuable modelling for their future professional practice.

Students can add a fresh perspective to agency conversations and feel valued for their contributions; their understandings of things that are not steeped in long-term experience are considered fresh and less influenced by historical standards of practice, rather than as naïve or inexperienced. This can be an irreplaceable contribution to agency conversations and may boost student confidence.

The Process of Research As Daily Practice

The process of Research As Daily Practice is not prescriptive and not necessarily ordered. To start using the strategy, determine a systematic way to answer any questions that come from your work by doing what makes sense and is in line with the ways in which you work. You can use the following sequence.

1. Identify a question or issue based in the work you do. This is the question of inquiry, the central issue that animates the research. It should be significant and make a difference in the work.

2. Ask if anyone else in your agency or practice is asking about the same question. This invites perspectives on the central issue from various stakeholder viewpoints. This is part of data generation. Understanding how others think about or approach the issue helps expand thinking around the issue creating a connection with others.

3. Discuss how others understand the issue to build more breadth and depth and to build and keep momentum. Each person will have a somewhat different understanding of the issue and their own level of energy with which to engage. This furthers data generation.

4. Go to the literature. Read widely regarding the issue, is in a sense, reaching out to others who have been engaged with the issue from many different places, times, and contexts to further your understanding. This is another step in data generation. The wider the literature search, the greater likelihood that you will find perspectives that differ from your own. The aim here is to deliberately find alternatives that expand thinking rather than confirming what is already known.

5. Use case or meeting notes to identify ideas that are present in professional documentation. This is a way to mine what is already known about the issue, giving us a chance to see how our ideas to this point are embedded in the documentation. Again, more data generation. Our written renditions of the issues can be viewed as a history-taking of the issue and an indication of how the issue has been taken up by our agency protocols and expectations.

6. Compare and contrast, sift through, examine, and take notice of what we have assembled, that is, analyze the data. During this step, you may see how you had become stuck on the central question and imagine a wider variety of options than you thought possible.

7. Examine the newness you have brought forward from your data generation and analysis. Use the work and our conversations to conceptualize anew, to take new actions regarding your issue of concern. What you do and change may be small scale or large, but it is the change that is exciting. You are not finished; you need to go full circle and examine the new strategies you are experimenting with in order to see their utility and effect(s), and perhaps modify as needed. We have often found that our original articulations of the issues of concern become reshaped into more focused or expanded versions through this process.

There are many ways that Research As Daily Practice might be used. We identify four types of questions or issues that could be raised in an agency and identify specific questions that could be used to advance inquiries through the first two steps in the process. The subsequent steps will not be specified for these four specific questions or issues because the steps that follow will be more common across questions.

Step 1: Identify a problem, question, or issue of concern.

☐ Practitioner: The majority of client families on my caseload report parent-child conflict in which the kids are tyrannical, controlling the house and their family members, and running away or inconsolable when things do not go their way. I have ways to discuss conflicts between parents and children that have worked in the past, but they do not seem as effective as they used to be. In addition, the level of aggression and violence seems to be much higher recently. Given that my ideas may not be constructive, the consequences in terms of violence among family members alarms me. If I cannot find ways of helping them out of this, there is real danger. I feel like I should do more, but when my old ways do not work, I am at a loss.

- Agency administrator: The number of clients who are no-shows has risen steadily over the last 12 months. This puts a stress on everyone and reduces our ability to reach as many clients as we possibly can. We are not sure how to address this, but we know we must do something other than just hope it gets better or create punitive policies for clients who do not show up.

- Teacher: The switch to online education has been extremely stressful and the worst part of it is teaching students who refuse to have their screens on. I cannot tell if they are even there, much less how much they are learning or what their growing edges are. Am I the only one who is befuddled and stressed by this? Is my concern legitimate or is this just the "new normal" for online education?

- Policy writer: Writing policies for social services in times of financial cutbacks poses some real challenges. We have always worked to create policies that focus on enhancing the work we do and appreciate how these policies affect our staff. The economic pressures on our agency are such that policies are increasingly centered on maximizing organizational output with reduced funding. We seem to be drifting away from providing the most beneficial services and programs to our community in favor of becoming leaner in what we do. Marketplace concerns are overriding our goal of serving our community. This feels wrong but we want to stay in business, so it doesn't seem like we have any options.

Step 2: Ask if anyone else in the agency or practice is having similar concerns.

- Practitioner: At a clinical rounds meeting a practitioner asks, "Is anyone noticing a similar trend?" or "Is anyone else struggling with this?"

- Agency administrator: In an agency staff meeting, the administrator asks, "We would like to open up a discussion about how we can better address the issue of client no-shows. We believe this is a burden for everyone to some degree, so input from everyone is important."

- Teacher: At a teacher's meeting, the teacher asked: "Am I the only one struggling with the students not turning their screens on when I teach online? Has anyone found some good ways to approach this? Am I concerned about something that I shouldn't be? Could we have a discussion about this?"

- Policy writer: In an agency-wide meeting, a policy writer explains, "As policy writers, we are feeling pulled away from creating new and better services for our community in favor of writing policies that focus mostly on ways of keeping our costs down. We are not opposed to cost-effectiveness, but this seems to be going too far. We feel more like bureaucrats and accountants rather than innovators for community betterment. Are there ideas you have on how to keep our focus on our community?"

Questions like those found in the examples invite others in the organization to acknowledge issues or difficulties being experienced and to share their own ideas. In addition to generating some useful ideas or initiatives, the process opens the door to collectively face issues experienced within the agency and to offer support to one another.

Step 3: Discuss with colleagues their understanding of the issues. We hope that you can see the continuation of the inquiry process into sharing multiple ways of seeing these issues or dilemmas from different stakeholders. (We would like to note that we are not searching for answers or solutions to the dilemmas, we are serious about the inquiring steps and believe they are necessary to shaping and designing change. We have often found that short-circuiting these inquiring steps to be costly and/or demoralizing). Discussions with colleagues often start with questions; examples of questions that help start conversations follow.

☐ What words and phrases do we hear from stakeholders as they consider these issues? Do we hear a variety of things or are we hearing the same thing over and over?

☐ What words and phrases do we use repeatedly use when we talk about these issues?

☐ What kinds of rules, traditions, and voices are we loyal to as we examine these dilemmas? Who or what influences our preferred patterns or expectations?

These questions (and others like them) encourage us to look for patterns in how we and other stakeholders are shaped in our thinking and actions by prior experiences, traditions, and standards. These questions focus our attention on how the difficulties or dilemmas we face may be influenced by others' expectations of us. This may make change challenging if the idea of changes to practices may be discouraged by loyalty to particular people or methods, disciplinary expectations, or established standards or policies.

Step 4: Go to the literature. This is a useful step regardless of the issue. Not all knowledge is located in the professional literature, but it does convey a significant amount of the shared wisdom in a field or on a topic. The literature includes research, theoretical writing, theses and dissertations, creative writing, and writing from related fields. The following are examples of questions you can ask when you review the research.

☐ What terminology is repeated in the literature on this topic?

☐ What themes seem to be consistent?

☐ Are there important distinctions within the literature on how something is understood or evaluated?

Our disciplinary backgrounds are important to our understandings about our work. Tracing professional literature and research in various related fields regarding how we conceptualize our work may reveal some possibilities for variability or may reassert understandings that guide us into places of impasse within our work. We may notice some dead ends in the ways we have learned to work with clients, supervisors, colleagues, and the larger community from prior training or reading. It is possible that we may find some built-in biases or pre-understandings that may be unwarranted. Noticing these stoppages may help us see how we might improvise or develop new practices from where our disciplinary training has left off. These places may be sites of innovation that could contribute to and extend our prior knowledge for ourselves and our colleagues. What we find in the literature can be woven into our agency conversations to build/expand them.

Step 5: Go to your case notes, agency reports, memos, and other professional documentation to identify discourses that are "invisibly" present.

☐ What kinds of unexamined or taken-for-granted conceptualizing and conversing show up in our professional documentation?

☐ What themes run through the way we write about our work? How has our work been conveyed to the public over time?

These questions stimulate thinking about the kinds of pre-understandings that went into forming the written documentation and by extension, the observations and behaviors that these were attempting to capture. This is taking a reflective position, inviting a more contextualized examination of a text that can provide much explicit and implicit information. Principles of practice and reporting are built into the ways we write about and record what we do so they are excellent places to reflectively examine what we stand for and who we are.

Step 6: Compare and contrast, sift through, examine, and take notice of the various ways to approach and understand our concern.

☐ What kinds of unexamined or taken-for-granted conceptualizing and conversing have occupied our thinking to date?

☐ What accounts for our preferred courses of action?

In asking ourselves these questions we recognize that we have been operating from within a set of choices; perhaps we did not recognize the available possibilities. We may have been operating under some assumptions or pre-understandings that inhibit what we were trying to accomplish. We might find ourselves acting under the influence of particular ways of seeing and thinking that prevents us from seeing in another way.

Step 7: What newness/freshness does this examination offer in terms of conversing, conceptualizing, and intervening within our current situation?

☐ What new ways of thinking and joining with others are more apparent to us now?

☐ What new questions can we create that can help us expand our understanding of our area of concern even further?

With these questions, we consider some of the information that grew out of this process. By this point, we may recognize that new ideas and conceptualizations are emerging from our data and that interesting new questions have surfaced. New questions may stimulate this process to begin again. In this sense, there is an "action research" cycle feel to Research As Daily Practice. It is a never-ending process that continues to spawn new ideas and initiatives.

Narrative Example of the Steps

Agencies typically have procedures for gathering information about new clients. This information may include demographics of the client's life, history, financial situation, presenting problem(s), and other personal questions. In the following example, Dan, who worked for a home-based family therapy and social service agency, had a set of questions that he was required to ask during the first meeting with the family. There were about 30 questions, and the answers were written on an assessment form.

When using this assessment procedure, a family expressed surprise regarding one of the questions. While the presenting problem for this family was a teenager who was doing poorly in school and "running around with bad kids," this question surprised the family: "when giving birth to [your son], was it a difficult childbirth?" The mother could not understand what the answer had to do with the current situation, and Dan did not himself know the relevance of this question—he was only asking it because it was on the form.

When Dan returned to the agency office, he asked other workers about the intake question. They explained that they did not understand why the question was on the form, but asked it because they were told to. All the workers felt uneasy about the question and felt it to be invasive, especially given the presenting reason Dan was working with them.

Dan asked the director of the agency about the reasoning for the assessment question. The director expressed surprise that the question was on the form because it had been added years ago to accommodate a doctoral researcher who had done her research in the agency two years earlier. The director suggested removing the question. Dan asked if it would be important to review all assessment questions to check for their current relevance. The director agreed and there were a series of meetings to look at which questions were no longer relevant and whether new questions would be useful.

The workers began by applying an overall question to each item on the assessment form: "What do we want an assessment to do and does this question contribute to that?" The group developed the following criteria for assessment questions that would be helpful in working with families: directly relatable to the presenting problem(s), easily understood by families (e.g., no professional jargon), phrased in ways that are supportive to the family, and few in number. This process of examining assessment questions which was started by a client's question evolved into a broad review of assessment at the agency. This was a surprising, but welcome, development—one that was not anticipated at the beginning.

Dan and his colleagues researched assessment forms from other agencies through literature searches, and their discussions included considering other ways of performing assessments through a conversation that did not involve writing down answers to questions. The group decided to have a list of preferred questions that needed answering in intake meetings, but each practitioner could choose how to collect those answers — using a form or another means.

This process led to a general review of all documentation at the agency, with the intention of streamlining and updating written records. This also led into a discussion of the pros and cons of digitalizing records. This question of whether or not to move toward complete utilization of computers for paperwork became a new round for Research As Daily Practice.

Conclusion

We see our chapter as an invitation to agencies to muster the resources they possess in ways to profit from their staff and the work they already do. Research need not be an external initiative that is costly and time-consuming. By valuing their staff, their positioning in the community, their work, and their experiences, the agency has all the requisite parts to create a Research As Daily Practice initiative that can support innovation and promote the well-being of their staff in the process.

Additionally, Research As Daily Practice helps create an environment that maximizes the practicum value of the organization for students. Universities that seek practicum sites for their students would be excited to provide their students with the opportunities to learn in agencies that use "*what* they do to continuously examine their practices." Research components in student learning contracts could be easily addressed in these settings. For a social work program, having a practicum site that provides a well-rounded educational field experience that includes both the micro and the macro would be ideal. Using Research As Daily Practice would be a valuable way for an agency to demonstrate how responding to ongoing critical challenges to their work is routinely built into the fabric of the organization.

Practicum students become relevant participants along with the staff of the agency in Research As Daily Practice initiatives by bringing in ideas from the outside, in particular the world of the university. This is an example of how a practicum student can create added value to the agency at a time when the thought of including a practicum student could feel like a drain of resources for an agency. Regular inclusion of practicum students from different faculties or different universities can add multiple dimensions to an agency because in a Research As Daily Practice setting, students can support the agency and help it grow. For students, being integrated in the agency in this setting affords them with the opportunity to experience more fully and deeply a sense of what work will be like in agencies after they graduate and enter the workforce, as well as what they can innovate.

The central thesis of this chapter is that research is already being done in social service agencies by social workers. A dominant discourse in our professional worlds has placed research into a special category that renders it significantly unavailable to those who do not have the requisite credentials and financing. We seek to expand that limited perspective to include everyone, including clients (who could actually be considered "researchers into their own lives"). Seeing research in our daily practices creates an awareness of a resource that has always been there, even if it has been largely unseen.

Discussion Questions

1. Seeing research and practice as the "same process, but languaged differently" may seem counter-intuitive given traditional social work texts and understandings. What are three compelling reasons why this understanding could make sense and be useful. What are three compelling reasons why it might not make sense or be useful?

2. List three activities in your practicum that could be understood as either practice or research. What words seem key in distinguishing an activity that is called practice and one that is called research?

3. Given your understanding of Research As Daily Practice, what are two issues that you would find worthwhile in using the strategy?

4. For an agency or colleague who has not heard of Research As Daily Practice, what are three key elements that you think would be important to highlight in presenting the idea to them?

5. What are ways that the principles and processes of Research As Daily Practice could be extended to include clients or customers of the social agency?

REFERENCES

Friedman, S. (Ed.). (1995). *The reflecting team in action: Collaborative practice in family therapy.* The Guilford Press.

St. George, S., Wulff, D., & Tomm, K. (2015a). Research As Daily Practice. *Journal of Systemic Therapies, 34*(2), 3–14. https://doi.org/10.1007/978-3-319-49425-8_890

St. George, S., Wulff, D., & Tomm, K. (2015b). Talking societal discourse into family therapy: A situational analysis of the relationships between societal expectations and parent-child conflict. *Journal of Systemic Therapies, 34*(2), 15–30. https://doi.org/10.1521/JSYT.2015.34.2.15

Wulff, D., & St. George, S. (2014). Research As Daily Practice. In G. Simon & A. Chard (Eds.), *Systemic inquiry: Innovations in reflexive practice research* (pp. 292–308). Everything is Connected Press.

Wulff, D., & St. George, S. (2020). We are all researchers. In S. McNamee, M. M. Gergen, C. Camargo-Borges, & E. F. Rasera (Eds.), *The Sage handbook of social constructionist practice* (pp. 68–76). Sage.

Wulff, D., St. George, S., & Tomm, K. (2015). Societal discourses that help in family therapy: A modified situational analysis of the relationships between societal expectation and healing patterns in parent-child conflict. *Journal of Systemic Therapies, 34*(2), 31–44. https://doi.org/10.1521/jsyt.2015.34.2.31

Wulff, D., St. George, S., Tomm, K., Doyle, E., & Sesma, M. (2015). Unpacking the PIPs to HIPs curiosity: A narrative study. *Journal of Systemic Therapies, 34*(2), 45–58. https://doi.org/10.1521/jsyt.2015.34.2.45

NOTES:

NOTES:

Maneuvering the Macro: A Guide to Macro-Level Field Placements for Social Work Students, Field Instructors, and Field Liaisons

Julie Mann-Johnson, Anne-Marie McLaughlin, Brenda Vos, and Maddie Wandler

> What is the spirit of social work? It was founded upon genuine human pity, upon the desire to relieve suffering, to give food to the hungry and shelter to the homeless; unless we can get back to that, underlying as it does, all the subdivisions and subtleties into which we have developed our activities, and take hold of this great world-situation, we will fail in an essential obligation, in a sense we will be traitors to our original purpose. (Jane Addams, 1920, as cited in Thompson et al., 2019, pp. 41–42).

Changes made at the macro level of social work practice are significant and have ripple effects with the potential to touch the lives of many individuals. There is theoretical consensus within the social work profession that macro practice produces these ripple effects by engaging across systems and working with individuals, groups, communities, organizations, and societies (Canadian Association of Social Workers [CASW], 2020). Even so, many social work students, educational programs, professional associations, and social workers maintain a myopic lens of social work practice by focusing on the micro-level with little attention directed towards macro work that may include policy development, research, analysis, advocacy, administration, and mobilization that attempts to influence systems towards social justice.

With a focus on field placement opportunities, this chapter situates macro practice within generalist practice, explores the benefits of macro-level practice, suggests a definition, reviews the literature on existing tensions in the field and classroom, and identifies the competencies required for macro-level social work practice. Opportunities for skill development and transferability will be highlighted along with suggestions and resources for learning activities for students. Considerations for field instructors and faculty liaisons will also be discussed with opportunities to best support students in these types of field education placements.

Generalist Practice

Social work has long struggled with its dual focus of helping people and changing society (McLaughlin, 2002). Generalist practice arose in response to a perceived drift away from the dual focus and towards a narrower interest in individual methods and models of practice focused on the needs, problems, issues, and concerns of individuals (Miller et al., 2008). In contrast, generalist practice encompasses a multimethod-multilevel approach to practice that best prepares social workers to understand and respond to the interrelated complexities of individuals, communities, and social systems. In Canada and elsewhere, undergraduate social work education prepares students for generalist practice (Canadian Association for Social Work Education [CASWE], 2021; Lavitt, 2009). Generalist practitioners not only work with individuals but also with systems and structures. Key features of generalist practice include a person-in-environment lens, which situates an individual's experience in the context of their environment in both assessments and interventions occurring at multiple levels. It also features multiple roles, including but not limited to educator, advocate, mediator, planner, organizer, and administrator. This chapter focuses on these roles at a macro level. A strong understanding of macro-level practice, and the transferability of its skills across levels of practice will assist students in the development of a strong social work identity that integrates micro, mezzo, and macro practice.

What is Macro Practice, Anyway?

The social work profession and social work education often speak of and describe social work practice as fitting within three levels of practice: micro, mezzo, and macro. These classifications, influenced by social work meta-theories such as systems theory and ecological approaches, underpin generalist social work practice (Greenfield, 2010). Yet pressure to specialize has forced some practitioners and educators to depart from the generalist perspective in favour of either mezzo, macro, or micro practice, with an overwhelming majority favouring the latter (Apgar, 2020). This challenge will be explored in further depth within this chapter. While the authors of this chapter agree that good social work practice engages across all three levels, for the ease of analysis, reflection, and learning, we will parse out macro-level practice with a definition, further discussion from the literature, and case examples.

Typically, the following definitions have been used to differentiate levels of practice: micro is direct practice with individuals, families, and/or small groups; mezzo is practice with organization, teams, and/or other formal groups; macro is community organizing, policy, and/or administration (Mattocks, 2018). Holtz Deal et al. (2007) describe macro-oriented social work as "management and community practice" (p. 43) in their discussion about graduate student field practicum experiences, identifying that macro-oriented field placements take place in communities and organizations. Field placements that have a management concentration are considered macro-level yet are also referred to as "social work administration" roles (Ezell et al., 2004).

The term "policy practice" is also used to refer to macro-level social work activity as an area requiring attention within social work curricula (Apgar & Parada, 2018). Other ways to differentiate practice have considered the proximity of practice to individuals, for example whether the type of support provided to individuals would be considered direct or indirect practice (Hunter & Ford, 2010). Direct practice may include regular contact with vulnerable individuals and families, while indirect practice may include administration, program development and implementation, networking, policy development and analysis, political work, and community mobilization (Hunter & Ford, 2010). Direct practice and indirect practice are frequently used to distinguish micro- and macro-level practice. Mezzo-oriented placements involve elements of both direct and indirect practice (Hunter & Ford, 2010). See Table 7.1 for a side-by-side comparison of various areas of practice within direct and indirect practice.

Table 7.1

MICRO	MACRO
DIRECT	INDIRECT
• Individual casework • Counselling with individuals, families, and groups • Individual resource provision • Advocacy with individuals • Individual assessment • Outreach	• Administration • Program development • Program implementation • Networking • Policy development • Policy analysis • Political work • Community mobilization • Public education and prevention programs

Practice that involves the ability to engage with larger systems in the socioeconomic environment (Long et al., 2006 as cited in Miller et al., 2008), such as at the global, societal, community or organizational level, is described as a distinguishing feature of macro-level social work (Miller et al., 2008). Encompassing an understanding of systems is also noted in LaTosch and Jones' (2012) conception, highlighting that macro-level work addresses systems that govern and impact lives, looks at entire communities, and identifies key areas for change. Apgar (2020) summarizes macro work as "social work [that] focuses on structural solutions to eradicate systemic inequities and prevent social problems" (p. 711).

Here, we propose a functional definition for macro-level social work based on the literature and our practice experience. We suggest macro-level social work practice is social work practice in policy development, research, analysis, advocacy, administration, and organizing and mobilization that aims to influence systems. We consider the aspect of "aiming to influence systems" to be a vital component of macro social work practice. This notion not only incorporates systems theory and its ecological perspectives, which are vital to social work's professional base, but also echoes social work's obligations and commitments to social justice, social change, and influence. Consider the case study and the role social workers have to play to influence the system.

Table 7.2: Case Study

Fozia is a social worker who works with a provincial government department that is focused on the provision of supports to people with disabilities. Her role as a policy analyst is varied and includes networking with other government departments with whom people with disabilities might interact with, meeting with advocacy groups, responding to citizen concerns, and advising her government department on policy responses to current issues.

In the course of her work and while attending inter-department meetings, it has become apparent that young adults who transition into adult disability services from children's services experience lengthy wait times while their extended health coverage transfers into adult programs. They may have accessed extended health care coverage as children from a different government department but must reapply for new coverage as adults. This application may take six months to process, leaving these individuals without coverage for prescription medication and other rehabilitation health services like occupational therapy. Lobby groups, advocates, and internal government service providers have also identified this as a problem.

Together with colleagues in the children-serving ministries, Fozia is leading a working group to address this issue through policy and operational responses. They make recommendations to their respective ministries to create a streamlined response to these applications to ensure these individuals experience no interruption in coverage and health supports. These recommendations also further educate legislators in the barriers and challenges experienced by individuals while they transition between program areas.

This work shows the influence that Fozia is having on multiple systems to impact individuals transitioning to adult disability services.

Tensions of Macro Practice in the Context of the Social Work Profession, Education, and Field Placements

Despite the theoretical consensus in the social work profession that social work spans individual, organizational, and systemic levels of practice (CASW, 2020), there are tensions surrounding the relative importance of each domain in social work education and in the profession. These tensions were embedded in the beginning of social work in the late 19th and early 20th centuries and persist today. The Charity Organization Society (COS) and the Settlement House Movement (SHM) are frequently cited as two strands from which the social work profession emerged (Brieland, 1990; Dore, 1999; Haynes & White, 1999). Although both aimed at improving social conditions, they offered different explanations for the root cause of social issues and different strategies for addressing them (Germain & Hartman, 1980 as cited in Thompson et al., 2019). While the COS is described as micro-oriented by focusing on problems, causes, and solutions at the individual level, the SHM was more macro-oriented in viewing social systems and institutions as the cause of human suffering, and therefore as the target of change (Shdaimah

& McCoyd, 2012). Individual casework theory and practice are thus associated with the COS, while social work with groups, organizations, and social systems is associated with the SHM. These two schools of thought continue to inform the landscape of social work practice today.

Although the COS and SHM are associated with differing perspectives, some argue that these two schools of thought were not as polarized as it may seem (Dore, 1999; McLaughlin, 2002; Thompson, et al., 2019). In their article, Thompson and colleagues (2019) provide multiple examples of how Mary Richmond and Jane Addams, cited as the leaders of the COS and the SHM respectively, acknowledge the importance of both micro and macro social work in fulfilling the purpose of the profession. However, the divide between micro and macro social work in theory and practice only grew with the rise of the political and economic ideology of neoliberalism. Van Heugten (2011) described how under neoliberalism "needs become wants for which individuals are responsible, and health and social welfare are commodities that should be delivered in such a way as to best support economic imperatives" (p. 182). In other words, neoliberalism suggests that individuals are responsible for meeting their own needs, state intervention and funding should be limited, and economic profitability should be prioritized—ideas that are all antithetical to macro social work practice.

Neoliberal policies have greatly impacted social work as a profession—including individual social workers and those they serve—through cuts to social spending that have forced public sectors to do more with less. With fewer resources and increased demands, organizations are pressured to prioritize efficiency and outputs, which has numerous implications on social service delivery and the workforce (Strier, 2019). One notable implication on service delivery has been an increased emphasis on interventions that are evidence-based, standardized, and quickly produce measurable outcomes (Heron, 2019). Consider how such characteristics are more suited to interventions that target individuals as the site for change compared to the dynamic and time-consuming process of systemic change. Implications for the workforce include increased caseloads, poorer working conditions, agency downsizing, and an increase in temporary work contracts (Preston & Aslett, 2013; Strier, 2019). These conditions contribute to a fragmentation of social work practice, where social workers are no longer valued for their capacity to work within and across systems, but rather for their ability to perform a distilled set of tasks (Heron, 2019). For example, with so many pressures and demands and not enough resources, social workers are expected to focus on specific individual needs and sets of tasks, and to otherwise refer clients out to other services, contributing to the fragmentation of the profession into specific subdivisions (Strier, 2019). With how neoliberal ideology is influencing the social sector, it is difficult to imagine how and where macro social work practice fits in. Despite the prevalence of the neoliberal ideology and discourse in Canada, social work regulatory bodies, codes of ethics, and standards of social work practice, education, and training consistently acknowledge micro and macro social work as interrelated and equally important (CASW, 2005; CASWE, 2021; Health Professions Act, 2000). Unfortunately, this is not always reflected in social work education or in the field. Nor does it reflect the desires of many social work students (Apgar, 2020).

The overt focus on micro over macro social work practice in the workforce has produced tensions that manifest in social work education. According to the findings of Austin and colleagues

(2005) and Weiss-Gal (2008), social work students preferred clinical practice, a common application of micro social work, to macro social work. Reasons for this preference included concerns about the job market, employability in higher paying positions, job security, and the ability to become licensed (Apgar, 2020). Research also indicates that students attribute fewer learning opportunities including less client contact and fewer relevant assignments to macro-level field placements (Holtz Deal et al., 2007). It therefore appears that students' preference for micro-level practice may be related to a belief that they will not gain a set of skills of similar value valuable through macro-level practicums, potentially harming their chances of securing a position in the workforce and obtaining their license. Considering the aforementioned ways in which neoliberalism is shaping the social work field, their concerns are not unfounded. Conversely, however, one study in the United States surveyed recent social work graduates with micro or macro concentrations and found no differences between the two groups of graduates in terms of salary or ability to secure a job after graduating (de Saxe Zerden et al., 2016).

Student preferences shape social work education programs; therefore, if programs seek to attract and maintain student enrollments, they must appeal to student preferences for micro practice. For example, only 21% of surveyed social work programs ($n = 240$) in the United States offer macro (community development, organization or planning, administration, and policy) specializations while approximately half offer micro (clinical or direct practice) specializations (CSWE, 2019, p. 10). The CASWE (2021) is the regulatory body of baccalaureate and master level social work programs across Canada. With the ability to deny or withdraw accreditation from any social work degree program in Canada, the CASWE has significant control over the components of social work education. The CASWE's (2021) accreditation standards for social work program curriculums include components of both micro- and macro-level social work; however, social work students are often taught about these areas of practice in isolation from one another (Austin et al., 2005). Social work courses, faculty, curriculum, and entire graduate programs are often separated into three distinct topic areas: direct (or clinical) practice, policy, or research (Shdaimah & McCoyd, 2012, p. 24). This structure of social work education inadvertently reinforces the conceptual divide between micro- and macro-level social work, impeding students' ability to integrate the two in their minds and in practice. Instead, students may perceive a choice between micro- and macro-level social work, and after choosing to pursue one, may neglect rather than integrate the other.

Table 7.3: Question for Reflection and Discussion

How has your social work education reinforced or challenged the divide between micro and macro practice?

There is No Micro Without the Macro!

Consider how this conceptual divide between macro and micro in social work impacts the pursuit of social justice. Without an understanding of how macro-level factors shape individuals' daily lives, a social worker's intervention is more likely to focus on individual change, rather than opportunities for systemic change (Shdaimah & McCoyd, 2012). If systemic factors impacting the individual are socially unjust, the social worker may find themselves supporting the person to adapt to a social injustice. Take child welfare practice as an example. Failure to consider structural or macro issues such as poverty or racism or evaluating a family's functioning without this context leaves social work without the ability to challenge social injustice, arguably harming individual wellbeing over time (Shdaimah & McCoyd, 2012). Conversely, a social worker engaged in policy creation or research, without any knowledge of the daily lived experiences of individuals impacted by said policy or research is unlikely to produce an outcome that will meaningfully improve people's daily lives and is more likely to cause harm (Shdaimah & McCoyd, 2012). Heron (2019) similarly warns of how fragmenting the social work profession and practice into specific specialized services will have "deeply troubling implications for the social justice purpose of social work practice" (p. 79). In summary, it is important to consider how teaching and learning about micro and macro social work practice integrated together, rather than isolated from each other, may support future practitioners' competency in pursuing social justice in all areas of practice. Take a moment to consider how bridging micro and macro practice may support your social work learning and development by considering the discussion outlined in Table 7.4.

Table 7.4: Discussion on Micro and Macro Practice

Take the example of a child with a learning difference. The child and her family may experience varying levels of distress that require individual accommodations. Social workers may assist them to acclimate to, and cope with, workplace or school settings. However, such settings are impacted by the Individuals with Disabilities Education Act (as amended in 1997, P.L. 105-117), by insurance reimbursement schemes, and by the laws and secondary legislation that regulate them. In school settings, the No Child Left Behind Act of 2001 (P.L. 107-110) also influences what schools are able and willing to do for children with disabilities, including whether or not they will work with families to retain such students. Family resources (financial, social, and emotional) will interact with the official and unofficial policy-related mandates and practices. Even diagnoses may be impacted by policies that define which services will be provided based on diagnostic categories. (Stone, 1985, as cited in Shdaimah & McCoyd, 2012, p. 25)

Consider Stone's (1985) example of providing individual support to a child living with a learning disability (as cited in Shdaimah & McCoyd, 2012, p. 25). On an individual level, a social worker may support the child in developing coping skills for issues at school and home, but the child's ability to thrive is also constrained by family resources, school policies, and government laws and legislation.

QUESTION: How can social workers integrate micro and macro practice in the pursuit of social justice in this case?

Macro Practice in Field Education

Market demands—and resulting student demands—for micro-focused social work impact field education in several ways. With clinical practice and research favoured over macro social work, fewer faculty with a keen macro interest are hired, resulting in less integration from classroom to field education for students and a drift in the curriculum to better accommodate clinical interests (Rothman & Mizrahi, 2014). Field education in social work consists of multiple stakeholders, including field education coordinators or liaisons, field or seminar instructors, field supervisors, and most importantly, the student. Each stakeholder holds influence over the success or failure of any particular placement. How each stakeholder perceives or values social work practice at the macro-level may be transmitted to students and other stakeholders. Developing and securing new practicums requires time and focus, and with clinical practice frequently being the priority, students may be rightly concerned that the availability and support for macro-level practica are lacking (Apgar, 2020). The emphasis on micro-level practice in social work field education also complicates the evaluation of student competencies in macro-level settings because most learning agreements and student evaluations emphasize technical skills that are often more easily observed in micro practice (Regehr et al., 2012a; Regehr et al., 2012b). Ideas for how to navigate this emphasis on micro practice in macro field placement evaluations will be provided later in this chapter.

This section of the chapter has provided an overview of tensions surrounding macro practice in the field of social work, and how they have shaped the current landscape of social work field education today. It is important for social work students reading this to be aware of such tensions and how they may influence one's ability to effectively pursue social justice. One notable impact of these tensions has been an emphasis on micro-level social work practice in the classroom and the field. Consider how increased integration of macro-level social work into the curriculum and beyond could help alleviate some of these tensions, for example, through expanded practicum opportunities and more inclusive evaluation tools. It is important that students, social work education programs, and agencies think critically about if and how they perceive an ideological divide between micro and macro social work practice and how it may unknowingly limit valuable teaching and learning. The following sections offer information and strategies to help integrate micro and macro social work, both internally and in practice.

The next section begins this process by exploring how the ideological divide between micro- and macro-level social work fails to recognize the many skills and competencies gained through macro-level field education that transfer across all levels of social work practice and produce an effective and well-rounded social worker. According to Bridges (1993), transferable skills allow a person "with some knowledge, learning, understanding or skill gained in one cognitive domain and/or social context to adapt, modify or extend it in such a way as to be able to apply it to another" (p. 50). As you read through the following section on macro-level competencies and skills, consider how these competencies and skills may be transferable within and beyond macro social work practice domains.

Macro-Level Competencies and Skills

Preparing social work students to become proficient practitioners requires not only equipping them with the necessary theories, skills, and competencies, but also providing them with practical opportunities to develop and integrate these macro social work skills and behaviours relevant to the field. Macro practice requires an orientation to systems and structures and their impacts on individuals, families, and communities. This section focuses on some key competencies for macro-level practice.

Competencies are the essential practice knowledge, skills, values, abilities, and behaviours that guide professional practice and conduct (Applewhite et al., 2018; Gamble, 2011). Social work competencies are informed by the core values and principles set forth by the CASW's Code of Ethics (2024) and described by the Council on Social Work Education (CSWE) in the United States as professional "practice behaviours" (CSWE, 2008) learned in the classroom and applied, cultivated, and sharpened in field education. Although macro-level social work practice focuses primarily on systems-level functions, macro-level social workers may also be involved with direct individual interventions and supports. As such, macro-level competencies encompass knowledge, skills, and abilities across all practice levels. Several attempts have been made to define and categorize these macro competencies (Applewhite et al., 2018; Gamble, 2011; Kim et al., 2021; Regehr et al., 2012a; Thompson et al., 2019). The description of competencies one identifies with may depend on what aspect of macro practice one is pursuing (for example, policy practice, administration, management, or community development; Applegate et al., 2018). A review of several studies aimed at establishing key skill areas or competencies for macro social work practice was conducted. In this section, we present seven key competencies noted by the CSWE's macro practice guide (2018) and other literature that we believe are relevant to the macro arena and transferable across all levels of social work practice: learning and growth, reflexivity and relationships, leadership, critical thinking, analysis, planning and implementation, professional communications, values and ethics, and research. In describing each of these competences, we will present self-check lists for you to consider as you reflect on your competencies in these areas.

Learning and Growth

Social work is a broad and dynamic profession consisting of increasingly complex and ever-changing settings and demands. Macro-level social workers encounter evolving societal and economic systems, socio-political landscapes, domestic and global policy, and legislative changes, as well as a growing body of evidence-based practice and theoretical approaches (Reisch, 2016). To meet these challenges and respond to the needs of professional practice, Regehr et al. (2005) suggest important traits for macro-level social workers including a keen interest in learning and a commitment to personal and professional growth. As well, the CASW Code of Ethics (2024) requires or encourages social workers to contribute to the ongoing development of the profession and current and future social workers and to advance professional knowledge. Core competencies in this domain include being self-reflexive, enthusiastic, enterprising, and proactive in seeking learning opportunities and facing challenges. According to Mertz et al. (2008), opportunities for social workers to be promoted to senior or management positions tends to occur from within their agencies. However, most social work administrators are not equipped for macro-level practice and thus are not systemically prepared for their administrative jobs. As such, there is a need for ongoing learning and development of macro practice competencies in order to fulfill their administrative duties and responsibilities.

Table 7.5: Self-Check List

SELF-CHECK LIST
☐ Seek learning opportunities
☐ Identify learning goals
☐ Be self-directed
☐ Be self-aware
☐ Be curious
☐ Keep organized

Reflexivity and Relationships

Recognizing power-dynamics and fostering collaboration and inclusivity in creating social change are fundamental to macro-level social work practice. Social workers should be skilled relationship builders, and macro-level social workers proficiently engage with clients; colleagues; stakeholders, including communities; organizations; and systems and exemplify respect and empathy for marginalized populations. This starts by understanding ourselves in reflection and extends to reflecting upon the broader social context in reflexive practice by defining who the client is. A client can be a person, a group of people, a community, an organization or all of these. This distinction and reflection become important in macro-level work. See Table 7.7 for a scenario that highlights the potential tensions and considerations in deciding who is the client.

Regehr and her colleagues (2012b) describe macro-level practitioner traits as warm, considerate, culturally sensitive professionals who are compassionate and passionate about community development and advocacy. Competencies in this domain include interpersonal skills, respect, flexibility, adaptability, self-reflexivity, and motivation.

Table 7.6: Self-Check List

SELF-CHECK LIST
☐ Develop and use engagement stills
☐ Be self-aware and critically reflective
☐ Exemplify integrity
☐ Be respectful
☐ Be adaptable and flexible
☐ Maintain professional boundaries
☐ Be supportive
☐ Be inclusive

Table 7.7: Scenario for Reflection and Discussion

Scenario for Reflection and Discussion

Noel is completing a practicum with a municipal government department focused on affordable housing for young adults. Part of this work has involved facilitating and coordinating a steering committee of local youth-serving agencies, government departments, housing advocates, and young adults with lived experience. Recently, she presented a literature review focused on current research on the impacts of harm reduction strategies in housing programs for young adults. The steering committee had interest in harm reduction programming in this community and had decided at the last meeting that they would make a number of recommendations based on their research. Noel committed to drafting and sharing the recommendations. A week later, an email directive came from the mayor's office stating that the municipality will not be adopting harm reduction initiatives. An election is being announced later this year and harm reduction has become a divisive topic in the community. The current mayor has announced publicly that they do not support harm reduction.

Noel feels conflicted and unsure what to tell the steering committee, how to support them, or how to continue. She meets with her field instructor for supervision and her field instructor asks who her client is. Noel quickly responds that the steering committee is her client, but upon reflection is not sure. She feels as though the mayor's office believes they are her client, but perhaps her clients are the young adults in her community.

Who is Noel's client and how might that impact her practice?

Leadership

A fundamental value of the social work profession is the pursuit of social justice and positive social change (CASW, 2024). The ability to motivate and inspire people to social action are distinguishing leadership attributes. According to Reisch (2016), social action and leadership are the embodiment of macro-level practice throughout the profession's history. As leaders of groups, communities, organizations, and societies, macro social workers should be able to draw on their relationship-building acumen to inspire and educate others to strive for positive and transformative change (CSWE, 2018). Competencies in this domain include possessing institutional knowledge and understanding about systems and communities and relevant policies, being attentive to research innovations and prevailing and evolving theories, and the ability to educate and have supervision and management skills to develop and mentor others, including colleagues and future social workers (CASW, 2020).

Table 7.8: Self-Check List

SELF-CHECK LIST
☐ Identify opportunities for self and others/ organizations
☐ Identify strengths and ways to contribute
☐ Integrate diversity and nurture solidarity to build capacity
☐ Inspire and motivate others
☐ Leed peers/others by example
☐ Expose and redress power differentials
☐ Be compassionate and empowering of others

Critical Thinking, Analysis, Planning, and Implementation

Possessing an aptitude for connecting policy to practice and practice theory to policy development is essential across all social work practice domains, including macro-level practice (McKenzie & Wharf, 2016, pp. 10–11). Macro social workers should be discerning practitioners who are curious about the complexities and barriers of social injustices. In line with a person in environment perspective, they should appreciate the importance of clients' environments and social systems, and explore deeper understandings of the challenges and issues relevant to their field of work and those they support (Kim et al., 2021). They should seek to confront and dismantle oppressive structures and neutralize power dynamics in thoughtful, creative, and constructive ways that incorporate the voices of those from the margins (CSWE, 2018). Macro social workers possess traits that are mindful, perceptive, and holistic in their thinking and approach. Competencies in this domain include strong conceptual and analytic ability and familiarity with diverse socioeconomic, political, and theoretical perspectives, such as critical theory, feminist theory, and anti-oppressive theory.

Table 7.9: Self-Check List

SELF-CHECK LIST
☐ Can see the broader picture
☐ Be able to understand, articulate and implement action
☐ Possess a good understanding of policies and practices
☐ Be able to critically evaluate practice
☐ Maintain an inquisitive stance and ask relevant questions
☐ Be attentive to power differences and giving to primacy to marginalized voices
☐ Be open and responsive

Professional Communications

Strong communication skills are key to establishing and galvanizing trust and creditability when engaging in dialogue with service users, decision makers, and power holders to articulate needs, interventions, and strategies, as well as to disseminate research findings that impact a group, organization, or population (Hardina & Obel-Jorgensen, 2009). Macro-level practitioners are often called to present and exchange information in written, oral, and media formats. They should be attentive listeners who are attuned to the voices of stakeholders, but especially to those who have been ignored or silenced. Competencies in this domain include proficiency in sophisticated writing, ability to confidently deliver accurate information, and to compel, influence and activate positive change (Regehr et al., 2012b).

Table 7.10: Self-Check List

SELF-CHECK LIST
☐ Recognize and use appropriate tone and language
☐ Be insightful
☐ Be a dynamic and engaging presenter
☐ Be clear and accurate
☐ Be attentive and mindful of the audience
☐ Engage in active listening

Values and Ethics

Social workers across all levels adhere to the fundamental values set forth in the CASW (2024) code of ethics and must be committed to engaging in ethical practice. Macro-level practitioners must endeavour to influence and accomplish large-scale positive and transformative change in an ethical manner from a critical and anti-oppressive lens that gives primacy to marginalized voices and epistemologies such as Indigenous wisdom and knowledge (CASW, 2024; CSWE, 2018) Competencies in this domain include integrating the core principles of the Code of Ethics (CASW, 2024), applying an anti-oppressive framework, and recognizing diversity and intersectionality as part of their work with marginalized people and communities.

Table 7.11: Self-Check List

SELF-CHECK LIST
☐ Have a clear sense of personal values and social work identity
☐ Be culturally competent
☐ Upohold human rights, social justice and be commited to social change
☐ Be committed to working with marginalized groups/populations
☐ Possess a solid understanding of professional and agency values and ethics
☐ Be sensitive to diversity
☐ Be committed to antioppressive practice

Research

Inherent to the social work profession is the obligation to "contribute to the ongoing development of the profession" (CASW, 2024, p. 24). Potts and Brown's (2015) assertion that "committing to anti-oppressive research means committing to social justice and taking an active role in that change" (p. 17), speaks to the mission and vision of macro social work practice. Research contributes to the knowledge base of the profession by fostering professional curiosity and cultivating innovation. Competencies in research cross all sectors of social work but are prominent in macro-level practice as relational work that nurtures solidarity and requires political listening and critical reflexivity (Potts & Brown, 2015, p. 29). They include the ability to identify an issue, asking critical and relevant questions, designing, planning, and implementing strategies to address the issue, analyzing data and findings that centre participants' values, and following research protocols (Data, 2018).

Table 7.12: Self-Check List

SELF-CHECK LIST
☐ Be knowledgeable and informed on findings to inform evidence-based practice
☐ Engage in critical analysis and challenge dominant structures, ideas and policies to activate social change
☐ Continually question, evaluate and analyse research data to further advance knowledge-base and influence policy
☐ Committed to collaborating with and organize stakeholders to engage in research activities that inspires social justice efforts

As stated earlier, macro-level practitioners must recognize the structural and systemic factors that disproportionately impact and exclude certain individuals and groups and aims to redress these inequities across all levels and settings. Macro-level practitioners should utilize the multifaceted skills, knowledges, and approaches they learned in class and strengthened in field practicums to shape policy and program development, research, analysis, advocacy, administration, and mobilization that attempts to influence social and political systems towards social justice.

In this section, we have described skills and competencies relevant to macro-level social work: social work practice in policy development, research, analysis, advocacy, administration, and organizing and mobilization that aims to influence organizational, political and social systems.. Although the skills and competencies described relate to macro-level practice, they are transferable and acquirable across all domains of social work practice. Acknowledging this transferability of skills and competencies supports a generalist practice framework and may empower social work practitioners to shift flexibly within and between levels of their social work practice in pursuit of social justice. The next section of the chapter includes concrete examples of the transferability of skills and competencies across social work practice settings, activities for recognizing and cultivating transferable skills and competencies in macro-level contexts, and practical strategies for implementing a generalist practice framework into elements of macro social work field education.

Context for Success

Entering your field practicum is an exciting time in the learning journey and it is important to structure it in a manner that can ensure success. We discuss how the learning contract, learning activities, and integrative seminar can be made most relevant to macro-level practicums. The learning contract and intentional learning activities creates accountability and clarity for all who are involved in supporting the practicum. The integrative seminar is the opportunity to connect classroom knowledge with field experiences and create the "aha moments" that are so critical to the development of one's social work identity.

The Learning Contract

Field education experiences are typically guided by a learning contract document or agreement. The learning contract is generally developed by the student with the input of their field instructor with the field instructor's practice and setting expertise. The contract brings together the expectations of the school, the expressed learning needs of the student and program, and the unique aspects of the practice setting, while being flexible and outlining a baseline level of competencies and expectations (Regehr et al., 2002). Learning contracts clearly establish learning goals and the criteria for assessing progress and performance (Fox & Zischak, 1989).

Students have identified that completing these contracts can be a challenge when entering macro-level field placements; they sometimes describe feeling excluded in the process of creating learning contracts in comparison to their peers in a micro-level setting (Mann-Johnson et al., 2022). This is even though overarching learning objectives are described broadly to include varied levels of social work practice at the micro-level, and macro practice. For example, learning objectives related to professional identity require students to "adopt a value perspective of the social work profession" (CASWE, 2021, p. 13). This value perspective is relevant at both the micro and macro-level. Similarly, learning objectives related to colonialism and recognizing "multiple expressive and experiences of colonialism" (CASWE, 2021, p. 14) are relevant and available in micro and macro settings. Yet, students placed in macro settings describe feeling of being excluded from these learning contracts.

Learning Activities

There are great learning activities available in macro-level settings. Of the seven macro-level competencies identified in the previous section, what competencies do you think these activities could help develop?

- Facilitate a working group, steering committee, focus group.
- Build relationships with stakeholders.

- Write a grant application.
- Create a resource, info sheet, or practice guide.
- Draft a briefing note.
- Complete a jurisdictional scan.
- Complete a needs assessment.
- Draft a social work job description.
- Engage in research on a social issue relevant to the scope of practice.
- Identify who the client is.
- Ask what the role of social work is at the organization.

Table 7.13: Questions

What other learning activities reflect macro-level practice?

What are the competencies that the learning activities above can help develop?

Refer to the self-check lists from the previous section; where are the areas you need to build competence and what are the activities that could help you do that?

Integrative Seminar

The CASWE's accreditation standards require students to participate in an integrative seminar class during their practicum. These courses can be graded, for-credit courses; in some cases, or the courses are ungraded and the hours count toward total practicum hours. Regardless of the format, students can use these opportunities to share their practicum learning experiences with other students, hear from peers about their practicum experiences, and integrate their practicum activities with classroom learning, including theories and knowledge.

We have heard from students in macro placements that when they find they are the only student with a macro placement in a class filled with clinical or direct practice practicum students, they feel significantly disadvantaged because of the need to explain their work or approaches to other students and the focus of classroom discussions generally being of a micro-focus. Students who felt like their macro practicum was an exception in a classroom of students doing micro practicums, felt their learning was lessened and found it challenging to integrate their learning alongside their classmates in micro settings through classroom discussions. Conversely, students who were placed in seminars with other students in macro practicum settings reported feeling greater clarity in their roles as social workers and an ability to integrate social work theory into their practice. The ability to integrate experience in practicum with theory learned in class is bolstered when they can engage in dialogue with other students placed in macro settings and experiencing the same opportunities In situations where seminar classes include students placed in micro and macro settings, discussions should equally highlight practice considerations in both areas.

The role of your faculty liaison and seminar instructor is an important support to your learning and integration. In mixed seminars—those that include micro and macro placed students—social work students can learn from each other, observe overlaps, and have the opportunity to recognize how skills transfer across levels. Your faculty liaisons can challenge the micro/macro divide by highlighting the commonalities between micro and macro practice within classroom discussions. Table 7.14 suggests possible questions to provoke seminar discussions that minimize the divide between micro and macro practice.

Table 7.14: Questions for Seminar

Identify the system(s) in which you are practicing.
From the practicum examples shared in this chapter, what are the theories that informed practice across systems?
Student A shared an example of an ethical dilemma in a macro setting and student B shared an example of an ethical dilemma in a micro setting. What are the similarities?
In the examples shared by the students, who was the client in each example?

Case examples

Anna

Anna is a fourth year, Bachelor of Social Work student completing her senior practicum in a provincial government ministry. Her field instructor is a social worker who oversees a job development program that includes a large grant program. In the first half of her practicum, she shadowed meetings and reviewed grant descriptions and application processes. At the midpoint of her practicum, Anna sat on a committee that reviewed grant applications and made funding decisions. She participated in conversations, including uncomfortable ones that presented ethical dilemmas in resource allocation. She and her field instructor often discussed what social work brings to these conversations and how they can both lead these conversations in a manner that advocates for equity. As a final learning activity in her practicum, Anna was asked to submit a mock grant application; she sat in with a "committee" that included her field instructor and colleagues, and they provided her feedback on her grant application.

Table 7.15: Questions

What competencies in Anna developing in this macro practice?
Which of these competencies are transferable across settings?
Who is Anna's client?

Rahim

Rahim is completing a practicum with a unit that supports child welfare practice and outcomes through policy changes and practice supports like training and manuals provided to direct service caseworkers. Rahim, his field instructor, and their team have drafted and developed several resources and practice guidelines related to promoting ongoing family contact for children and youth placed in alternative care settings during the COVID-19 pandemic. In order to develop these, Rahim interviewed key contacts in other provincial child welfare programs to ask how they were facilitating family contact. Rahim was also responsible for completing a literature review focused on the emotional impacts of reduced family contact on various developmental stages considering trauma, loss, and grief. This information, along with information gathered at meetings with the health system and a town hall meeting with caregivers, was used to inform practice resources that were distributed via email as well as several online learning sessions. Rahim was asked to draft a few sections on these resources and led a section of the online learning session.

Table 7.16: Questions

What competencies did Rahim develop in this macro practicum?
What competencies are transferable across settings?
Who was Rahim's client?

Table 7.17: Transferable Skills

COMMUNITY COUNSELLOR	COMMUNITY PLANNER
Provide counseling to individuals, couples, and groups.	Facilitate meetings with agency staff, and community stakeholders.
Facilitate therapeutic groups.	Facilitate focus groups and public forums to gather community feedback on current policies and desired changes.
Develop and deliver psychoeducational workshops.	Develop and deliver presentations to disseminate research findings.
Advocate for clients' best interests with other professionals, groups, and organizations.	Participate in research activities, including literature reviews, evaluation, and funded research.
Network with community agencies to build and nourish working relationships.	Advocate for policy changes based on the public's best interests.
Effective oral and written communication including case reports and summaries, and outcome reporting.	Network with potential local, provincial, and national partners to develop and build on existing relationships.
Regular practice evaluation and contributing to program evaluation.	Effective oral and written communication including reports to disseminate research and information and grant applications to fund programs.

The principle of transferable skills between micro and macro practice is apparent as we look at the comparison of the job advertisements in Table 7.17. While the social work position listed on the left is considered micro in focus and the position on the right is considered macro, think about the similarities of the required skills for each job.

Concluding Thoughts

Macro practice and field education in macro settings strengthen social work identities and connect us to the spirit of social work described by Jane Addams (1920) quoted at the beginning of this chapter. Considering the ability of macro practice to influence social change, it is essential for social workers and social work students to engage in this type of practice in the pursuit of social justice. Changes at macro levels influence large systems and ensures justice for individuals. By maneuvering within the macro, students gain valuable competencies across levels of practice to then truly engage in the spirit of social work across all levels.

REFERENCES

Alberta Kings Printer. (2024). Health Profession Act, SA 2000. C. H-7, s. 27. https://www.qp.alberta.ca/documents/Acts/h07.pdf

Apgar, D. (2020). Increasing social work students' participation in macro specializations: The impossible dream? *Advances in Social Work*, *20*(3), 709–724. https://doi.org/10.18060/24045

Apgar, D., & Parada, M. (2018). Strengthening competency in policy practice: An experiential model for student learning. *The Journal of Baccalaureate Social Work*, *23*(1), 145–158. https://doi.org/10.18084/1084-7219.23.1.145

Applewhite, S. R., Kao, D., & Pritzker, S. (2018). Educator and practitioner views of professional competencies for macro social work practice. *International Social Work*, *61*(6), 1169–1186. https://doi.org/10.1177/0020872817702705

Austin, M. J., Coombs, M., & Barr, B. (2005). Community-centered clinical practice: Is the integration of micro and macro social work practice possible? *Journal of Community Practice*, *13*(4), 9–30. https://doi.org/10.1300/J125v13n04_02

Bridges, D. (1993). Transferable skills: A philosophical perspective. *Studies in Higher Education (Dorchester-on-Thames)*, *18*(1), 43–51. https://doi.org/10.1080/03075079312331382448

Brieland, D. (1990). The Hull-House tradition and the contemporary social worker: Was Jane Addams really a social worker? *Social Work*, *35*(2), 134–138. https://doi.org/10.1093/sw/35.2.134

Canadian Association for Social Work Education. (2021). *Educational policies and accreditation standards for social work education*. https://caswe-acfts.ca/wp-content/uploads/2021/04/EPAS-2021.pdf

Canadian Association of Social Workers. (2024). *CASW code of ethics, values and guiding principles 2024*. https://www.casw-acts.ca/en/casw-code-ethics-2024

Canadian Association of Social Workers. (2020). *CASW scope of practice statement*. https://www.cswe.org/getattachment/d778d922-bf29-49c4-bef0-28873937f41f/2018-statistics-on-social-work-education-in-the-united-states-ver-2.pdf/

Council on Social Work Education. (2018). *Specialized practice curricular guide for macro social work practice: 2015 EPAS curricular guide resource series*. https://www.cswe.org/CSWE/media/Curricular-Guides/Macro-Social-Work-Curricular-Guide.pdf

Canadian Association of Social Workers. (2019). *2018 Statistics on social work education in the United States*. https://www.onlinemswprograms.com/wp-content/uploads/sites/55/2021/06/2018-Statistics-on-Social-Work-Education-in-the-United-States.pdf

Data, R. (2018). Decolonizing both researcher and research and its effectiveness in indigenous research. *Research Ethics*, *14*(2), 1–24. https://doi.org/10.1177/1747016117733296

de Saxe Zerden, L., Sheely, A., & Depard, M. R. (2016). Debunking macro myths: findings from recent graduates about jobs, salaries, and skills. *Social Work Education, 35*(7), 752–766. https://doi.org/10.1080/02615479.2016.1188915

Dore, M. M. (1999). The retail method of social work: The role of the New York school in the development of clinical practice. *Social Service Review, 73*(2), 169–190. https://doi.org/10.1086/514413

Ezell, M., Chernesky, R., & Healy, L. (2004). The learning climate for administration students. *Administration in Social Work, 28*(1), 57–76. http://doi.org/10.1300/J147v28n01_05

Fox, R., & Zschka, P.C. (1989). The field instruction contract: A paradigm for effective learning. *Journal of Teaching in Social Work, 3*(1), 103–116. https://doi.org/10.1300/J067v03n01_09

Gamble, D. N. (2011) Advanced concentration macro competencies for social work practitioners: Identifying knowledge, values, judgment and skills to promote human well-being. *Journal of Community Practice, 19*(4), 369–402. https://doi.org/10.1080/10705422.2011.625914

Greenfield, E. (2010). Developmental systems theory as a conceptual anchor for generalist curriculum on human behaviour and the social environment. *Social Work Education, 30*(5), 529–540. https://doi.org/10.1080/02615479.2010.503237

Hardina, D., & Obel-Jorgensen, R. (2009). Increasing social action competency: A framework for supervision. *Journal of Policy Practice, 8*(2), 89–109. https://doi.org/10.1080/15588740902740074

Haynes, D. T., & White, B. W. (1999). Will the 'real' social work please stand up? A call to stand for professional unity. *Social Work, 44*(4), 385–391. https://doi.org/10.1093/sw/44.4.385

Heron, B. A. (2019) Neoliberalism and social work regulation: Implications for epistemic resistance. *Canadian Social Work Review, 36*(1), 65–81. https://doi.org/10.7202/1064661ar

Holtz Deal, K., Hopkins, K. Fisher, L., & Hartin, J. (2007). Field practicum experience of macro-oriented graduate students: Are we doing them justice? *Administration in Social Work, 31*(4), 41–58. https://doi.org/10.1300/J147v31n04_05

Hunter, C. A., & Ford, K. A. (2010). Discomfort with a false dichotomy: The field director's dilemma with micro–macro placements. *Journal of Baccalaureate Social Work, 15*(1), 15–29. https://doi.org/10.18084/basw.15.1.4077u45512526222

Kim, H., Sussman, T., Khan, M. N., & Kahn, S. (2021). 'All social work takes place in a macro context': The gap between international social work training and practice. *International Social Work, 42*(1), 1–15. https://doi.org/10.1177/0020872821993524

LaTosch, K., & Jones, K. (2012) Conducting macro-level work in a micro-focused profession. *Practice Digest, 2*(1), 1–3. https://www2.simmons.edu/ssw/fe/i/LaTosch.pdf

Lavitt, M. (2009). What is advanced in generalist practice? A conceptual discussion. *Journal of Teaching in Social Work, 29*, 461–473. https://doi.org/10.1080/08841230903253267

Mann-Johnson, J., MacLaughlin, A.,Vos, B., & Wandler, M. (2022). Meeting the needs of students placed in macro-level practicum settings [Unpublished manuscript].

Mattocks, N. O. (2018). Social action among social work practitioners: Examining the micro-macro divide. *Social Work, 63*(1), 7–16. https://doi.org/10.1093/sw/swx057

McKenzie, B., & Wharf, B. (2016). *Connecting policy to practice in the human services.* (4th ed.). Oxford University Press Canada.

McLaughlin, A. M. (2002). Social work's legacy. Irreconcilable differences? *Clinical Social Work Journal, 30*, 187–198. https://doi.org/10.1023/A:1015297529215

Mertz, L. K. P., Fortune, A. E., & Zendell, A. L. (2007). Promoting leadership skills in field education: A university-community partnership to bring macro and micro together in gerontological field placements. *Journal of Gerontological Social Work, 50*(1-2), 173–186. https://doi.org/10.1300/J083v50n01_12

Miller, S. E., Tice, C. J., & Harneck Hall, D. M. (2008). The generalist model: Where do the micro and macro converge? *Advances in Social Work, 9*(2), 79–90. https://journals.iupui.edu/index.php/advancesinsocialwork/article/view/203/198

Potts, K., & Brown, L. (2015). Becoming an anti-oppressive researcher. In S. Strega and L. Brown (Eds.), *Research as resistance: Revisiting critical, Indigenous, and anti-oppressive approaches*, (2nd ed., pp. 17–41). Canadian Scholars' Press.

Preston, S., & Aslett, J. (2014). Resisting neoliberalism from within the academy: Subversion through an activist pedagogy. *Social Work Education, 33*(3), 502–518. https://doi.org/10.1080/02615479.2013.848270

Regehr, C., Regehr, G., Leeson, J., & Fusco, L. (2002). Setting priorities for learning in the field practicum: A comparative study of students and field instructors. *Journal of Social Work Education, 38*(1), 55–65. https://doi.org/10.1080/104 37797.2002.10779082

Regehr, C., Bogo, M., Donovan, K., Lim, A., & Regehr, G. (2012a). Evaluating a scale to measure student competencies in macro social work practice. *Journal of Social Services Research, 38*(1), 100–109. https://doi.org/10.1080/01488376.2 011.616756

Regehr, C., Bogo, M., Donovan, K., Lim, A., & Anstice, S. (2012b). Identifying student competencies in macro practice: Articulating the practice wisdom of field instructors. *Journal of Social Work Education, 48*(2), 307–319. https://doi. org/10.5175/JSWE.2012.201000114

Reisch, M. (2016). Why macro practice matters. *Journal of Social Work Education, 54*(3), 258–268. https://doi.org/10.1080/ 10437797.2016.1174652

Rothman, J., & Mizrahi, T. (2014). Balancing micro and macro practice: A challenge for social work. *Social Work, 59*(1), 91–93. http://www.jstor.org/stable/23719548

Shdaimah, C. S., & McCoyd, J. L. M. (2012). Social work sense and sensibility: A framework for teaching an integrated perspective. *Social Work Education, 31*(1), 22–35. https://doi.org/10.1080/02615479.2010.541237

Strier, R. (2019). Resisting neoliberal social work fragmentation: The wall-to-wall alliance. *Social Work, 64*(4), 339–345. https://doi.org/10.1093/sw/swz036

Thompson, J. B., Spano, R., & Koenig, T. L. (2019). Back to Addams and Richmond: Was social work really a divided house in the beginning? *Journal of Sociology and Social Welfare, 46*(2), 3–22. https://scholarworks.wmich.edu/jssw/ vol46/iss2/1/

University nuhelot'įnethaiyots'į nistameyimâkanak Blue Quills. (2019). *Honouring sacred relationships: Wise practices in Indigenous social work.* Alberta College of Social Workers. https://acsw.in1touch.org/uploaded/web/RPT_ IndigenousSocialWorkPracticeFramework_Final_20190219.pdf

van Heugten, K. (2011). Registration and social work education: A golden opportunity or a Trojan horse? *Journal of Social Work, 11*(2), 174–190. https://doi.org/10.1177/1468017310386695

Weiss-Gal, I. (2008). The person-in-environment approach: Professional ideology and practice of social workers in Israel. *Social Work, 53*(1), 65–75. https://doi.org/10.1093/sw/53.1.65

NOTES:

NOTES:

NOTES:

Developing a Theoretical Framework for Practice

Heather I. Peters

Developing a theoretical framework for social work practice is one of the key aspects of social work education, although many students, and even educators and practicing social workers, are not clear on what this means or how to go about it. One of the perceived tensions between theory and practice is that of theories versus skills. Students often enter social work programs wanting to learn skills to allow them to work effectively with clients, whereas educators can appear to be more interested in teaching theories. While the two are closely connected, bridging the gap between them can be challenging. This chapter describes how theories and skills necessarily go hand-in-hand and lays out a process to support students in developing their own theoretical framework for practice in a way that will make clear how this framework informs, and is crucial to, one's social work practice and the use of practice skills.

Gap Between Theory and Practice

Social work academics have been discussing the gap between theory and practice and describing it as a common challenge in the social work discipline for decades (Bogo & Vayda, 1998; Mullaly, 2007; Mullaly & Dupré, 2019; Peters, 2010; Pilalis, 1986; Reynolds, 1942, 1963). Students commonly experience difficulties in integrating various theories with practice when they begin field work (Bogo & Vayda, 1998; Vayda & Bogo, 1991). In addition, social work programs often struggle with how to assist students in making this link (Boisen & Syers, 2004).

There are two related tensions in discussions of theory and practice that come up during social work practice and in field placements. First is the age-old debate of which comes first: theory or practice. In this case, it is typically academics stating that theory should guide practice, while practitioners less disposed to theory suggest that personal experiences of practice should guide future interventions (Lee, 1982; Smith, 1971). Others suggest that practitioners utilize theory even if they are not aware of it (Mullaly, 2007; Mullaly & Dupré, 2019; Reay, 1986). This happens as practitioners examine their experiences for patterns that they then use to guide their future actions. Through this process, people essentially develop informal theories of their own making, which then guide their practice (Mullaly & Dupré, 2019). These experiential theories are rarely articulated let alone subjected to analysis and research. Using self-created and unexamined theories can, at the least, lead to somewhat disorganized work with clients, and at the worst, can cause damage and distress (Mullaly, 2007; Mullaly & Dupré, 2019; Robbins et al., 1999). Thus, this chapter lays out a perspective of how and why it is crucial that theory inform one's practice and use of practice skills.

The second debate around theory and practice is whether one should use a specific theoretical approach in which the practitioner has expertise, or if practitioners should use aspects of various theories that are relevant to them and their work (Poulter, 2005; Robbins et al., 1999). The latter eclectic approach to a theoretical framework where a practitioner mixes and matches pieces of theories that work for them is also problematic. This approach often arises from a superficial understanding of theory and can result in the misuse of theory in practice settings (Mullaly, 2007; Robbins et al., 1999). Using theories in this way can result in an approach that is inconsistent and inaccurately applied, potentially resulting in distress for clients rather than being of benefit to them. Yet using only one theory to guide practice can be somewhat constraining and is frustrating when a different theory may be better suited to a particular social issue. Students are taught to be flexible and responsive to clients' needs and to be prepared to do things differently if something does not work for a client. Why would this not also be true for the use of theories? The development of a theoretical framework for practice seeks to strike a balance between these perspectives, where one grand or overarching theory is the foundation of one's practice, and a number of practice theories are used within that context. This is explained further on in this chapter.

Social work is not alone with these dilemmas; these problematic understandings of theory and practice can pose issues in other professional disciplines as well. The potential devastating effects of the misuse, or lack of use, of theories is important to understand. It is necessary to utilize practice theories which are well-established and which have been analyzed, thoroughly detailed, and studied to ensure that they are internally consistent, predictive, and have positive outcomes (Hammond et al., 2020). The term "evidence-based practice" is relevant here, as the theories used in practice need to be demonstrated to have the desired outcome that is beneficial for clients. It also means that social workers are responsible to ensure that they understand theory, how it guides their practice, and that they can articulate a theoretical framework for practice.

ACTIVITY AND REFLECTION 1

Ask social workers and others at your field placement how they use (or do not use) theories in their practice and which theories they use and why (or why not). Reflect on their responses in your field journal and summarize what you learn on the next page.

A Brief Theoretical History of Social Work

The social work profession has drawn on theories from a number of other disciplines in its search for a unifying theory for the profession (Lundy, 2011). Theories and information from disciplines such as psychology, sociology, anthropology, women's studies, and more have influenced social work at different times, and many are often still utilized in the context of social work practice. The variety of theories that have influenced social work has led to a great diversity in how social work is practiced. As a relatively new discipline in the late 1800s and early 1900s, social work explored many theories and types of practice (Lundy, 2011). An understanding of the history of social work practice is necessary to clarify the two approaches that ended up vying to be the unifying approach in social work.

An approach to social work that blames individuals evolved out of the English Poor Laws of the 1500s whereby poverty was addressed with punishment for the purpose of ensuring that people had the "proper" motivation to seek employment (Carniol, 2005). In the late 1800s, the Charitable Organization Society (COS) developed in Britain and quickly spread to North America (Carniol, 2005; Reynolds, 1963). The Poor Laws informed this perspective of social work such that COS workers focused on identifying the flaws of individuals seeking support services in an effort to determine if they were deserving of help. The focus of these charitable and religious organizations, although more "friendly" than the Poor Laws' focus on punishment, continued to address poverty and other social issues by "fixing" the individual and by distinguishing between those they determined to be deserving or undeserving of help (Carniol, 2005; Finkel, 2006; Hick, 2002; Lundy, 2011).

The late 19th century also heralded the development of the settlement house movement in both Canada and the United States, with a shift in perspective that understood poverty, and other social issues, as embedded in societal structures (Finkel, 2006; Hick, 2002; Lundy, 2011; Reynolds, 1963). This social service movement sought to identify structural and systemic barriers facing the people they worked with, thus striving to change structures and the system, more so than individuals. Since then, social work has been divided between two streams, the first of which focuses on assisting individuals in meeting their needs and coping with their environments, and the second, which seeks political and social reform to address the root causes of poverty and other issues (Lundy, 2011). The separation between the two streams of social work has never been completely clear cut. For example, the settlement houses, in addition to addressing social structures, also sought to "reform the poor" (Finkel, 2006, p. 86). Other movements also encompassed social justice thinking to various extents, including the urban reform and social gospel movements (Guest, 2006). Yet these two distinctions are important.

These two historic ways of practicing social work are connected to the types of theories that have informed the discipline over the years. Theories to support individual change and theories to understand systemic issues and promote structural change have all became enveloped into the social work field and are still relevant today.

ACTIVITY AND REFLECTION 2

PART A

Watch the 30-minute video *Theories in Social Work Practice* (citation found in the resources section at the end of this chapter and can be accessed through your university's library). In your journal, reflect on which theories you would like to use in your social work practice and why, as well as any theories you would not want to use and why not.

PART B

Think about the theories you have studied in your social work education and field placement, thus far. List as many theories as possible in the space below. We are going to use this list as the basis of additional activities further on in this chapter, so try to come up with 15 or so theories from as many diverse disciplines as possible. Feel free to refer back to other chapters in this text, to another theory textbook, or draw on the video *Theories in Social Practice* to add more theories to your list.

Organizing Theories: Structural or Casework

At first glance, a long list of theories can be confusing when one is trying to develop a theoretical framework for practice. There are many theories, and most of them sound interesting and appear to address relevant aspects of people's lives. Combined with the knowledge that an eclectic approach to using bits and pieces of various theories is not considered good practice (Mullaly, 2007; Robbins et al., 1999), it can be overwhelming to see so many potentially beneficial theories and wonder how to choose which to use in practice. Understanding the connection between theories and the two historic streams of social work is a starting point for organizing theories.

There are two streams of social work theories, the first which focuses on social structures and the second which focuses on individuals and families. It is the focus on social structures, coming out of the settlement houses, that is connected to the current development of structural social work theory, anti-oppressive theory, and other social justice perspectives in social work that have an emphasis on structural or systemic change (Carniol, 2005; Lundy, 2011; Mullaly & Dupré, 2019). In contrast, the casework perspective, coming out of the COS, is typically connected to current clinical and micro approaches with more of a focus on supporting individuals and families in personal change. These two streams are still evident in social work theories and practice today (Lundy, 2011; Mullaly & Dupré, 2019).

Mullaly and Dupré (2019) describe a method of organizing theories that will be used here. They call the theories related to casework and the COS the conventional (or traditional) approaches. The theories related to settlement houses and a structural analysis are called progressive approaches to practice. The social work profession and academic discipline has increasingly become aligned with progressive approaches as social workers recognize that challenging oppression is a political act. However, this does not mean that conventional approaches are "wrong", or are off-limits for practice. According to Mullaly and Dupré, "although the conventional approaches . . . have historically reinforced the status quo, they can be used in progressive ways" (2019, p. 5). Thus, while it is important to decide whether to practice from a conventional or progressive framework, there are ways to incorporate work with individuals into progressive approaches.

ACTIVITY AND REFLECTION 3

In this exercise, connect each theory you listed in Activity and Reflection 2, Part B. above, with either a progressive approach, which seeks to change structures, or a conventional approach, which focuses more on individual growth and change. Rewrite the theories from Activity and Reflection 2 into the most relevant category in the box on the next page.

PROGRESSIVE APPROACHES	CONVENTIONAL APPROACHES	UNCERTAIN

In the 1960s, one of the proposed theories to unify the social work discipline was systems theory (Lundy, 2011; Mullaly & Dupré, 2019). Instead of focusing solely on the individual or family, systems theory identifies the environment within which the person or family is located as important to understanding and working with people. While this addition of the environment to theories focused on the individual or family was a significant step forward, there is a general consensus in the social work discipline that ultimately the theory did not go far enough to recognize structures of oppression, nor did it propose structural change (Lundy, 2011; Mullaly & Dupré, 2019). Mullaly and Dupré (2019) add systems theories to the conventional approaches, albeit in a type of sub-category to acknowledge the environmental context.

Table 8.1 lays out a sampling of theories in these three different categories. It is grounded in the discussion above and is based on Table 8.1 in the Mullaly and Dupré text (2019, p. 6). The theories listed here are a small sampling of the numerous theories that could be included.

Table 8.1: Progressive and Conventional Approaches to Social Work in Perspective

PROGRESSIVE APPROACHES	CONVENTIONAL APPROACHES	
	Conventional approaches focused on person in environment	Conventional approaches focused on individual change
• structural social work theory • Marxist theory • critical race theory • critical social work theory • feminist theory • post-colonial theory • Indigenous theory • Afri-centric theory • just therapy	• systems theory • ecosystems theory • strengths perspective • trauma-informed perspective • family systems theory	• behavioural therapy • cognitive behavioural therapy • psychosocial therapy • casework • psychodynamic therapy

ACTIVITY AND REFLECTION 4

Compare the theories here and the categories they are placed in, with your responses in Activity and Reflection 3. For a deeper understanding of progressive and conventional approaches and their connections to theory, read the chapter titled The Social Work Vision, in the textbook *The New Structural Social Work: Ideology, Theory and Practice* (Mullaly & Dupré, 2019). In your journal, reflect on how to understand the differences between theories consistent with a progressive approach and those consistent with the two types of conventional perspectives. Make connections to the Mullaly and Dupré (2019) chapter in your journal writing.

Organizing Theories: Grand or Practice

This next section of the chapter explores a second way of organizing theories. Having two ways of organizing theories may be confusing at first, so I use the analogy of organizing vegetables to explain it. One way to organize vegetables is to put all the root vegetables in one group and all the vegetables grown above ground in another group. Alternatively, vegetables could be grouped by colour, causing the groupings to change. These two ways of organizing vegetables can both be useful in different contexts; it does not mean that one is better than the other. Likewise, using two ways to organize theories does not mean that one is right and one wrong, nor that one is more important or useful than the other. The need for two ways to organize theories will become clear as we move through the next sections. These are important elements of developing a theoretical framework for practice.

Many theoretical analysts, across disciplines, have described another way of organizing theories; they distinguish between levels of theory, or grand theories and practice theories (Fook, 1993; Hammond et al., 2020; Marchant, 1986). Grand theories are those that describe an overarching understanding of society, social issues, and how the world works. As these theories try to explain many issues and contexts at a broad level, they are sometimes seen as being more abstract or even vague, possibly even confusing (Hammond et al., 2020). Practice theories, also known as middle-range theories (Hammond et al., 2020), are narrower in scope and typically focus on a specific issue or concept.

An example of a grand theory is critical theory, which came out of Marxist theory and seeks to connect society, social relationships, and economics, among other things (Mullaly & Dupré, 2019). An example of a practice theory is the stages of change theory developed by Prochaska and Di Clemente, which was developed to specifically explain one formulation of addictions and posits ideas on how to better motivate people to reduce or stop their substance use based on what stage of change they are at when in counselling (Prochaska et al., 1992; Prochaska & DiClemente, 1983). Critical theory is complex and abstract and speaks to people in the context of society, nation states, and globalization, while the stages of change theory is very specific, smaller in scale, and focused on an individual's struggle with the issue of substance use.

ACTIVITY AND REFLECTION 5

The fifth exercise asks you to think about the theories you listed in Activity and Reflection 2, Part B and identify if they are a grand theory or a practice (or middle-range) theory. Using your list of theories from Activity and Reflection 2, Part B, place each theory in the column below with which it has the best fit. Notice as you do this, that the theories will not be in the same groups as they were in Activity and Reflection 3 or Table 8.1 above.

PROGRESSIVE APPROACHES	CONVENTIONAL APPROACHES	UNCERTAIN

Levels of Practice: Connecting Grand Theories, Practice Theories, and Skills

Fook (1993) connected grand theories, practice theories, and skills in a format that described these as levels of theories and skills. Level one is that of grand theories, level two is practice (or middle-range) theories, and level three is skills or activities used in social work practice. In her book, Fook (1993) connected radical (also known as critical or structural) theory to social work practice by linking these three levels. It is in identifying these linkages that we begin to develop a theoretical framework for practice.

A theoretical framework for practice needs to include a number of elements. First, it needs to include at least one grand theory that provides an overarching explanatory understanding of society and social problems. Second, it needs to contain a number of practice theories that are directly related to the choice of grand theory so that the framework is internally consistent.

Keep in mind that, as discussed earlier, it is problematic to incorporate too many theories into one's practice (Robbins et al., 1999). It takes time to learn about a theory in enough depth to use it accurately in one's professional work. Incorporating too many theories initially means a person is likely utilizing bits and pieces of various theories in an eclectic fashion, rather than understanding them in depth and using them in a consistent way. Proceeding with an eclectic approach can be damaging to clients rather than beneficial. We can know a few things in great depth, or many things in a superficial way, but especially when new to practice it is not possible to quickly become an expert in many theories. Therefore, when starting out in the social work profession it is better to start with a fewer number of theories in order to ensure an adequate depth of knowledge of the theories to be able to use them effectively and accurately. As a person uses these theories through the years, and continues with their professional development, over time they will be able to add more practice theories to their framework in a slow, studied, and consistent manner, ensuring that each new theory fits into the framework in a coherent way. I suggest that students start with one grand theory and a small number (three to five) of related practice theories. Table 8.2 is an example of a grand theory and five practice level theories consistent with that grand theory.

Table 8.2: An Example of a Theoretical Framework for Practice that is Internally Consistent

GRAND THEORY	PRACTICE THEORIES CONSISTENT WITH THE GRAND THEORY
• critical theory and/or structural theory	• feminist counselling • anti-racism theory • anti-oppression education or community development • theories addressing oppression • policy analysis framework

Critical and structural theories have at their core an analysis of power, privilege, and oppression and seek to challenge structures and systems that create or maintain oppression (Fook, 2002; Mullaly & Dupré, 2019). It is possible to see in this example that the practice theories in the second column of Table 8.2 fit well with critical theory and/or structural theory. Yet, while social work practice from a critical or structural framework may indicate the need to work at a macro level, practitioners can work from these perspectives even while working in micro or clinical contexts. In this case, there are other aspects of clinical work and approaches that we may want to bring into this framework too. Casework is necessary in clinical practice, and a practitioner may want to incorporate strengths-based or problem-solving approaches as well. However, casework, strengths-based and problem-solving approaches grew out of a conventional framework, while critical and structural theories are progressive approaches. This is where having the framework, and the grand theory, in place is key. In this context, we could incorporate these conventional approaches while ensuring that they are implemented from and within a progressive framework. For example, instead of utilizing casework as an approach to working with clients, we can identify that casework is a skill or activity that we use, within a progressive framework, to organize, plan and document our practice with clients. To acknowledge the progressive theoretical framework, a social worker would maintain casework records and case planning in a progressive manner such as: ensuring the documentation of experiences of oppression and privilege by the client; planning for consciousness-raising activities to educate clients on the structural nature of the social problems they are experiencing (such as racism, heterosexism, sexism, ableism, classism, ageism, etc); connecting clients with others experiencing similar social problems; actively challenging structural barriers and documenting such barriers as structural for clients (rather than a personal flaw) in case notes; advocating for clients; encouraging clients to lobby for structural change; etc. In this way casework is not a practice approach, which is inherently conventional in nature, but aspects of casework are adapted and molded into a progressive theoretical framework. The literature has identified challenges to incorporating conventional approaches into a progressive theoretical framework, but it is important, possible and necessary to work through the challenges (Baines, 2000, 2003). In the previous example, one way to address this challenge is to first not utilize conventional approach at a theoretical level, but rather to identify the techniques within the approach that are useful, and second to articulate the ways in which those techniques can be utilized in a progressive manner. Without this second step we risk simply wanting to be progressive without actually doing it, and accidentally sliding into a conventional practice.

Finally, the last piece to incorporate into our framework is that of skills or activities that we use in social work practice. The grand theory provides the overarching structure to our social work practice and keeps us on track, ensuring that our practice is connected and consistent. The grand theory informs and influences our choice of practice theories. Both the grand and practice theories in turn create the foundation for how we use practice skills, what kinds of questions we ask clients, and what awareness-raising and educational focuses we have in sharing information with clients, groups, and communities.

Table 8.3: Brief Example of a Progressive Theoretical Framework for Practice

GRAND THEORY	PRACTICE THEORIES	PRACTICE SKILLS AND ACTIVITIES
• critical theory and / or structural theory (some use these interchangeably with anti-oppressive theory)	• feminist counselling • anti-racism theory • anti-oppression education or community development • theories addressing all types of oppression • consciousness-raising • policy analysis framework	• questions related to experiences of oppression and privilege and the effects on the client • challenging structures that maintain oppression • developing policies to further inclusivity and challenge oppression

Table 8.4: Brief Example of a Conventional Framework for Practice

GRAND THEORY	PRACTICE THEORIES	PRACTICE SKILLS AND ACTIVITIES
• humanist and or psychodynamic theory	• client centred perspective • problem-solving theory • strengths-based theory • psychotherapy	• questions related to thoughts and feelings • support the client to grow and live a fulfilling life

Ultimately, the choice of which grand theory and practice theories to use is yours to make. As a discipline, social work's contribution to practice and study is to bring together people, communities, societies, environments, and structures to create a unique understanding of how society works and the barriers to well-being. In Canada, social work education through the Canadian Association of Social Work Education (CASWE; 2014) is clear that understanding issues of oppression at micro, mezzo and macro levels is key to our understanding of the world and our practice. This is consistent with Mullaly and Dupré's (2019) description of a progressive vision of social work and with other discussions in the literature (Baines, 2000; Campbell 2003a, 2003b). Thus, I suggest that social workers ought to set as their foundation a grand theory that is consistent with this progressive vision; practice theories need to be consistent, not in conflict, with that approach. However, the choice is yours.

ACTIVITY AND REFLECTION 6

PART A

The short (three minute) video called *Counseling Theory vs. Techniques* helps explain how to incorporate practice theories or techniques from various theories into your overall theoretical orientation or framework. Watch the video here: https://www.youtube.com/watch?v=S3yBPuf46Jo

PART B

Based on this chapter and your knowledge of theories, create your own theoretical framework for social work practice. Choose one grand theory, three to five practice theories that are theoretically and philosophically consistent with your grand theory, and identify related skills and activities consistent with your overall framework. Describe how your choice of grand and practice theories will influence which skills you will use in practice as well as how you will use those skills differently. Record your theoretical framework here and reflect on why you made the choices you did in your journal.

To determine if the practice theories you have chosen are related to each other, look to see if they are in the same column in Activity and Reflection 3 or Table 8.1. Grouping theories into conventional or progressive categories is the starting point for understanding if they are related to each other (in the same column) or are not (in different columns). Theories that are not related to each other may be in conflict with each other. To prevent this, the starting point is to identify, and refer back to, the overarching grand theory. The next step is to acknowledge which components of non-related approaches are being used, and then identify what will be done to ensure these techniques are being utilized in manner consistent with the grand theory and your overall framework (as per the example given in text before Table 8.3). Describe how you will do this in your journal reflections. (For more information on grand versus practice theories and on ways to incorporate techniques from one approach into a different theoretical framework approach see Fook 1993 and Mullaly and Dupré 2019, especially chapter 1 on a social work vision).

GRAND THEORY	PRACTICE THEORIES	PRACTICE SKILLS AND ACTIVITIES
REFLECTIONS SUMMARY:		

Conclusion

Your field placement is an excellent opportunity to explore numerous theories and ways in which to bring theories into your social work practice. Remember that this is the start of your theoretical framework; begin small and seek to develop a depth of understanding of the theories you identify. The framework you develop now is just a beginning of your work and does not have to be the final framework you will use in your practice. Just as theories are dynamic and grow and develop, so your own theoretical framework will grow and develop over time through your professional practice and with continuing professional development.

Discussion Questions

1. Have you heard social workers or other practitioners talk about the use of theory in their practice? Do they support having a theoretical framework, and can they identify the one they use? Or do they prefer to make practice decisions based on their personal experiences or an eclectic use of theory? Give examples of each of these.

2. Working with other students, share your responses and categorizing decisions to Activity and Reflection 3 and how each of you organized the theories. Discuss why you put the theories in particular categories. Focus on theories some people were not sure how to categorize and on differences of opinion about where theories best fit. Explain your thinking to each other and try to agree on where the theories fit best.

3. What are the key differences between grand theories and practice theories? List some grand theories and some practice theories. Which grand theories best fit with which practice theories? Share your thoughts with others; where you disagree with each other, explain your thinking and try to agree on the best fit. Why do you need both grand and practice theories in your theoretical framework?

4. Choose a topic or social issue, such as working with a client with addictions, or a client experiencing racism. First work from a casework or personal change theoretical perspective and come up with a list of six to eight questions that you would ask of the client. Second, work from a structural change perspective and identify another list of six to eight questions you would ask the client. How and why are these questions different from each other? Are there any questions that overlap with both approaches (i.e. can the same question be asked with either approach)? Why or why not? Discuss how one's theoretical framework guides the choice of questions you use with a client.

5. Share your draft theoretical framework for practice with other students. Discuss why each of you have chosen your particular theories and framework. How does your framework influence or speak to the type of practice you want to do? How do people with different frameworks complement each other? How much room is there for different frameworks across the social work profession, and is there a point at which the differences could be problematic?

RESOURCES

Lary, B. (Producer), & Lary, B. (Director). (2005). *Theories in social work practice.* [Video]. Promedion.

Dean A. (2017, May 18). *Counseling theory vs. techniques* [Video]. YouTube. https://www.youtube.com/watch?v=S3yBPuf46Jo

The video *Counseling Theory vs. Techniques* helps explain how to incorporate practice theories or techniques from various theories into your overall theoretical orientation or framework (three minutes long).

Mullaly, B. & Dupre, M. (2019). Chapter 1: The social work vision. In *The new structural social work: Ideology, theory, and practice.* Oxford University Press.

REFERENCES

Baines, D. (2000). Everyday practices of race, class and gender: Struggles, skills and radical social work. *Journal of Progressive Human Services, 11*(2), 5–27. https://doi.org/10.1300/J059v11n02_02

———. (2003). Race, class, and gender in everyday talk of social workers: The ways we limit the possibilities for radical practice. In W. Shera (Ed.), *Emerging perspectives on anti-oppressive practice* (pp. 43–64). Canadian Scholars' Press Inc.

Campbell, C. (2003a). Anti-oppressive theory and practice as the organizing theme for social work education: The case in favour. *Canadian Social Work Review, 20*(1), 121–125. https://www.jstor.org/stable/41670001

———. (2003b). Struggling for congruency: Principles and practices of anti-oppressive social work pedagogy. National Library of Canada, Ottawa. https://research.library.mun.ca/10259/

Carniol, B. (1992). Structural social work: Maurice Moreau's challenge to social work practice. *Journal of Progressive Human Services, 3*(1), 1–20. https://doi.org/10.1300/J059v03n01_01

———. (2005). *Case critical: Social services and social justice in Canada.* (5th ed.). Between the Lines.

Canadian Association of Social Work Education. (2014). *Standards for accreditation.* https://caswe-acfts.ca/wp-content/uploads/2013/03/CASWE-ACFTS.Standards-11-2014-1.pdf

Finkel, A. (2006). *Social policy and practice in Canada: A history.* Wilfrid Laurier University Press.

Fook, J. (1993). *Radical casework: A theory of practice.* Allen & Unwin Pty. Ltd.

Fook, J. (2002). *Social work: Critical theory and practice.* Sage Publications.

Guest, D. T. (2006). Saving for a rainy day: Social security in late nineteenth century and early twentieth-century Canada. In R. B. Blake and J. A. Keshen (Eds.) *Social fabric or patchwork quilt: The development of social policy in Canada* (pp. 25–44). Broadview Press.

Hammond, R., Cheney, P., & Pearsey, R. (2020). *Introduction to sociology.* http://www.freesociologybooks.com

Hick, S. (2002). *Social work in Canada: An introduction.* Thompson Educational Publishing, Inc.

Lundy, C. (2011). *Social work and social justice: A structural approach to practice* (2nd ed.). Broadview Press.

Marchant, H. (1986). Gender, systems thinking and radical social work. In H. Marchant and B. Wearing (Eds.), *Gender reclaimed: Women in social work* (pp. 14–32). Hale & Iremonger.

Marchant, H., & Wearing, B. (1986). *Gender reclaimed: Women in social work.* Hale & Iremonger.

Mullaly, B. (2007). *The new structural social work* (3rd ed.). Oxford University Press.

Mullaly, B. & Dupré, M. (2019). *The new structural social work* (4th ed.). Oxford University Press.

Peters, H. (2010). Situating practitioners' experiences in a model of theory-practice integration. In S. F. Hick, H. I. Peters, T. Corner, and T. London (Eds.), *Structural social work in action: Examples from practice* (pp. 39-57). Canadian Scholars' Press Inc.

Prochaska, J.O., DiClemente, C.C., and Norcross, J.C. (1992). In search of how people change: Applications to addictive behaviors. *American Psychology, 47*(9), 1102–14. https://psycnet.apa.org/doi/10.1037/10248-026

Prochaska, J.O. and DiClemente, C.C. (1983). Stages and processes of self-change of smoking: Toward an integrative model of change. *Journal of Consulting and Clinical Psychology, 51*(3), 390–5. https://psycnet.apa.org/doi/10.1037/0022-006X.51.3.390

Reynolds, B.C. (1963). *An uncharted journey: Fifty years of growth in social work.* The Citadel Press.

NOTES:

NOTES:

NOTES:

Striving for Equity, Diversity, and Inclusion in Social Work Field Education: From the Personal to the Political

Emmanuel Chilanga and Jill Hanley

Schools of Social Work in Canada, as institutions of higher learning and as members of the Canadian Association of Social Work Education (CASWE), are expected to promote principles of equity, diversity and inclusion (EDI) in all aspects of their work from the classroom, to working conditions, to field education (Tamtik & Guenter, 2019). The goal of EDI is to eradicate prejudice and discrimination on the basis of prohibited grounds of discrimination in the Canadian Human Rights Act and to strive for fair treatment and opportunity for all. Canadians are protected from discrimination based on disability, gender identity or expression, religion, ethnic origin, race, colour, age, sex, sexual orientation, marital status, family status, genetic characteristics, and conviction for an offence for which a pardon has been granted (Commission, 2018). To ascribe to the Canadian Human Rights Act, most universities have put in place EDI committees to support combatting discrimination and to promote social justice. However, research shows that issues remain prevalent as students from minority groups continue to face discrimination in accessing education (Mathieu et al., 2022).

Discrimination is not only prevalent in educational institutions; studies show that it is also staggering in social institutions. For instance, a recent study indicates that 38.8% of Canadians reported experiencing discrimination based on race and ethnicity before and during the COVID-19 pandemic (Statistics Canada, 2022). Discrimination and intolerance have negative health and socioeconomic impacts on the people who are affected and indirect negative impact on society (Drabish & Theeke, 2022). As such, there is a need to support community members, including students who are experiencing discrimination.

To support government anti-discrimination efforts and to uphold its social justice commitment, social work education in Canada is committed to help students acquire EDI competencies to mitigate social exclusion and promote justice in their current and future working spaces. This is reflected in curriculum in Canadian social work schools where social justice and anti-oppressive course content are mandatory (Bhuyan et al., 2017). Given that social work field education is an indispensable component of social work education in Canada, commonly referred to as social work's signature pedagogy (Ayala et al., 2018; Drolet et al., 2021), ensuring that it is done according to EDI principles is essential. Field education provides an opportunity for students to foster social work competencies by integrating classroom theories, research, and knowledge into practice—ideally each with EDI at its core. Students are mentored by social work field supervisors in agencies that support people from diverse social backgrounds who are often not treated with equity and inclusion principles. Students need to be equipped with cultural and rights-based competencies that will prepare them to work effectively with marginalized community members from different backgrounds (Banks et al., 2021). This chapter has been written to help prepare social work students with the knowledge and skills that will help them to understand and implement EDI in their field practicum. It introduces EDI and prepares social work students to mitigate discrimination during their field education through an EDI lens.

Understanding EDI

The use and application of the concepts of equity, diversity, and inclusion have taken a center stage globally. There is widening recognition of social injustices imposed upon historically marginalized groups, such as Indigenous Peoples, Black people, the 2SLGBTQ+ community, and people with disabilities. Despite many of these groups having equal legal rights, inequities persist in society. Interest in EDI is growing as some individuals, institutions, and governments aim to tackle these injustices. Social work students need to have an understanding of EDI concepts in order to better prepare for field practicum.

Equity

Scholars have defined the term equity in different ways. On a basic level, equity implies fairness, impartiality, or justice (Kikhi & Gautam, 2021). The concept focuses on people's awareness of the circumstances that create an unequal starting position of individuals in relation to others in society and finding ways to mitigate the disparity. For example, a child born into poverty does not generally share the same conditions for potential educational achievement as a child born into wealth. There are various systemic and cultural factors that create inequality by posing barriers for marginalized populations and equity acknowledges that people have different needs, experiences, and opportunities.

People at times use the term *equality* and *equity* interchangeably. In fact, these two terms do not have the same meaning and their implementation can lead to different outcomes among underprivileged populations. The word equality refers to the state or quality of being equal and it corresponds to quantity, degree, value, rank, or ability (Kikhi & Gautam, 2021). Equality means each person, or groups of people, are given the *same* opportunities or resources. Equity recognizes that each person begins with different circumstances; even if people are given the same opportunities, some individuals may not reach an equality with their peers or within society.

Going back to our example of education, children with different socioeconomic backgrounds may have equal access to free public school, but unequal resources at home so that, ultimately, their educational outcomes will be very different. An equitable access to education would offer extra supports for children that require them. The distinction between equality and equity can be summarized using Paula Dressel's quote: "The route to achieving equity will not be accomplished through treating everyone equally. It will be achieved by treating everyone justly according to their circumstances" (Dressel et al. 2020).

To conceptually understand the difference between equality and equity using some imaginary ideas, read the example in the box:

> Deborah and Maureen are both 1.5-meters tall and are given the opportunity to pick 50 apples from a 4-meter-high tree. They are each given a 2-meter ladder and a bag to collect the fruit. On observation, the trunk of the tree leans towards Deborah, making it easier for her to access the fruit. In contrast the branches on Maureen's side of the tree are tilted upward as the tree trunk leans away from her. Second, the branches on Deborah's side have numerous apples while Maureen's branches have fewer than 50 apples.

This is an example of equality: both Deborah and Maureen have been given the same resources (ladder and bag) to access the opportunities (apples). However, their circumstances are different, which creates imbalance in the opportunities they can access. What are the impacts of the tree leaning more towards Deborah and also the fruits being more available on her side of the tree?

We can bring equity to the scenario by giving Maureen a ladder that is taller than Deborah's. However, the situation would still favour Deborah as the fruits are not equally distributed in the tree. To ensure full equity after both girls can reach to the top of the tree, they must work in a tree where the fruit is evenly distributed in the branches.

Achieving Equity and Equality in Social Work Field Education.

Imagine that you are working as a practicum student at Organization Y that provides food hampers to recent immigrants. Today, Maureen and Deborah come to collect their food hampers. Maureen has five children between one and fourteen years old, while Deborah has only one child who is twelve years old. Your field supervisor gives each of them 1 kg of rice, a loaf of bread, and a packet of vegetables.

QUESTIONS

1. What is your field supervisor trying to achieve in this context?

   a. Equality in distributing the food hampers?

   b. Equity in distributing the food hampers?

2. Since you have a good picture of the situation of the two women, how would you share the food hampers?

In the broader context, there is a need for deliberate policies that can remove systemic barriers and biases to enable all individuals to have equitable access to resources from service providers. In the context of social work field education, practicum students need to develop a strong understanding of the systemic barriers that service users from underrepresented groups face in accessing social and other services in agencies. By using an equity rather than diversity lens, practicum students can promote fairness by creating a tailored support for all community members regardless of their social location. For example, the intersectionality of poverty and HIV seropositive status can create barriers to accessing housing for HIV-positive service users compared to HIV-negative service users as illustrated in the following activity.

Franklin is an HIV-positive service user, while Richard is an HIV-negative service user. They are both struggling to raise money to rent an apartment after their work was terminated because of the COVID-19-related financial difficulties. They separately went to a community organization that offers accommodation support to homeless clients. The organization has adequate funds to subsidize one-year private apartment leases for both service users. You are assigned to support each client in finding a one-bedroom apartment. You provide them with a letter to the landlords assuring them that your organization has available funds to subsidize the lease. In Franklin's letter to the potential landlord, with his consent, you state that he needs a house because he is finding it difficult to take his antiretroviral therapy. In Richard's letter, you did not mention a medical condition. Within a week, Richard secures accommodation. But four months later, Franklin has yet to secure accommodation.

QUESTIONS

1. Why might Franklin still be struggling to secure an apartment despite receiving the same subsidy from the organization as Richard received?

2. How might the disclosure of Franklin's HIV status in the letter to landlords impact his chances of accessing accommodation compared to Richard?

3. If you were the practicum student, how might you support Franklin in his search for housing from an equity perspective?

It is important for social work students to know the difference between equality and equity as the concepts can guide them in their practice based on the specific circumstances of service users. Equity focuses on the fair and respectful treatment of all people and is a process towards achieving equality in society.

Diversity

Diversity refers to all the dimensions of human identity that make everyone unique (Byrd, 2014). It considers differences in characteristics such as race/skin colour, religion, place of birth, economic status, ethnicity, ability, sex, sexual orientation, gender, and age. Diversity also includes characteristics such as values, perspectives, behaviours, lived experiences, worldviews, and perceptions that shape an individual's relationships with others. Diversity is associative, meaning that it is manifested through the composition of groups, teams, and organizations: It is measured on a collective basis. These dimensions of human identity have a significant impact on how service users are treated within social service organizations.

There are four basic dimensions of diversity according to Gardenswartz's and Rowe's (2003) diversity circle scheme that can inform social work practicum students when working with different community members in an organization. The first is personality traits that involves behaviours such as openness to experience, conscientiousness, and agreeableness. The second is internal dimension traits which include demographic attributes of community members such as their age, gender, sexual orientation, physical ability, ethnicity, and race. External dimension is a third dimension to consider and it includes the external layers such as service users' geographic location, income, personal habits, recreational habits, religion, educational background, work experience, appearance, parental status, and marital status. Organization level is the fourth dimension of diversity that includes components like functional level strategies like actions and goals. EDI should be considered at all levels of organizational department, or group; work seniority; work location; union affiliation; and management status. Social work students need to ensure that the breadth of their EDI actions and conversation be informed by the diversity circle scheme because it uses the intersectionality of all of the attributes of diversity that are either an advantage or disadvantage to people

Inclusion

Social work students need to be aware of the concepts of social exclusion and inclusion as they may inform their professional conduct in class or during their practicum. Social exclusion describes a situation when some individuals are not given an opportunity to participate fully in social, political, economic, and cultural life, which undermines their wellbeing (Gingrich & Lightman, 2015). Groups that are socially marginalized may not be able to secure financially sustainable employment, build strong social networks, or comfortably access public services, among other things. This exclusion has a negative impact on their health and wellbeing.

Watch *Social Exclusion*, a YouTube video, to understand the concept and negative impact of social exclusion.

Shannon, S. (2016, November 13). *Social exclusion*. [Video]. YouTube. https://www.youtube.com/watch?v=FuYVRUdt35o

In Canada, efforts are being made to promote social inclusion and belonging in academics and institutions that provide social services (Gaudry & Lorenz, 2018; Selimos & George, 2018). It is therefore important that social work students preparing or are in practicum acquire skill sets that can enhance social inclusion among the people they work with. This section conceptualizes and highlights ways that social inclusion can be promoted in local agencies.

Social inclusion refers to a process of increasing the involvement of marginalized groups through enhanced opportunities, access to resources, voice and respect for rights (Cordier & Martin, 2020). Promoting inclusion requires deliberate efforts to make marginalized individuals feel that their contribution to the organization is valued and that they enjoy the same rights and opportunities as all others. Social inclusion is associated with a sense of belonging and has a positive mental health outcome for individuals (Michalski et al., 2020). Social work students require the ability to foster the social inclusion of diverse populations during their practicum time.

In a macro practice social work practicum setting, students can plan social inclusion activities that offer opportunities for socialization and relationship-building among community members. For instance, in organizations that promote integration, a student can plan activities based on the parameters that are provided in the textbox below (Townsend et al., 2021).

1. Plan activities that can encourage community members to have regular contact with each other, such as cooking lessons, community gardens, and recreational activities.

2. Community members must be included in planning the activities. This helps to ensure that the common interest of stakeholders is recognized and promotes inclusion.

3. The designed activities should provide opportunities for community members to interact with each other.

4. Address participation barriers that some members may encounter, including a lack of transportation, medical challenges, and safety concerns.

ACTIVITY

1. In your social work practicum, what programs you can suggest and/or develop that could promote an inclusive environment?

....

....

....

2. Outline the activities that can be used to promote social inclusion in the suggested programs.

....

....

....

3. Describe the barriers that can undermine the implementation of your inclusion program among the service agency's clientele.

....

....

....

4. How can the barriers be addressed in a way that enhances social inclusion?

....

....

....

Challenges to EDI

Systemic Discrimination

Systemic discrimination refers to patterns of policies and practices that are part of the institutional structures that create and perpetuate disadvantages to marginalized people (Phillips-Beck et al., 2020). It is prevalent in both public and private institutions such as police, healthcare, education, justice, and political systems. People who hold a privileged position, such as politicians, police officers, and policy makers, are more likely to dismiss the existence of systemic racism that undermine its intervention for justice institutions in Canada (Ng & Lam, 2020). As a social work practicum student, it is important to be critical and point out institutional policies that disadvantage some groups over others.

Watch the video *What Systemic Racism in Canada Looks Like*, which discusses the manifestation of systematic racism in Canada.

CBC News. (2020, July 9). *What systemic racism in Canada looks like* [Video]. YouTube. https://www.youtube.com/watch?v=7GmX5stT9rU

After watching the video, reflect on the following questions:

QUESTIONS

1. Why do you think politicians in the video denied that there is no racism in Canada?

2. Explain why many Black and Indigenous people are more likely to be incarcerated than white people in Canada?

3. The video suggests that there is antiracism symbolism or gestures among policy makers, but there are limited practical strategies of addressing the problem. Do you agree with this position?

4. What can you do to address systemic racism in your practicum and workplace?

Bias

Bias refers to unfair prejudgment in favor of or against people who are members of one group as compared to another without based on reality (Wang & Jeon, 2020). Biases develop over the course of a lifetime, beginning at a very early age through exposure to direct and indirect messages by the media, peers, family, and society as a whole. These learned associations cause people to have feelings and attitudes about other people based on diverse characteristics that include race, ethnicity, age, gender, sexual orientation, and socio-economic status.

The biases and prejudices faced by visible minority groups in Canada and the United States is a problem of public importance. Studies in these two countries have shown that there is bias against visible minorities when it comes to job hiring (Hodson et al., 2021). In addition, anti-Indigenous, anti-Black, anti-Hispanic, and anti-gay/lesbian bias is prevalent among healthcare providers (Kitching et al., 2020; Mateo & Williams, 2020). Bias and discrimination against visible minorities has also been documented in Canadian security systems such as the police. For instance, anti-Black police bias and discrimination has been reported during police stops and in pre-charge diversion programs (Samuels-Wortley, 2022; Wortley & Owusu-Bempah, 2022).

Watch the video *Toronto Police Chief Apologizes After Report Highlights Systemic Racism* to understand systematic racism in the police force in Toronto.

The National. (2022, June 15). *Toronto police chief apologizes after report highlights systemic racism* [Video]. CBC News. YouTube. https://www.youtube.com/watch?v=ikG9yWRVwbI

Based on the information that can be presented by the clients, service providers may have both positive and negative biases. For example, they may respond positively towards community members who belong to privileged groups and hesitantly to members of less privileged groups. It is important for social work students in practicum to understand and check their biases.

> Paul is a Black social work student who is doing his practicum at an organization that supports a diverse population of people accessing harm reduction services. His supervisor noted that Paul usually spends more time with and provides more support to Black service users than those from other racial backgrounds.

QUESTIONS

1. Why might Paul spend more time with Black clients than others?

2. How might positive or negative bias be at play for Paul, for service users, and for Paul's supervisor?

3. How can Paul's practicum supervisor help him avoid bias and prejudice when Paul decides how much time to spend with Black service users?

Microaggressions

When working with community members, social work practicum students should guard their behavior against microaggressions. Microaggressions are the intentional or unintentional normalization of verbal, behavioral, or environmental indignities that communicate derogatory, hostile, or negative prejudicial slights and insults toward marginalized groups (Torino et al., 2018). A student may perceive microaggressions as innocent, harmless comments, but they reinforce stereotypes and are a form of discrimination.

> Watch the video *Microaggressions in Everyday Life* and answer the questions that follow.
>
> Wing Sue, D. (2010, September 8). *Microaggressions in everyday life* [Video]. YouTube. https://www.youtube.com/watch?v=xAIFGBlEsbQ

QUESTIONS

1. In your own words, what does microaggression mean to you?

2. Do you have examples of microaggressive language that you have heard? Give some examples.

3. Based on the video *Microaggressions in Everyday Life*, how do you think the supervisor could compliment Michael?

4. Why do you think the female manager experienced discrimination and bias in the meeting with the President?

Tokenism

Social work practicum students also need to guard their behavior and action against tokenism. Tokenism refers to a context where an institution makes a symbolic effort of including people from underrepresented groups in order to give an impression of practicing equality (Mugo & Puplampu, 2022). In their social work practicum, a student may create a committee to inform program improvements that includes people from minority groups to show that there is visual diversity and avoid criticism of not promoting social justice and fairness. What is needed is to have tangible actions such as empowering minority members in the group to meaningful contribute to the discussions and implementation stages.

Striving to Achieve EDI on Different Levels

During your field placement, you can think about EDI on different levels. In order to contribute to EDI through your work, you need to be aware of how your own actions might inadvertently work against EDI. It's impossible to eradicate all bias or discrimination from our work, but as social workers, it is our responsibility to strive towards this goal. Let's reflect on how EDI might play out along different lines within field practice.

The Population in Your Field Setting

Very often, social work settings have the mandate to serve populations that struggle with EDI. For example, a community health centre may offer homecare services to older adults with disabilities. Several things can help you analyze the situation:

- Consider the ways that older adults with disabilities might not have equity in different aspects of their lives, such as access to health services, access to public transportation and public buildings, and access to leisure activities.

- Evaluate the types of diversity that would exist among older adults with disabilities, for example, sexual orientation, immigration status, and ethno-racial background. Ask yourself how these elements of their identities might intersect with their experiences as older adults with disabilities.

- Ask yourself what factors would facilitate or hinder older adults with disability's social inclusion given their experiences of equity and diversity.

Reflect on how EDI plays out in the lives of the people with whom you work in your practicum. By being conscious of EDI, you can take concrete steps to adapt your practice to promote EDI and avoid compounding inequity and social exclusion. For example, an EDI analysis such as that given above can help you to identify subgroups of older adults with disabilities who might require particular support. You might do special outreach to make sure low-income older adults know your services are free or to let queer older adults know that your agency welcomes to them.

Organizational Culture and Practices

Social work students also need to reflect upon the organizational culture and practices in their field settings that relate to EDI. There are many ways that we organize our services, behave among ourselves or with service users or members, and even decorate our space that can signal either positive or negative EDI messages to people visiting our agency.

- Ask yourself whether the services offered by your field setting are equitably accessible. For example, are there expensive fees? Do the opening hours work for people who cannot take time off work? What happens if a client does not speak English or French?

- Consider whether your services or your way of working are adapting to the diversity of the population you want to serve. People of different ages, cultural backgrounds, physical abilities, trauma experiences, substance dependency, and other factors of diversity may want to access your services. Is your organization equipped to adapt to diverse needs?

- Finally, analyze whether your organization actually is welcoming and inclusive of diverse populations. Do the staff and board reflect the diversity of the population? Are there signals in the decoration, music, food, language, or other elements of the space that diversity is recognized and welcomed? Are decisions made in collaboration with community members?

If we continue with our example, among the older adults with whom you would like to work, a number of them are not permanent residents or citizens of Canada and who, therefore, are ineligible for your services. Organizational practices of insisting on presentation of a medical services card before opening a file will exclude many people with precarious immigration status. This could lead you and your supervisor and colleagues to ways to advocate and ensure the necessary support for older adults with precarious immigration status.

Your Experience as a Field Education Student

Finally, as a student in field education, you also need to expect that EDI applies to you. Just as you need to strive to ensure EDI is present in your emerging practice skills, it is legitimate to ask your school and your field setting to consider your learning experience from an EDI lens.

- Regard different elements of your identity and social location that might influence your experience of field education. These elements may positively or negatively affect your privilege in your field setting. For example, do you share the same ethno-racial background as your supervisor? Are you juggling full time studies with raising young children? Do you have learning disabilities? Are you managing mental health challenges?

- Consider whether you are treated equitably in your field setting, given your identity and social location. Are accommodations possible for your learning disability? Does your supervisor listen carefully if you raise concerns about microaggressions and work with you to address racism? Are students of different genders offered comparable opportunities within their field education?

- To sum-up, if equity and diversity are taken into account, you will hopefully feel that you have social inclusion in your field setting, a sense of belonging, and an appropriate sense of power. Social inclusion within a field setting means that you are a respected member of the group, your needs are considered, and you contribute toward the collective well-being.

As a student, working in a setting where you feel your own experience is being considered from an EDI perspective puts you in a better position to work towards EDI in your practice with a more diverse community. It is an important skill for a social worker to be aware of EDI issues in their own work and to be able to raise it constructively with supervisors and colleagues.

Conclusion

Over the years, there has been scholarly and practical attention paid to social work field education in Canada. Social work educators can find stronger ways to prepare students to acquire the competencies needed to gain and apply an EDI social justice lens in field settings. This chapter supports students to acquire and understand concepts that they can use to promote human rights and social justice when they are in their field practicum. Through vignettes, we have contextualised the meaning of equity, diversity, and inclusion in social work field education.

REFERENCES

Ayala, J., Drolet, J., Fulton, A., Hewson, J., Letkemann, L., Baynton, M., Elliott, G., Judge-Stasiak, A., Blaug, C., Gérard Tétreault, A., & Schweizer, E. (2018). Restructuring social work field education in 21st century Canada: From crisis management to sustainability. *Canadian Social Work Review / Revue Canadienne de Service Social, 35*(2), 45–65. https://doi.org/10.7202/1058479ar

Banks, S., Tuggle, F., & Coleman, D. (2021). Standardization of human rights–based workforce induction curriculum for social work field supervisors. *Journal of Human Rights and Social Work, 6*(1), 4–13. https://doi.org/10.1007/s41134-020-00152-y

Bhuyan, R., Bejan, R., & Jeyapal, D. (2017). Social workers' perspectives on social justice in social work education: When mainstreaming social justice masks structural inequalities. *Social Work Education, 36*(4), 373–390. https://doi.org/10.1080/02615479.2017.1298741

Byrd, M. Y. (2014). Diversity issues: Exploring 'critical' through multiple lenses. *Advances in Developing Human Resources, 16*(4), 515–528. https://doi.org/10.1177/1523422314544297

Canadian Human Rights Commission. (2018). *People first—The Canadian Human Rights Commission's 2017 annual report to parliament*. Government of Canada. https://policycommons.net/artifacts/2194217/people-first/2950196/

Cordier, R., & Martin, R. (2020). The challenges of defining and measuring social inclusion. In P. Liamputtong (Ed.), *Handbook of social inclusion: Research and practices in health and social sciences* (pp. 1–22). Springer International Publishing. https://doi.org/10.1007/978-3-030-48277-0_18-1

Drabish, K., & Theeke, L. A. (2022). Health impact of stigma, discrimination, prejudice, and bias experienced by transgender people: A systematic review of quantitative studies. *Issues in Mental Health Nursing, 43*(2), 111–118. https://doi.org/10.1080/01612840.2021.1961330

Dressel, P., Minkler, M., & Yen, I. (2020). Oppressions/intersectionality. *Political And Economic Determinants of Population Health and Well-Being: Controversies and Developments, 467.*

Drolet, J. L., Alemi, M. I., Bogo, M., Chilanga, E., Clark, N., St. George, S., Charles, G., Hanley, J., McConnell, S. M, McKee, E., Walsh, C. A., & Wulff, D. (2021). Transforming field education during COVID-19. *Field Educator, 10*(2), 1–9. https://fieldeducator.simmons.edu/article/transforming-field-education-during-covid-19/

Gaudry, A., & Lorenz, D. (2018). Indigenization as inclusion, reconciliation, and decolonization: Navigating the different visions for indigenizing the Canadian Academy. *AlterNative: An International Journal of Indigenous Peoples, 14*(3), 218–227. https://doi.org/10.1177/1177180118785382

Gardenswartz, L., & Rowe, A. (2003). *Diverse teams at work: Capitalizing on the power of diversity.* Society for Human Resource.

Gingrich, L. G., & Lightman, N. (2015). The empirical measurement of a theoretical concept: Tracing social exclusion among racial minority and migrant groups in Canada. *Social Inclusion, 3*(4), 98–111. https://doi.org/10.17645/si.v3i4.144

Hodson, G., Ganesh, N., & Race, T. (2021). Double-pronged bias against black women: Sexism and racism (but not right-wing ideology) as unique predictors. *Canadian Journal of Behavioural Science / Revue Canadienne Des Sciences Du Comportement, 53*(4), 507–513. https://doi.org/10.1037/cbs0000227

Kikhi, K., & Gautam, D. R. (2021). *Comprehending equity: Contextualising India's north-east.* Taylor & Francis.

Kitching, G. T., Firestone, M., Schei, B., Wolfe, S., Bourgeois, C., O'Campo, P., Rotondi, M., Nisenbaum, R., Maddox, R., & Smylie, J. (2020). Unmet health needs and discrimination by healthcare providers among an Indigenous population in Toronto, Canada. *Canadian Journal of Public Health, 111*(1), 40–49. https://doi.org/10.17269/s41997-019-00242-z

Mateo, C. M., & Williams, D. R. (2020). Addressing bias and reducing discrimination: The professional responsibility of health care providers. *Academic Medicine, 95*(12S), S5. https://doi.org/10.1097/ACM.0000000000003683

Mathieu, J., Fotsing, S., Akinbobola, K., Shipeolu, L., Crosse, K., Thomas, K., Denis-LeBlanc, M., Gueye, A., & Bekolo, G. (2022). The quest for greater equity: A national cross-sectional study of the experiences of Black Canadian medical students. *Canadian Medical Association Open Access Journal, 10*(4), E937–E944. https://doi.org/10.9778/cmajo.20220192

Michalski, C. A., Diemert, L. M., Helliwell, J. F., Goel, V., & Rosella, L. C. (2020). Relationship between sense of community belonging and self-rated health across life stages. *SSM–Population Health, 12,* 100676. https://doi.org/10.1016/j.ssmph.2020.100676

Mugo, S., & Puplampu, K. P. (2022). Beyond tokenism and objectivity: Theoretical reflections on a transformative equity, diversity, and inclusion agenda for higher education in Canada. *SN Social Sciences, 2*(10), 209. https://doi.org/10.1007/s43545-022-00509-2

Ng, E., & Lam, A. (2020). Black lives matter: On the denial of systemic racism, White liberals, and polite racism. *Equality, Diversity and Inclusion 39,* 729–739. https://doi.org/10.1108/EDI-09-2020-297

Phillips-Beck, W., Eni, R., Lavoie, J. G., Avery Kinew, K., Kyoon Achan, G., & Katz, A. (2020). Confronting racism within the Canadian healthcare system: Systemic exclusion of First Nations from quality and consistent care. *International Journal of Environmental Research and Public Health, 17*(22), Article 22. https://doi.org/10.3390/ijerph17228343

Samuels-Wortley, K. (2022). Youthful discretion: Police selection bias in access to pre-charge diversion programs in Canada. *Race and Justice, 12*(2), 387–410. https://doi.org/10.1177/2153368719889093

Selimos, E. D., & George, G. (2018). Welcoming initiatives and the social inclusion of newcomer youth: The case of Windsor, Ontario. *Canadian Ethnic Studies, 50*(3), 69–89. https://doi.org/10.1353/ces.2018.0023

Statistics Canada, General Social Survey—Social Identity. (2022). *Discrimination before and since the start of the pandemic.* Government of Canada. https://www150.statcan.gc.ca/n1/en/pub/11-627-m/11-627-m2022021-eng.pdf?st=lW_XFgtI

Torino, G. C., Rivera, D. P., Capodilupo, C. M., Nadal, K. L., & Sue, D. W. (2018). *Microaggression theory: Influence and implications.* John Wiley and Sons.

Townsend, B. G., Chen, J. T-H., & Wuthrich, V. M. (2021). Barriers and facilitators to social participation in older adults: A systematic literature review. *Clinical Gerontologist, 44*(4), 359–380. https://doi.org/10.1080/07317115.2020.1863890

Wang, Q., & Jeon, H. J. (2020). Bias in bias recognition: People view others but not themselves as biased by preexisting beliefs and social stigmas. *PLOS ONE, 15*(10), e0240232. https://doi.org/10.1371/journal.pone.0240232

Wortley, S., & Owusu-Bempah, A. (2022). Race, police stops, and perceptions of anti-Black police discrimination in Toronto, Canada over a quarter century. *Policing: An International Journal, 45*(4), 570–585. https://doi.org/10.1108/PIJPSM-11-2021-0157

NOTES:

NOTES:

NOTES:

Addressing Discrimination Against Minority Groups in Social Work Practice and Field Education

Saleema Salim

We live in a globalized world that promotes human coexistence yet continues to be driven by conflict. Minority groups experience difficulties due to discriminatory factors such as physical and mental abilities; age; culture; sexuality, gender identity and sexual orientation; race; ethnicity; language; religion and spiritual beliefs; political opinions; socio-economic status; poverty; class; family structure; relationship status; and nationality (or lack thereof). Our responsibility as social workers is to recognize how ideology, laws, policies, regulations, customs, and practices can lead to inequalities and prevent people of certain backgrounds from receiving equitable treatment. It is essential that social workers address institutionalized discrimination and oppression against minority groups in their practice by focusing on ethical imperatives because the profession has an obligation to challenge and dismantle systems of oppression that perpetuate inequality and injustice. By actively addressing institutionalized discrimination, social workers uphold the core values of the profession, including social justice and respect for dignity. The skills needed to do this are often learned in field education.

Respect for human individuality and the richness of diversity entails being compassionate, empathetic, caring, and striving to improve the well-being of minority groups. As expressed by Roy Henry Vickers, a First Nations artist of Tsimshian descent, we all possess unique talents, and when we come together to share and exchange these gifts, our collective wealth grows. Cultural competence is considered an important component of respecting others because it requires respecting the dignity of all people in a fair and equitable manner—this is in line with the principles of social work. According to Este (2007), cultural competence is defined as accepting and respecting differences, continuing self-assessment, carefully observing the dynamics of differences, expanding knowledge and resources, and adapting services to meet the needs of diverse populations. To demonstrate cultural competency, social workers should "ensure that their work does not reflect personal or organizational biases or prejudices" (Fisher, 2013, p. 60).

As the Canadian Association of Social Workers (CASW; 2005) states, "Social workers have a responsibility to maintain professional proficiency, to continually strive to increase their professional knowledge and skills, and to apply new knowledge in practice" (p. 5). Unfortunately, there remains a lack of cultural competency among social workers serving diverse groups of people (Este, 2007).

In this chapter, we explore minority groups' experiences of discrimination that can have a negative impact on their social and psychological well-being. In this chapter, you will learn about different types of discrimination and the ways discrimination against minority groups is located in social work practice and field education. Tips and strategies for addressing and overcoming discrimination are provided.

Discrimination

The Canadian Human Rights Commission defines discrimination as any action or decision that treats a person or a group unfairly because of their race, age, or disability (Canadian Human Rights Commission, n.d.) Helly (2004) identifies several types of discrimination, such as direct discrimination, institutionalized discrimination, indirect discrimination, usual discrimination, and systemic discrimination, that can occur against minority groups. The details of the types of discrimination are presented in the following section.

Direct discrimination occurs when members of a minority group are denied a right or a freedom. This manifests in many ways. For example, in Canada, 1,798 hate crimes against various minority groups were reported to the police in 2018 (Moreau, 2020). Moreover, over 47% of hate crimes between 2010 and 2013 against Muslims targeted Muslim women who wore the hijab or niqab (Statistics Canada, 2013).

Oxford defines institutional racism as extending beyond government: "Institutional racism is described as discrimination or unequal treatment based on membership in a particular ethnic group (typically one that is a minority or marginalized), arising from systems, structures, or expectations established within an institution or organization." (Oxford, n.d.). This concept encompasses various institutions such as universities, social work organizations, and others. Institutionalized discrimination occurs when a minority group is purposefully excluded through the use of governmental laws and regulations because of their cultural identity (Poynting & Perry, 2007). For example, during the 2015 Canadian general election, Stephen Harper stated that, if re-elected, his government would consider banning the niqab for public employees (Niqab Ban, 2015). The Harper government had previously attempted to prohibit the wearing of niqabs during Canadian citizenship ceremonies. The niqab is a type of face covering worn by some Muslim women. Quebec's government went even further in 2013 by proposing the Charter of Quebec Values, which would have prohibited public employees from wearing or displaying religious symbols (Niqab Ban, 2015). While bans of this type purport to treat all Canadians equally, they are inequitable because they promote the religion of one group of Canadians in major institutions while excluding the culture of others. If the Canadian ban were to be enacted, Muslim women in Canada who wear niqabs as part of their cultural practice would be forced to give up this aspect of their identity in order to participate in society.

Indirect discrimination occurs when an unequal effect is produced for a minority group by a measure put in place for people in general (Waddington & Heniks, 2002). A frequent example of indirect discrimination is when a university's academic calendar requires all students to attend classes or take exams on those days when people from minority groups celebrate their festivals. This privileges one group's celebrations over those of another. For example, the festival of the Eid among Muslim groups is as significant as Christmas for Christian groups, although only Christmas is officially recognized. As such, Muslim students are often required to attend classes, appear for exams, or attend evening classes during the month of Ramadan instead of celebrating their festivals. Minority groups often sacrifice their way of life because of the absence of accommodations. This is a form of indirect religious discrimination.

Resource: Watch Video 10.1 and 10.2, which demonstrate how minority groups are discriminated against in Western countries based on their religious beliefs. The videos are about the European Union (EU) and Quebec bans on religious symbols. These videos illustrate how Muslim women were restricted from working by a ban on religious symbols imposed by legislation. While these policies do not indicate the name of a specific group, it shows that this policy is for everyone. However, the videos show which groups of people benefit from such policies and which groups face difficulties. Usual discrimination relates to negative attitudes and behaviours toward a minority group among individuals and private organizations (Helly, 2004). For example, a landlord might have leasing rules that make renting a home unreasonably difficult for new immigrants. This may be a case of discrimination based on both race and national origin. Another example is racial profiling, which occurs, for example, when airport security personnel unfairly scrutinize Muslim minority groups due to their religious identity or race.

Video 10.1

Al Jazeera English. (2017, March 14). *Concerns of discrimination after EU's court ban on religious symbols* [Video]. YouTube. https://www.youtube.com/watch?v=sftc8GieBvo

Video 10.2

WION. (2020, March 9). *Gravitas: Why Muslim families are leaving Canada's Quebec* [Video]. YouTube. https://www.youtube.com/watch?v=MtZvdaO8hOg

Systemic discrimination refers to the policies and practices embedded within an organization's structure that create or perpetuate social exclusion and disadvantage for certain groups of people (Sheppard, 2010). They appear to be neutral on the surface but may discriminate against persons based on race, ethnicity, or religion, among other factors. It impacts the general population of minority groups through conscious or unconscious bias in proposed policies, programs, and decisions.

Unconscious bias occurs when people make conclusions based on generalizations and preconceived ideas rather than on objective measures. In other words, unconscious bias is "the attitudes or stereotypes that affect our understanding, actions, and decisions in an unconscious manner. These biases, which encompass both favourable and unfavourable assessments, are activated involuntarily and without an individual's awareness or intentional control" (Tyner, 2019, p. 31). Sometimes systemic discrimination is intentional, such as when Muslim girls are expelled from school because they wear a hijab or bans are placed on niqabs at citizenship ceremonies (Golnaraghi & Mills, 2013).

Online Training Activity

To learn more about unconscious bias, you may wish to strengthen your ability to recognize and describe bias, and further understand the methods for mitigating the influence of bias that are relevant to health and social services through this online training module (see CIHR's Bias in Peer Review module, n.d.)

The majority of discrimination types remain invisible to the general population. Typically, discrimination becomes apparent only to those individuals who experience it. Many minority groups are conscious of specific types of discrimination directly aimed at them. Moreover, many people fail to comprehend that discrimination often occurs unintentionally, meaning that individuals may not actively intend to discriminate against others, but it still happens nonetheless. Discrimination can be deeply ingrained in societal norms, attitudes, and systems, which may lead to biased behaviors or decisions even without conscious awareness. An important component of understanding discrimination is recognizing that it can occur between different groups. Groups may not see discrimination that happens to other groups, leading to a lack of awareness or acknowledgment of the problem. This intergroup discrimination can perpetuate inequalities and divisions within society.

Additionally, discrimination between groups is something that new social workers might not understand or know is a problem. Without awareness of these dynamics, social workers may struggle to effectively address discrimination and advocate for marginalized communities in their practice. The impacts of discrimination are experienced on a personal level such as negative consequences for their mental and sometimes physical health (Fernando et al., 2013; Pascoe & Richman, 2009). Many minority groups report experiencing discrimination in Western countries. This includes intentional avoidance, encountering ignorance, being called degrading names, or being unfairly scrutinized by security personnel or police because of their ethnic, cultural, or religious identity (Nagra & Maurutto, 2016; Pasha-Zaidi, 2015).

Diversity and Discrimination

Canada is a multicultural country where people of diverse cultural backgrounds and races generally live together peacefully. Every year, thousands of people immigrate to Canada with the belief that their culture will be honoured. Unfortunately, Reitz and Bannerjee (2006) found that visible minorities in Canada experience much greater levels of discrimination and inequality than immigrants of European origin.

The word "respect" comes from a Latin root that suggests the idea of seeing or viewing (Egan, 2014). One of the core values of social work is respect for clients, which forms the foundation of all helpful interventions (Egan, 2014). As per the CASW (2024) Code of Ethics, "social workers enhance their relationship with diverse service users by engaging in ongoing learning related to cultures, beliefs and practices and respecting their rights to receive services free of bias or judgement" (p. 8) regardless of any differences, such as age, culture, abilities, sexuality and gender identity, sexual orientation, race, ethnicity, language, religion, spiritual beliefs, political opinions, socio-economic status, poverty, class, family structure, relationship status and nationality. Unfortunately, this is not always seen in practice or in field education settings. Due to a lack of knowledge about minority cultures, social workers often fail to maintain attitudes of respect for other cultures in their practicums and practice (Jani et al., 2016).

Table 10.1: Questions to Understand Yourself

It is important for social workers to understand themselves. You are invited to reflect on your self-identity and your purpose in social work to gain a deeper understanding of your own perspectives and biases.

Who am I?

For example, as a social worker, I am a compassionate advocate dedicated to promoting social justice, equality, and empowerment for individuals and communities facing adversity. I recognize that my identity is multifaceted, shaped by my personal experiences, values, beliefs, and cultural background.

Why am I here?

For example, I am here in the field of social work because I am passionate about making a positive difference in people's lives and contributing to social change. I believe that every individual deserves to be treated with dignity and respect, and I am committed to working collaboratively with clients to address their needs, strengthen their resilience, and enhance their well-being.

Respect for others begins with an understanding of oneself. As outlined in Table 10.1, you may ask yourself questions to gain a deeper understanding of yourself.

The questions about identity will help you gain a deeper understanding of yourself and how your identities might affect your interactions with others. Social workers are responsible for respecting the cultures of diverse minorities. Cultural respect does not simply mean accepting differences it requires us to embrace human differences. In order to develop respect for the cultures of diverse minorities, we need a solid understanding, empathy, intellectual curiosity, and a willingness to engage in an open and honest manner. In addition, we need to develop the capacity within ourselves for compromise, an appropriate degree of humility, and a genuine effort to welcome human differences. The absence of these capacities means that diverse minorities face discrimination in many Western societies, including Canada. Students can use the questions in Table 10.2 to gain an understanding of their knowledge and gaps related to respecting diverse cultures.

Experiences of Discrimination Among Minority Groups in Social Work Practice and Field Education in Canada

Cenat et al. (2022) examined the prevalence of racial discrimination and major racial discrimination experienced by Black Canadians between the ages of 15 and 40. The study found that the majority of people in this group have experienced racial discrimination daily. Additionally, nearly half of the participants reported experiencing major forms of racial discrimination, including in employment, policing, education, housing, banking, and healthcare.

Social work practitioners also experience discrimination in their social work practice. Lilly et al. (2018) report that Black social work students experience microaggressions on a frequent basis. Black practitioners, for example, report disturbed sleep; fatigue; loss of energy; significant weight loss or gain; feelings of worthlessness; recurrent thoughts of death, including suicidal ideation; restlessness; irritability; muscle tension; excessive worry; hypervigilance; and avoidance as a result of microaggressions (Brown, 2020). This suggests that racism against Black social workers may be particularly challenging, given the intersectionality of race and professional identity.

In Weinberg and Fine's (2022) study of social workers in Ontario and Nova Scotia, many participants reported instances where clients refused to accept a racialized social worker as their practitioner. For example, a Black practitioner recalled an incident in which a client stated they did not want Black girls to take care of them. A child welfare worker explained that when clients were in conflict with her, they immediately used racial comments or connotations to say they did not wish to work with her.

Weinberg and Fine (2022) found that institutional racism prevents professionals from enjoying the same employment opportunities as those belonging to non-racialized groups. For example, they found that a number of participants expressed difficulties in finding work. As the example, one participant indicated that she was Indigenous in her cover letter and applied as a social worker to a child welfare agency five times. Each time, she was told that they did not need anyone or that she did not meet the job qualifications. She subsequently applied for the position without declaring her Indigenous identity and was invited for an interview.

Several Muslim social work female students also reported facing systemic and racial discrimination when applying for practicum placements (Salim, 2022). One Muslim participant mentioned that she and a non-Muslim colleague were worried about finding field placements because they lacked Canadian experience. However, her colleague easily obtained a practicum placement. In contrast, the Muslim woman applied to numerous field agencies but was not successful in securing a placement. Upon reflection, she determined that the issue did not relate to her lack of Canadian work or practice experience but rather to systemic and racial discrimination.

Table 10.2: Questions for Respecting Diversity

Answer the following questions to help you reflect on your own opportunities and challenges in demonstrating respect for cultural differences.

How would you know if sociopolitical influences, such as poverty, oppression, stereotyping, stigmatization, discrimination, prejudice, and marginalization might have affected your client who belongs to a minority group?

How could you understand the situation of your client who belongs to different culture without oversimplifying their experience or assuming it is the same as others from their cultural background?

Practice Example

Please read this case study and respond to the question in Table 10.3.

Table 10.3: Case Study

Nasima is a 12-year-old girl who lives with her nine-year-old sister and her widowed mother in a block of flats in the inner city of Calgary. An officer from the Calgary Education Board (CEB) has noted that neither Nasima nor her sister Sofia have been attending school regularly. He visited their home but found that the mother could not speak English and the children's English was insufficiently developed to provide explanations for their school absences. He returns with a colleague who speaks Urdu and finds out that the mother and children had only been in the country for one year when the father died from cancer. The family has no immediate family in the city, and an auntie who lives in Airdrie has done a little to support them. Nasima has felt the burden of responsibility to protect her mother against the racist violence and bullying they have suffered from their neighbour upstairs due to their visible Muslim identity. The neighbour has made negative verbal comments and thrown rubbish, excrement, and other things onto their balcony; her children have persistently called members of Nasima's family terrorists, and when Nasima and Sofia have tried to go to school or to the park to play with other kids, they have been the victims of spitting, name-calling, and jostling on their way to the park by their neighbour's children, as well as being made fun of in front of the other children, which makes them cry.

You have been contacted by the CEB officer. How will you help and support this family?

Table 10.4: Demonstrating Respect for Cultural Differences

Answer the following questions to help you reflect on your own opportunities and challenges in demonstrating respect for cultural differences.

How would you know if sociopolitical influences, such as poverty, oppression, stereotyping, stigmatization, discrimination, prejudice, and marginalization might have affected your client who belongs to a minority group?

How could you understand the situation of your client who belongs to different culture without oversimplifying their experience or assuming it is the same as others from their cultural background?

Develop Cultural Sensitivity by Overcoming Knowledge Gaps and Empathy Gaps

In social work education, we learn that empathy is an essential component of our practice to address discrimination. The empathetic person works with others within their context (Egan & Reese, 2019) and tries to inhabit the world of the 'other'. Through empathy, social workers gain a profound understanding of the other person's world and values (Parrott, 2010). Empathy, in other words, is the capacity to put oneself in another's situation in order to understand their situation, since our experiences are all different. It is an important aspect of social work practice and part of what it means to be human beyond our practice. Each human being has innate dignity: The foundation of human rights is based on equality and dignity. All humans have the right to be treated with respect regardless of class, race, gender, nationality, culture, sexual orientation, level of education, religion, and other factors. The International Association of Schools of Social Work (IASSW) supports human dignity as a social work value and a human right, which is reflected in social work education, strategies, policies, and research.

Empathy can be hampered without a foundation of knowledge or without a basic grasp of facts about diverse people and their perspectives. For example, the widespread ignorance of the faith, history, and cultural diversity of minority groups in much of the Western world creates a knowledge gap. Often, ignorance manifests itself in stereotypes that can breed intolerance and insensitivity, resulting in conflict. Knowledge gaps among social workers have the potential to lead to empathy gaps. Some social workers in Canada continue to struggle to be empathetic.

Developing empathetic openness and a sense of cultural sensitivity requires a strong intellectual commitment. This commitment can only come from a deep understanding of the subject. Our multicultural society demands that we not only enhance our own knowledge about diverse cultures, but it also requires that we build bridges of knowledge from one culture to the other so that we generate a diverse yet cohesive cultural society. The knowledge of diverse cultures in our society can increase one's ability to respect those who are different from us and understand cultures that we often ignore. It is not as easy as it sounds. It requires a willingness to study and learn across a wide range of cultures to develop greater cultural sensitivity. However, if we wish to serve a multicultural society as social workers, we must become acquainted with a wide variety of cultures. One way to achieve the commitment of gaining cultural knowledge is to work with diverse minority groups.

Some social work students try to avoid practicum placements that differ from their own cultures. This is unfortunate because a practicum with a minority group can be considered an opportunity to gain a deeper understanding of different cultures; even if one encounters challenges at first, students gradually gain a greater understanding of other people. As a result, students not only enhance their chances of getting more job opportunities, they also improve their knowledge and cultural competency. According to Salim (2022), a significant number of minority social work students indicated that social work students lack an understanding of minority cultures. In contrast to other social work students, those students who had completed a practicum with a minority group were more open-minded and respectful of both their similarities and differences.

Below is a case study of Sarah, a Canadian social work student. Through Sarah's experiences, we can explore the significance of cultural immersion, interpersonal relationships, and allyship in social work practice. Her deliberate choices in group settings and practicum selection provide valuable insights into fostering inclusivity, empathy, and advocacy for marginalized communities within diverse social contexts.

Please read the case of Sarah's engagement with minority students and respond to the questions in Table 10.6.

Table 10.5: Case Study

Sarah was a student in a social work undergraduate program. She obtained her diploma in social work from a Canadian college. During her diploma program, she completed a practicum in India as an international social work student and joined a non-governmental organization upon her arrival. Sarah's international practicum experience in India provided her with numerous opportunities to become familiar with the culture, food, languages, and worship practices of the people she worked with. She also participated in numerous cultural and religious rituals, including marriages, funerals, and other cultural and religious festivals. On her return to Canada, Sarah remained in contact with her friends in India, exchanging greetings and best wishes. During her studies, she actively participated in discussions about minority cultures, refugees, and immigrants. In class, there were three students who belonged to a minority group: one was from Africa, another from Pakistan, and the third was from India, and they all were friends of Sarah. In contrast, other students with White backgrounds had their own group circle, while Sarah spent most of her time with these minority students. During group presentations, many White girls approached Sarah, but Sarah chose to join groups where minority students were present. As part of the practicum selection process, Sarah selected immigrant and refugee services. Other White students, however, had different priorities, opting for placements that aligned more closely with their personal interests.

Table 10.6: Reflecting on Your Knowledge about the Culture of Others

> **Answer the following questions to gain a deeper understanding of your own knowledge about others.**
>
> What do I know about the culture of my client?
>
> Do I have sufficient knowledge to place myself in my client's situation, to understand what my client feels in their situation?
>
> Am I willing to acquire knowledge about the culture of my client? If not, what are the barriers stopping me from gaining this knowledge?
>
> Is empathy even possible without understanding my client's culture?

Resources

Gaine, C. (2010). *Equality and diversity in social work practice*. Learning Matters.
The book titled *Equality and diversity in social work practice* is a great resource for social work students to gain an understanding of equality and diversity in social work practices because several aspects of diversity are explored, including gender, sexual orientation, aging, disability, class, race, ethnicity, faith, and religion.

The International Association of Schools of Social Work. IASSW Vision & Mission Statement

https://archive.iassw-aiets.org/about-iassw/mission-statement/#:~:text=IASSW%20 vision%20is%20to%20promote%20and%20develop%20%E2%80%98Excellence,pursuit% 20of%20a%20more%20just%20and%20equitable%20world%E2%80%99.

It's essential to familiarize yourselves with the organizations that shape the profession globally. One such pivotal entity is the IASSW. As an international association comprising institutions of social work education, organizations supporting social work education, and dedicated social work educators, the IASSW plays a significant role in advancing the field worldwide. In this link, you will delve into the vision and mission statement of the IASSW, gaining valuable insights into its overarching goals and commitments.

Table 10.7: Reflecting on Your Competency in Demonstrating Respect for Cultural Difference

> **Answer the following questions to help you reflect on your own cultural knowledge and competency in demonstrating respect for cultural differences.**
>
> What were the factors that made Sarah more comfortable with minority students in the class as compared to students who were White?
>
> Which strategy did Sarah use to improve her cultural competency and gain a greater understanding of different cultures?
>
> What do you know about the different cultures that exist in Canada? What strategies have you employed to gain cultural knowledge, and what strategies would you like to propose to enhance your knowledge of different cultures?

Diversity Versus Assimilation or Homogenization

As social workers, we must ensure that our actions do not reduce difference to sameness, promote relativism, nor promote exclusion. Instead, we should strive to increase engagement with diverse minority groups. In the face of globalization, cultural identity is fundamental to societies that might otherwise be susceptible to the effects of disorienting change, homogenization, and disintegration.

Treating all people with respect, dignity, and fairness is fundamental to our relationship with the Canadian public and contributes to a safe and healthy work environment that promotes engagement, openness, and transparency. The diversity of people in Canada and of the ideas they generate are the source of our innovation. (Government of Canada, n.d.).

Despite this, there is a conflict between the two concepts: assimilation and pluralism. One concept suggests that immigrants should be assimilated into mainstream culture; that is, they should strive to conform to mainstream Eurocentric society by dropping what makes their cultures and religions unique. The other concept is pluralism, an alternative to assimilation that proposes that society should acknowledge and accept the differences brought by these groups and allow them to coexist alongside mainstream cultures. As social workers, our goal should be to work towards bridging the gap between cultures, balancing the needs of minority and majority groups, and creating inclusive spaces that provide opportunities for diverse minority groups. This effort requires collaboration and advocacy to foster a safe and equitable environment for all. In our role, we should not support the homogenization of diverse minority groups' practices, beliefs, and cultures. Instead, our roles and actions should demonstrate acceptance, respect, and an effort to understand diverse cultures and their values. The lack of basic knowledge about Muslims, for instance, has led to generalizations, assumes homogeneity, and stereotypes people, which leads to unethical practices (Mahdi & Paul, 2014). If we fail to respect minority cultures and try to homogenize the human race, we risk marginalizing underrepresented groups, which can lead to various forms of oppression, as well as economic and social repression. Indigenous Peoples are one example of this push for assimilation: In the 19th century, the Federal Government of Canada established the Residential School System through legislation. The system included policies that were designed to integrate Indigenous Peoples into settler societies. This system was designed to convert Indigenous children to Christianity while separating them from their traditional cultures based on the notion of the racial, cultural, and spiritual superiority of White settlers. About 150,000 First Nations, Inuit, and Métis children were forcibly removed from their homes and enrolled in residential schools through this system between the 19th and 20th centuries (Brady, 2013). The experiences of students in residential schools have had a long-term negative impact, not only on survivors but also on their extended families and communities. After decades of destruction, we have learned that the policies that were put in place had a negative impact on Indigenous Peoples in Canada.

Table 10.8: Assimilation vs. Inequality

Answer the following questions to help you reflect on your knowledge about the concepts of homogenization and assimilation and their impact on minority groups.

In your capacity as a social worker, how would you advocate on behalf of minority groups?

What do you know about the culture and religious practices of minority groups?

Do you believe that the concept of assimilation is imposed on minority groups? If so, please discuss the pros and cons of this concept.

Table 10.9: Resources on How to be Anti-Racist

> **Read the following resources to gain a deeper understanding of how to be anti-racist.**
>
> Government of Canada. (n.d.). *About the Public Health Agency of Canada*. Retrieved from https://www.canada.ca/en/public-health/corporate/mandate/about-agency.html
> By exploring the information provided on the Public Health Agency of Canada (PHAC) website, you will delve into the core values that guide the agency's operations. Rooted in principles of democracy, integrity, and excellence, PHAC is committed to upholding key values such as Respect for Democracy, Respect for People, Integrity, Stewardship, and Excellence. Through an examination of PHAC's values, you will gain valuable insights into the foundational beliefs that underpin the agency's efforts to safeguard and promote the health of Canadians.
>
> Buckley, M.E., Drewery, M., Jones, G. (2022). An antiracist approach to social work education at HBCUs. In Johnson, K.F., Sparkman-Key, N.M., Meca, A., Tarver, S.Z. (Eds.), *Developing anti-racist practices in the helping professions: Inclusive theory, Pedagogy, and Application*. Springer International Publishing.
>
> In social work education, the culture of whiteness has persisted and, in some instances, has remained unchallenged. In this chapter, the author outlines the historical context of racist theoretical frameworks, and perspectives used in social work education, critical race theory usage and implications in social work, social work education: A call for antiracist pedagogy. This knowledge can provide students a deep understanding on antiracist approach to social work field education.
>
> ***
>
> Centre for Integrative Anti-Racism Studies. (n.d.). *Dismantling anti-black racism in schooling, education, and beyond*. https://www.oise.utoronto.ca/home/sites/default/files/2023-11/abr_resource_guide-final.pdf
>
> Dismantling anti-Black racism in schooling and education is a resource guide compiled by Janelle Brady and Zainab Zafar. The booklet provides resources on the experiences of Black communities in Canada and the impacts of systemic anti-Black racism. The chapters focus on Black communities in Canada, Black feminism, anti-racism and anti-colonial theory, teaching and talking about race and racism, and affirming health and wellness.

Summary

Social workers need to understand the importance of multiple identities, subjectivity, and social context in their learning. This requires them to improve the ability and cultural competency to practice effectively with diverse populations (Council on Social Work Education [CSWE], 2022; Jani et al., 2011). Social work education emphasizes cultural competence since it entails having respect and treating individuals fairly. As social workers we demonstrate our commitment to respecting others and adhering to social work values in order to fulfill our professional responsibilities and obligations. We must integrate professional knowledge and values into field practice. Moreover, it is imperative that we foster a desire to explore and connect with individuals from diverse backgrounds, to enrich our understanding of ourselves, and to learn from others. In this chapter, we learned about diversity and the discrimination experienced by minority groups in Canada. The tips and strategies for addressing discrimination in social work practice and field education along with case studies and resources, provide ways for students to gain more knowledge about discrimination. This knowledge will contribute to the development of students' learning agreements, anti-discrimination training, policy development, the creation of a reporting mechanism for discrimination, academic research, and classroom instruction.

REFERENCES

Brady, M. J. (2013). Media practices and painful pasts: The public testimonial in Canada's Truth and Reconciliation Commission. *Media International Australia Incorporating Culture and Policy, 149*(1), 141–150. https://doi.org/10.3316/informit.740197338781209

Buckley, M.E., Drewery, M., Jones, G. (2022). An antiracist approach to social work education at HBCUs. In: Johnson, K.F., Sparkman-Key, N.M., Meca, A., Tarver, S.Z. (Eds.), *Developing anti-racist practices in the helping professions: Inclusive theory, Pedagogy, and Application* (pp. 173–196). Springer International Publishing. https://doi.org/10.1007/978-3-030-95451-2_10

Brown, S. L. (2020). *Racism by any other name: The lived experiences of Black social work practitioners and racial microaggressions* (Publication No.) Doctoral Dissertation, University. ProQuest Dissertations Publishing.

Canadian Association of Social Workers. (2024). Code of ethics. https://www.casw-acts.ca/files/attachements/CASW_Code_of_Ethics_Values_Guiding_Principles_2024_0.pdf

Canadian Human Rights Commission. (n.d.). What is discrimination. https://www.chrc-ccdp.gc.ca/en/about-human-rights/what-discrimination

Council on Social Work Education. (2022). Educational policy and accreditation standards. https://www.cswe.org/accreditation/policies-process/2022epas/

Cenat, J. M., Blais-Rochette, C., Morse, C., Vandette, M.-P., Noorishad, P.-G., Kogan, C., & Labelle, P. R. (2020). Prevalence and risk factors associated with attention-deficit/hyperactivity disorder among US Black individuals: A systematic review and meta-analysis. *JAMA Psychiatry* (Chicago, Ill.), *78*(1), 21–28. https://doi.org/10.1001/jamapsychiatry.2020.2788

CIHR. (n.d.) *Bias in peer review.* https://cihr-irsc.gc.ca/lms/e/bias/

Egan, G. (2014). *The skilled helper: A problem-management and opportunity-development approach to helping* (10th ed.). Brooks/Cole, Cengage Learning.

Egan, G., & Reese J.R. (2019). *The skilled helper: A problem management and opportunity development approach to helping* (11th ed.). Brooks/Cole, Cengage Learning.

Este, D. (2007). Cultural competency and social work practice in Canada: A retrospective examination. *Canadian Social Work Review/Revue Canadienne De Service Social, 24*(1), 93–104. https://www.jstor.org/stable/41669864

Fernando, M., Patricia, R., Cristina, G.A., María, J. F., & Pilar, S. (2013). Measuring dimensions of perceived discrimination in five stigmatized groups. *Social Indicators Research, 114*(3), 901–914. https://doi.org/10.1007/s11205-012-0179-5

Fisher, C. B. (2013). *Decoding the ethics code: A practical guide for psychologists* (3rd ed.). SAGE.

Gaine, C. (2010). *Equality and diversity in social work practice.* Learning Matters.

Golnaraghi, G., & Mills, A. J. (2013). Unveiling the myth of the Muslim woman: A postcolonial critique. *Equality, Diversity and Inclusion an International Journal, 32*(2), 157–172. https://doi.org/10.1108/02610151311324398

Government of Canada. (n.d.). About the Public Health Agency of Canada. https://www.canada.ca/en/public-health/corporate/mandate/about-agency.html

Helly, D. (2004). Are Muslims discriminated against in Canada since September 2001? *Canadian Ethnic Studies*, *36*(1), 24–47. https://ezproxy.lib.ucalgary.ca/login?qurl=https%3A%2F%2Fwww.proquest.com%2Fscholarly-journals%2Fare-muslims-discriminated-against-canada-since%2Fdocview%2F215636001%2Fse-2%3Faccountid%3D9838

The International Association of Schools of Social Work (IASSW). (n.d.). IASSW vision & mission statement. https://archive.iassw-aiets.org/about-iassw/mission-statement/#:~:text=IASSW%20vision%20is%20to%20 promote%20and%20develop%20%E2%80%98Excellence,pursuit%20of%20a%20more%20just%20and%20 equitable%20world%E2%80%99.

Jani, J. S., Osteen, P., & Shipe, S. (2016). Cultural competence and social work education: Moving toward assessment of practice behaviors. *Journal of Social Work Education*, *52*(3), 311–324. https://doi.org/10.1080/ 10437797.2016.1174634

Lilly, F. R. W., Owens, J., Bailey, T. C., Ramirez, A., Brown, W., Clawson, C., & Vidal, C. (2018). The influence of racial microaggressions and social rank on risk for depression among minority graduate and professional students. *College Student Journal*, *52*(1), 86–104.

Mahdi, J. Q., & Paul, J. (2014). Counselling Muslims: A culture-infused antidiscriminatory approach/Musulmans en counseling: une approche antidiscriminatoire tenant compte des références culturelles. *Canadian Journal of Counseling and Psychotherapy*, *48*(1), 57. https://cjc-rcc.ucalgary.ca/article/view/59301

Moreau, G. (2020). Police-reported hate crime in Canada, 2018. *Juristat*, 1–31.

Nagra, B., & Maurutto, P. (2016). Crossing borders and managing racialized identities: Experiences of security and surveillance among young Canadian Muslims. *Canadian Journal of Sociology*, *41*(2), 165–194. https://doi. org/10.29173/cjs23031

Niqab ban for public servants would be considered: Stephen Harper. (2015, October 6). *CBC News Online*. https:// www.cbc.ca/news/politics/stephen-harper-niqab-ban-public-servants-1.3258943

Oxford. (n.d.). Institutional racism. In Oxford Languages. https://www.google.com/search?sca_esv= 590699485&rlz=1C1CHBF_enCA823CA823&q=institutional+racism&si=ALGXSlZgIb9NAHU9uuSufEA_ sS933hFuHHdjCFavjejMtMIBzkzHl-26-AaXE4g81S2Qb2zN24q0b7d6yA3VNW4sd6bTkHOr5i 1JVQ6FoNGMqdWwf7gJPaQoOWgGi2eM4fmZX5yyMekp&expnd=1&sa=X&ved=2ahUKEwio jdmExo2DAxVRFjQIHXDFD30Q2v4IegQICRAP&biw=1812&bih=950&dpr=1.25%20)

Parrott, L. (2010). *Values and ethics in social work practice* (2nd ed.). Learning Matters.

Pascoe, E. A., & Richman, L. S. (2009). Perceived discrimination and health: A meta-analytic review. *Psychol Bull*, *135*(4), 531–554. https://doi.org/10.1037/a0016059

Pasha-Zaidi, N. (2015). Judging by appearances: Perceived discrimination among south Asian Muslim women in the US and the UAE. *Journal of International Women's Studies*, *16*(2), 70–97. https://vc.bridgew.edu/jiws/ vol16/iss2/5/

Poynting, S., & Perry, B. (2007). Climates of hate: Media and state inspired victimisation of Muslims in Canada and Australia since 9/11. *Current Issues in Criminal Justice*, *19*(2), 151–171. https://doi.org/10.1080/10345329.20 07.12036423

Reitz, J. G., & Bannerjee, R. (2006). Racial inequality, social cohesion and policy issues in Canada. In K. Banting, T. J. Courchene, and F. L. Seidl (Eds.), *Belonging? diversity, recognition and shared citizenship in Canada* (pp. 489–545). Montreal, QC: Institute for Research on Public Policy.

Rukavina, S. (26 February 2015). Quebec judge wouldn't hear case of woman wearing hijab. http://www.cbc.ca/ news/canada/montreal/quebec-judge-wouldn-t-hear-case-of-woman-wearing-hijab-1.2974282

Salim, S. (2022). "Experiences of Muslim female students in social work programs in western Canada." Unpublished doctoral dissertation, University of Calgary. https://prism.ucalgary.ca/server/api/core/ bitstreams/040c27cc-f9ef-44cd-8c4b-5e49529d3378/content

Sheppard, C. (2010). *Inclusive equality: The relational dimensions of systemic discrimination in Canada*. McGill-Queen's University Press.

Statistics Canada. (2013). Police-reported hate crimes in Canada. Statistics Canada. http://www.statcan.gc.ca/ pub/85-002-x/2015001/article/14191-eng.htm

Tyner, A. R. (2019). Unconscious bias, implicit bias, microaggressions: What can we do about them? *In GP solo,* (Vol. 36, Issue 4, pp. 30-33). American Bar Association.

Waddington, L. B., & Heniks, A. (2002). The expanding concept of employment discrimination in Europe: From direct and indirect discrimination to reasonable accommodation discrimination. *The International Journal of Comparative Labour Law and Industrial Relations, 18*(4), 403–427. https://doi.org/10.54648/5113464

Weinberg, M., & Fine, M. (2022). Racisms and microaggressions in social work: the experience of racialized practitioners in Canada. *Journal of Ethnic & Cultural Diversity in Social Work, 31*(2), 96–107. https://doi.org/10.1080/15313204.2020.1839614

NOTES:

NOTES:

NOTES:

11

Becoming a Spiritual Influencer Through the Heart and Soul of Field Practice

Heather M. Boynton and Indrani Margolin

This chapter offers students a spiritual model of practice for developing the knowledge, attitudes, and skills for integrating spirituality into one's professional identity and practice. Faculty and field supervisors can adopt this framework alongside students. There are various definitions in the literature regarding spirituality which speak to its complex and broad nature. Canda et al. (2020) professed that spirituality includes a sense of or search for connectedness to oneself, others, to nature and the universe. Further, that it has transcendent aspects of connection to a higher power of one's belief and entities that are spiritual or non-human. Boynton and Mellan (2021) conveyed that "spirituality involves identity and developmental concerns, and it has multiple dimensions and facets including love, gratitude, virtues of hope and forgiveness, joy, values, beliefs, and it comprises the cognitive, physical, emotional, experiential, social, environmental, existential, and supernatural dimensions" (p. 3). Spirituality exists along a continuum of beliefs and worldviews upon which every unique individual resides. Spirituality is highly intertwined with culture, and it is important for social workers to consider the ethnic and spiritual diversity of each client, family, or community. Given the Canadian context and the immense diversity of the global population spirituality requires attention and knowledge for social work practice as spirituality is expressed uniquely by each individual (see Boynton & DeVynck, 2022). It is important for social workers to consider that spirituality is fundamental in determining values, making decisions, and engagement in meaningful life activities and relationships, and one's worldview.

Field practicum is a time where students apply theory, knowledge, and skills in practice and develop a sense of who they are as social work practitioners. A practitioner's spirituality is key to, and even inseparable from, one's professional identity formation and requires "care full" contemplation and analysis. Therefore, it is paramount that students develop a professional sense and use of self with the consideration of spirituality, and reflective processes including discernment of one's own spirituality in relation to the profession's values. Attuning to the spiritual component of life for oneself and those we serve creates space for greater meaning-making, determining a sense of purpose, and for healing and connection.

Spirituality can play a pivotal role in practitioner strength and resilience and can mitigate compassion fatigue and burnout (Carneiro, 2019; de Diego-Cordero et al., 2022; Dezorzi & Crosetti, 2008) to which social workers are vulnerable. Self-care that includes daily or weekly spiritual activities, practices, or rituals is an important way of being that elevates energy and can help sustain social workers while supporting others who are encountering adversity. Additionally, spirituality can facilitate posttraumatic growth (PTG) and transcendence, that is moving beyond the ordinary, rising above oneself, the highest level of human consciousness (Maslow, 1971) for individuals, which is important for both the people social workers encounter in their work and in their own personal lives (Boynton & Vis, 2022). Seidlitz (2002) defined spiritual transcendence as "a perceived experience of the sacred that affects one's self-perception, feelings, goals, and ability to transcend one's difficulties" (p. 439). Social workers are encouraged to consider ways of facilitating spiritual transcendence within their own life and in the lives of those they encounter through their work.

This chapter presents a spiritually oriented and healing-centered model for education and practice that includes the knowledges, attitudes, and skills required in adopting a spiritually sensitive and informed approach to practice. This model is based on both authors' research and work over the past two decades. At the heart of our spirituality practice model is the assumption that all individuals have a spiritual worldview that integrates how they make sense of existence and mortality, and that as human beings living on earth, we interconnect with all that exists both on and beyond our world. The heart unity, in the middle of our model, permeates throughout the other areas and embodies our spiritual essence and core of our personal and professional selves as social workers within our professional body. Beneath our diversity is our shared humanity on earth and as social workers. The foundation of self and other compassion (an important concept known as *karuna* in Sanskrit) is recognizing our underlying unity. The concept of *ubuntu* is also resonant of this and is described by Mayaka and Truell (2021) as the belief that "an authentic individual human being is part of a larger and more significant relational, communal, societal, environmental, and spiritual world" (p. 650). Our approach is holistic involving culture, spirituality, social justice and action, and collective healing. Furthermore, the intersections of trauma and spirituality are recognized, and trauma is not viewed just as an individual isolated experience but considers the ways in which trauma and healing are also experienced collectively and over time.

The very first step for developing a spiritually sensitive and informed practice approach is to understand and conceptualize spirituality, and then to develop a greater awareness of one's own spirituality. The chapter will highlight why spirituality is important for practice and discuss the spiritual practice model (see Figure 13.1) starting from the outer circle which highlights the critical theoretical assumptions and aspects of practice that underpin this approach to social work. The inner sections speak to one's identity and personal development, and spiritually informed practice approaches at a personal and at a practice level. Our intention is that after reading this chapter, each social worker (developing and practicing) will fully embrace their own deep meaning-making, recognize their spiritual self, attune to the spiritual dimension of practice, and discover their role as a spiritual influencer through supporting spiritual aspects in the transformation of clients, families, communities, organizations, and institutions. Our ultimate hope is that this will be used to cultivate knowledge transcendence in our continually evolving social work practice and for a healthier world.

Why is Spirituality in Social Work Important?

Research has demonstrated that clients of all ages desire to have their religious and spiritual beliefs included in treatment. Spirituality has the potential to result in positive outcomes and improved health and wellbeing for clients (Boynton, 2016b; Oxhandler & Pargament, 2014). Attuning to spirituality is important as it aligns with anti-oppressive and strength-based approaches and is ultimately ethical practice. Social workers need to consider and acknowledge the many spiritual strengths and challenges of their own spirituality alongside the spirituality of the individual, family, or community as part of holistic practice.

In a survey of social workers in the United States, Oxhandler and Giardina (2017) found that close to half described how their own spiritual beliefs, practices, curiosity, and journey led them to explore spirituality with clients. They caution though that implementing spirituality into assessment and treatment with little training increases the risk for proselytizing or for social workers to impose their own beliefs onto potentially vulnerable clients. In a related study, Oxhandler and Ellor (2017) surveyed 469 social workers across the United States, including 69 field instructors, and found that although the participants were open to spiritual and religious explorations with clients, only half felt they had adequate training to do so. Additionally, many felt that spiritual sensitivity would improve their practice. In an international study of 15,067 culturally diverse social work students, Pandya (2018) found that spirituality was perceived by them as a core aspect of field practice and interventions. Despite this, students have felt ill-equipped to engage in spiritually oriented interventions and had fears of doing harm as a result (Kvarfordt & Herba, 2018; Kvarfordt & Sheridan, 2010; Oxhandler & Giardina, 2017; Oxhandler et al., 2015). In my own research (Boynton, 2016b), practitioners also expressed a lack of training and felt unprepared to address spiritual aspects of working with clients, and in my teaching practice, where I focus on spirituality, students have shared with me that they have more knowledge and feel more confident and skilled in addressing spirituality with people they work with. We hope that the content in this chapter will facilitate the development of your own evolving spiritually informed approach to practice.

We believe that spirituality could readily be included as a component of diversity and an extension of other areas of social justice and anti-oppressive practice. It is congruent with many theories such as narrative, existential, and humanistic theories, and it can be integrated into most interventions and, as such, could fit into coursework; it is particularly needed in skills classes. There are several pertinent journals from which content could be derived, including *the Journal for Religion and Spirituality in Social Work*; the *International Journal of Children's Spirituality*; *Spirituality and Aging*; *Religions*; *Social Work with Groups*; *Child and Adolescent Social Work*; and *Social Work and Christianity*. There also are several books on spirituality and social work that have been written over the past several decades and more continue to be released (for example Boynton & Vis, 2022; Canda, Furman & Canda, 2020; Crisp, 2017).

Social workers are increasingly taught to regard people holistically as bio-psycho-social beings and are beginning to recognize the missing spiritual nature of human identity in this approach. Kvarfordt et al. (2018) provided two rationales for including spirituality in the curriculum noting that the "attention to religion/spirituality aligns with the profession's commitment towards working effectively with diverse client systems and (ii) religion/spirituality are important aspects of human existence and, therefore, are key for understanding human development and behaviour" (p. 10). This is in alignment with the core learning objectives of the Canadian Association for Social Work Education (2021) accreditation standards where social work students are to have opportunities within their educational experience to "understand the complexities of ethical practice across various professional roles and activities and within spiritual, cultural and institutional contexts" (p. 16). Thus, curriculum and field practice experience should prepare students for practice realities where spiritual aspects of clients' lives will likely be encountered.

The Spiritual Practice Model

Our spiritual practice model provides a framework for incorporating spirituality into social work education and practice.

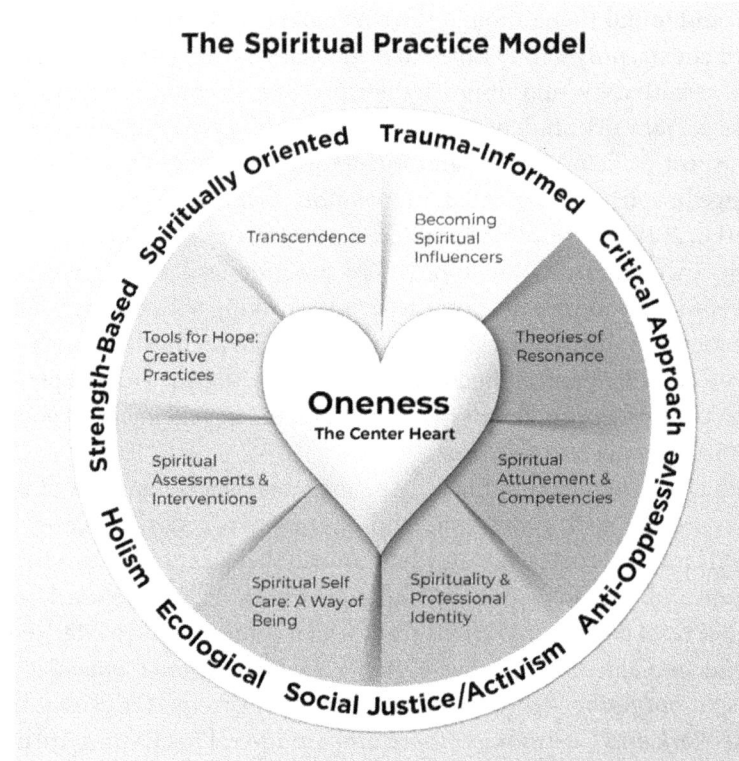

Figure 11.1:
The Spiritual
Practice Model

The Centre of the Circle

The center heart of the spiritual practice model depicts a paradigm of unity, which unifies the rest of the model. Ancient and Indigenous traditions and philosophies speak to the interconnectedness and unity of all forms of life and convey that the core of our spiritual essence is oneness. This concept of oneness refers to a Universal Consciousness that is individualized in every human being (Sen, 2016, see p. 39 & 76). This universal consciousness is intelligent and creative. Centering practices, such as meditation, enable an individual to experience a sense of connection with oneself and the sacred, divine, and Universal Consciousness.

The Outer Circle

The spiritual practice model embraces critical social work and anti-oppressive methods that challenge systemic power and privilege and honour diversity and difference. Spirituality and service to humanity and the world often drive social action and social justice concerns and are why many individuals enter the social work field. A spiritually informed approach to practice requires a trauma informed lens based on the intersections of spirituality, trauma, and grief and loss. An ethically grounded and spiritually oriented approach supports the work of decolonization and reconciliation. This critical approach employs reflective processes that are necessary at the micro, macro, and mezzo levels.

Using an ecological lens, which views people and the environment as interdependent and is integral to planetary well-being, social justice, and spirituality, social workers can begin to consider the broader issues of global concerns related to the environment, sustainability, and survival and well-being of all living beings including Mother Earth (Gray & Coates, 2013). A systems life model approach views individuals within their environments, which we argue include religious and spiritual contexts, and this model includes developmental and life transition components. By incorporating the ecological and systems approaches, our spiritual practice model adopts a philosophy of holism where we are part of something larger and beyond ourselves. The spiritual practice model accepts multiple ways of knowing, doing, and being. Additionally, the model is strength-based and seeks to identify and foster spiritual strengths, supports and resources, spiritual growth and transcendence where an individual moves beyond normal experiences and limits and can include connection with spiritual states or realms. Spiritual social work, like all effective social work, entails creating safety and active listening with curiosity, humility, and empathy, to deeply understand and demonstrate a willingness to be with a client, family, or community in their reality to reduce isolation and foster new perspective taking or looking at situations, events, or contexts from a different angle, or worldview.

The Middle Circle

The middle portion of the circle incorporates the theories discussed above and links to practice. It identifies the skills, knowledge, and attitudes required for the development of a spiritually sensitive and informed practice. The eight sectors offer guiding processes and tools that support development for spiritual social work practice.

Theories of Resonance

Our spiritual practice model is based upon perspectives of growth, self-actualization, and transcendence, as well as meaningful transformation that includes authenticity, creativity, and love. Theorists such as Frankl, Maslow, and Rogers evolved their conceptual models to include transpersonal perspectives recognizing the spiritual, transcendent, and cosmic connections in life. A transpersonal perspective considers human developmental processes and a continual transcendent process that goes beyond the egoic sense of self, and emphasizes connection to Universal Consciousness, God, or energy, and embraces wholeness or oneness and the spiritual dimensions of being and how individuals can move towards comprehensive modes of spiritual enlightenment (Canda & Smith, 2001; Wilber, 1997, 1998). A transpersonal view holds importance for the sacredness of the earth and the cosmos, recognizing the intimately intertwined nature of humans with everything in the local and nonlocal universe. Our model is informed by transpersonal theory, which we believe is pivotal for social work.

Spiritual Attunement and Competencies

Within social work, Canda et al. (2020) and Hodge (2018) have discussed the need for humility and competence regarding spiritual aspects that are of critical importance for providing spiritually relevant practice. Boynton (2016a) defined spiritual competence "as a human relational and intuitive capacity" for co-creating spiritually focused dialogue and a common understanding between those with "differing spiritual perspectives and worldviews within a safe therapeutic space" which includes "spiritual listening and attention" (p. 177) which is elaborated on below. Spiritual competencies for social work practice include developing awareness of self and others, creating safety for self and others, engaging in humility, considering the appropriateness of interventions, and attunement. These competencies are not necessarily all linear in nature and are ongoing processes. The first step in developing spiritual competencies requires developing an awareness of one's own spiritual worldview and biases through reflection and questioning.

ACTIVITY BREAK 1
We invite you to pause and contemplate the reflexive questions below, perhaps take some time to journal on each one. Do not immediately answer; let them simmer within you. You may even reflect on them over a period of days or weeks. Wait patiently for your heart's response as you continue your inquiry.

Critically Reflexive Questions

1. Who am I?
2. Why am I here?
3. What is my purpose or calling?
4. What are my guiding values?
5. What is my direction in life?
6. How did my spirituality develop and how was it informed?
7. Is faith or religion a part of my spirituality?
8. What are my beliefs surrounding life and death?
9. How do I view my existence in the world?

After reflecting on the questions in the box above think about how each informs your worldview. Ask yourself: How might my ways of knowing and understandings of the world influence my practice with others? How might I have assumptions, biases, or hold stereotypes of others? What is my spirituality and what does it include? Take some time to consider articulating your worldview and its influence on your practice. You may be asked by those you work with about your spirituality, so it is good to have some clarity for yourself and even to consider your response.

The next step is to understand the spiritual worldview of the individual, family, or community you are or might be working with. In order to do this establishing safety is important. Considering your own safety in practice involves your physical safety in the space you are in, awareness of your level of skills and continuing to build these, your emotional and psychological safety, and your spiritual safety. These dimensions are important for those you work with as well.

Practicing humility through creating safer spaces for others involves openness, curiosity, and inquiry, and honoring and accepting (see Boynton & Mellan [2021] for more on opening one's heart for sacred relationships). There are tools that can be used to explore the cultural domain such as the culturagram (see Yeshiva University, 2021) and spiritual aspects which are described later in the spiritual practice model. After assessing the worldview of who you are working with then consider whether the interventions are appropriate and how they align with the spirituality of the individual, family, or community. Many Western theories and practice approaches are not appropriate for all spiritual worldviews.

You may have heard of multiple intelligences or encountered the term emotional intelligence (EQ), which is the ability to understand and manage one's own emotions and to recognize and influence the emotions of an individual with whom one engages. Yet, you may not have heard of spiritual intelligence (SQ) which is now considered the highest level of intelligence and is paramount in relational and leadership activities. Zohar (2018) stated that SQ is an ability to access higher meanings, values, abiding purposes, and unconscious aspects of the self and to embed these meanings, values, and purposes in living richer and more creative lives. Signs of high SQ include an ability to think out of the box, humility, and an access to energies that come from something beyond the ego, beyond just me and my day-to-day concerns (para. 8).

Developing spiritual competencies also involves developing the capacity of SQ, and an intuitiveness and openness to spiritual realms. Wigglesworth (2012) identified 21 skills of SQ that are encompassed within four quadrants — awareness of self and knowing oneself; the universal and knowing the world; self-mastery, and social mastery; and spiritual presence. Cindy Wigglesworth discusses these skills in a TEDxTalk (see Wigglesworth, 2014). The development of SQ skills is necessary for social workers to embrace the spiritual component of practice and are a critical part of lifelong learning and self-transcendence. You can also watch a webinar on spiritual competency and diversity hosted by the U.S. Society for Spirituality and Social Work and the Canadian Society for Spirituality and Social Work (Franco & Lopez, 2022).

Spiritual Attunement

Hoskins (1999) offered 5 key areas of cultural attunement: acknowledging the pain of oppression, engaging in acts of humility, acting with reverence, engaging in mutuality, and maintaining a position of "not knowing". These are applicable for what we deem to be involved in spiritual attunement. We add to this by including engaging heart to heart with unconditional love, empathy, and compassion, and for those who hold a divine belief, having a soul-to-soul connection. Spiritual attunement refers to the capacity to be receptive to intuitive and collective knowledge and builds upon Ainsworth's (1977) attachment theory work in attunement. Attachment theory posits that an internal working model of self within relationships forms within the first five years of life and encompasses the child's expectations of how others will respond to their needs, out of which they develop a sense of safety in the world. Spiritual attunement extends this concept to spiritual relationships with oneself, others, and a higher power.

Spiritual attunement in the therapeutic relationship is an active relationship-building process that encompasses attending, spiritual listening and being receptive, and reflecting deeply. Within the relational practice of attunement social workers act with reverence (high regard, awe, and honour) towards others (Hoskins, 1999; Boynton & De Vynck, 2022). Spiritual attunement and receptivity involve being present with the interactional symbiosis or matching non-verbal communication and affect, and co-regulation through modelling a calming presence and speaking in a warm tone with open body language in the counselling process.

The Mandarin and Cantonese characters for listen means "I give you my ears, my eyes, my undivided attention [like the respect for a king] and my heart" (personal communication with Ik Chang, October 20, 2008). This is congruent with spiritual listening and takes active listening to its deepest level. In the act of spiritual listening, practitioners enter a field of vulnerability where a reciprocal process of bearing witness and creating trust can ensue. Spiritual listening also involves opening one's heart and accessing a deeper level of consciousness. Genuine and meaningful articulation of thoughts, feelings, meanings, and understandings can only occur through conversing heart to heart. Listening, even through silence, allows for knowing to arise (Hart, 2002) through presence, reflection, and introspection. This respectful connection, resonance and relational and intuitive capacity is integral in SQ and promotes safety in the therapeutic relationship. According to trauma expert Dan Siegal (2022),

When we attune with others we allow our own internal state to shift, to come to resonate with the inner world of another. This resonance is at the heart of the important sense of "feeling felt" that emerges in close relationships (para. 2).

This level of attunement involves a stance of unconditional love that unites our human family. Buddhists call this loving kindness; Martin Buber (1958) named it the "I-thou relationship." It is a sacred form of human expression and connection we can strive for as social workers.

When a social worker focuses on their own breath, bodily sensations, and feelings they center and calm themselves. These are some of the most potent ways that social workers can become aware of clients' unspoken thoughts and feelings. In trauma therapy, co-regulation through this attuning process of calming the body and mind is part of a caring and secure relationship. Through spiritual attunement social workers can become aware of the client's unspoken thoughts and feelings and are better positioned to hear and highlight spiritually themed content of strengths and struggles. This can provide clarity for direction in the counselling process as to which spiritual strengths might be resources for the client and any struggles requiring further support.

Spirituality and Professional Identity

Students reflect on and consider their desired areas of practice that connects to their strengths, talents, abilities, and capacities. This also includes the meaning and purpose of the work. The spiritual aspect is often implicit in this process; if students don't recognize it, they miss the opportunity to consider how they make meaning and decisions related to their own spiritual worldview and values. Many social workers were drawn into the social work field because of their spirituality, philosophical stance, and/or religious beliefs and values (Freeman, 2007; Hirsbrunner, 2012; Oxhandler & Giardina, 2017) and see their work as service in a divine sense.

Social work students need to know that the journey of reflecting on one's own spirituality and stage of spiritual development can be a delightful and empowering process, yet for some it can be challenging and distressing, and may require support from a spiritual leader, elder or counsellor. This can particularly occur if one has encountered tensions or struggles with religion or spirituality, spiritual abuse, and/or trauma as these can disrupt one's spiritual worldview and spiritual relationships, causing spiritual crises, wounds, pain, and injury (Boynton, 2016b; Boynton & Vis, 2011, 2017). De Vynck et al. (2022) highlighted that spiritual distress can arise when and individual struggles with a divine relationship, experiences painful feelings and strife surrounding doubts or disillusionment related to religion or spirituality or concerning moral and existential concerns. Attending to spiritual distress can aid with spiritual growth, development, and transformation (Exline & Rose, 2005). Not reflecting on one's own spiritual worldview and development can increase the potential for ruptures in the therapeutic relationship and transference, countertransference, or avoidance of critical areas for the client regarding spirituality might occur.

The social worker's self awareness is especially important when working with clients for whom spirituality is an important part of their life, an aspect of their identity, or is interconnected with the struggles for which they are seeking help (which may be explicit or implicit). For these clients, spirituality and/or religion should be a central component of therapeutic work and students need to learn to traverse these topics; this requires awareness of one's own spirituality and worldview and related potential biases and judgements. Therefore, answering the questions in Activity Break 1 are part of spiritual competency development which is important for new social workers.

As students learn through their academic program and practice experiences their developing professional identities are modified to align with new ideas, values, and beliefs. There can be times when one's own beliefs and values are tested and can involve a steep and challenging learning curve and assimilation of diverse theoretical and practice understandings along with values and ethics. If students are already prepared and have been through engagement in introspective and spiritual reflective processes in their academic career which might involve revising their spiritual worldview, they will be much better equipped to manage situations later in their professional career. In our experience of teaching students about spirituality, they often express relief, joy, and/or excitement that their new and emerging practice identity and professional development can embrace their spiritual self.

Spiritual Reflexivity in Practice

Spirituality can be a pivotal resource to draw upon in times of need for professional life. Therefore, we advocate for students to take the time at the end of each practicum day to contemplate the day's events, interactions, thoughts, and feelings in relation to spirituality, and for all social workers to do this as well. Intentional spiritual reflection makes room for the resolution of any unresolved conflict(s) at the practicum agency, incomplete work with clients, or the identification of new directions. Shocking or difficult realizations about self and others may have arisen and can be processed through spiritual reflection and transcendent meaning making involving a deep understanding one oneself and their existence in the world (Vis & Boynton, 2008). Furthermore, focusing on successes, interactions, understandings, and aspects of the work that students feel proud of can lead to greater self-esteem, competence, and mastery. Spiritually-oriented reflection expands upon social work reflective practice and fosters more authentic professional and personal aspirations. Reflection assists with congruence and alignment of one's spiritual beliefs and values, and with professional practice identity. Reflection on spiritual identity, as well as, conversations with peers, teachers, and practitioners, and spiritually focused interventions is a component of ethical practice.

Spiritual Self Care: A Way of Being

Engagement in activities that contribute to our health and wellness should not be done occasionally or forgotten in times of stress. They need to be integrated into a daily routine that demonstrates care of your sacred self. Self-care needs to be considered as a way of being and living, not an add-on or only done when under pressure or fatigued. Authentic and spiritual self-care is much more in depth — it is fundamental for resilience and necessary in our profession, particularly in work where trauma is encountered. The soul or authentic core of oneself requires nourishment like a child. Would you ever forget to feed a child in your care? This is the way to approach holistic and spiritual engagement or wellness. In fact, throughout our careers as social workers and professors, we have witnessed that individuals who have a balanced day or week and who have integrated activities to nourish the mind, body, and spirit regularly function more effectively than when living an unbalanced life. Ensuring non-negotiable time in your daily or weekly life for mind, body, and spiritual wellness demonstrates the value and honour you give to yourself and can bring peace and elation.

Spiritual self care as a way of being means to evaluate your needs, take stock of your desires, and to live your best life each day which can contribute to overall health and resilience, combat stress and burnout, and reduce the potential for compassion fatigue (Margolin, 2014). Just as we strengthen our muscles and body as we exercise, or we improve a skill through practice, our spiritual self-care practice increases our spiritual fitness and enhances all the aspects of our health and vitality.

Tygielski (2022, June 17) conveyed that engaging in daily repeated patterns of self care is like a musical rhythm that "helps maintain the song of our life" (para. 4). This author also highlighted the monthly and seasonal rhythms where we can target our focus of self-care. As the creator of your best life, what is the nourishing rhythm you want to play to allow you to flourish? You might consider adopting the mantra "nourish to flourish"! Like all visions, the choices that you cultivate today will be reflected in your circumstances and your future. Consider optimal choices for your wellbeing that offer the energy and balance for your whole being so that you can be fully present on a regular basis. Gillis (2013) conveyed that the ABC's of self-care are awareness (quieting, solitude, and understanding our needs), balance (eight hours of action, eight hours of play and eight hours of rest), and connection (meaningfully, interdependent connection to something beyond ourselves). How might you include activities that address awareness, balance, and connection in your life to avoid burnout?

Wright (2005) frames burnout as a spiritual crisis, which often is indicative of "spiritual aridity," or spiritual emptiness, which would then call for spiritual renewal, that is, awakening or reigniting our passions. They outline several areas where we can feed our spirit, such as engaging with soul friends (wise counsellors or mentors), soul communities (groups where we feel at home and that nourish our spiritual growth and development, which can include groups for reflective practice), soul foods (activities that offer inspiration, peace, creativity, and joy, such as engaging with music, poetry or scripture, or spending time in nature for renewal and revitalization), and soul works (practices to keep us in the flow of the divine that we engage in independently or in a group such as yoga, tai chi, meditation, etc.). Ask yourself, "How much soul time am I giving myself?" and "How will I care for myself to enhance wellbeing and living my best life?"

ACTIVITY BREAK 2

We invite you to pause and contemplate the reflexive questions below. Do not immediately answer. Let them simmer within you and patiently wait for the response.

Critically Reflexive Questions

1. How does spirituality fit into my daily life?
2. What are my own spiritual rituals, practices, and activities (e.g. in the morning, before meeting with clients or going into meetings, at lunchtime and breaks, or at the end of day. Examples include changing from work clothes and engaging in physical activity, spending time in nature or with animals, lighting a candle, connecting with others, creating, listening to music, praying, meditating, or visioning)?
3. When and how will I carve out time for solitude, reflection, contemplation, prayer, or meditation?
4. How do I want to harmonize the various aspects of my life?
5. How can I consciously open myself to receive inner or higher guidance to overcome obstacles in all aspects of my life?
6. What visions and steps do I need to realize my aspirations?
7. What am I passionate about? How do I activate my passion? How do I engage passionately?
8. How do I make self-care meaningful?
9. How will I make spiritual self-care an integral aspect of who I am?

Spiritual Assessments and Interventions

This section offers strategies and tools for addressing spirituality in practice through assessment and intervention processes. Attuning to spirituality and its inclusion offers hope for the clinician and the client and facilitates spiritual development. Providing clients with the skills and resources they require for coping facilitates PTG and is a means of empowerment (Hipolito et al., 2014) that can support a full and authentic life.

According to Margolin and Sen (2022), PTG refers to the positive transformations that individuals, families, and communities undergo in terms of their life priorities, sense of place, and self as they make meaning of loss after trauma. They further stated that,

> regardless of an individual's personal belief system, the processes of personal narrative reconstruction, re-evaluation and whole person development, are negotiated through spiritual routes . . . Life cannot grow without metamorphosis. The butterfly emerges directly from the imaginal cells of the cocooned destroyed caterpillar (Margolin & Sen, 2022, p. 199).

Boynton (2022) highlighted that individuals across the lifespan who experience PTG often feel stronger and enriched and emerge from trauma better able to manage future challenges, and spirituality is interconnected with this process.

Spiritual Assessments

Assessment is an integral part of initiating a relationship with a client. Social workers are trained to gather pertinent information to understand the client's context, risk level, and protective factors and use that information to support them with formulating goals. Using an eco-bio-psycho-social-spiritual approach ensures that a holistic view is applied. A strengths perspective is also important when conducting spiritual assessments and interventions with clients (Saleebey, 2013; Margolin, 2019). Canda et al. (2020, p. 355) offer four guidelines:

1. Open the topic.
2. More detailed exploration.
3. Establish relevance for the helping plan.
4. Identify the next step in a plan for action.

As the social worker attends to the client's responses it will become clear whether the client wants to "move from implicit to explicit discussion of spirituality and religion" (Canda et al., 2020, p. 355). Opening the topic creates an understanding of what spirituality means to the client and is part of creating a safe spiritual space. You can start with an opener such as *I would like for us to speak together about your personal spirituality, as this can be a source of strength and a resource or it may be a place of struggle. Would it be okay for us to talk about this area of importance and what this means for you and our work together?*

If a client agrees, then a social worker can proceed to conduct a spiritual assessment and gather more details. If the client appears hesitant or does not agree to discuss spirituality, then we recommend taking a more implicit approach. The questions in Activity Break 3 are drawn and adapted from Hodge (2013, p. 227) and Canda et al. (2020, p. 354).

ACTIVITY BREAK 3

We invite you to review the implicit spiritual questions in this activity. First, reflect on these questions yourself. Then practice with a peer or mentor prior to incorporating these tools into your work.

Implicit Spiritual Questions

1. What gives you a sense of meaning, purpose, or hope for your life?
2. When do you feel most fully alive and in the flow of life?
3. Who/what do you rely on most in life?
4. What rituals/practices are especially significant and bring you calm or joy?
5. At the deepest level of your being, what nourishes you?
6. What causes you the greatest despair/suffering?
7. When you are in pain (or afraid), where do you turn for comfort?
8. What strengths or gifts have supported you through past difficulties that could support you now?
9. Who are your most important mentors and why?
10. Is there a recent time that you experienced an "aha" moment or gained new insight? Please describe.
11. What are you most grateful for in life?
12. What are your most cherished ideals?
13. Who and what do you love most?
14. What are the deepest questions this current challenge ignites for you?
15. How does this situation shake your sense of what is true and right?
16. How does this situation shake your sense of being?
17. What are your hopes, goals, and aspirations?
18. How would you like to be remembered?

Conducting an explicit spiritual assessment can include a few brief questions or more involved questions and history-taking. There are various models that can be used to discuss spiritual and religious aspects with individuals as outlined by LaRocca-Pitts (2012). Social workers assess client's spiritual strengths including beliefs, values, practices, rituals, activities, resources, and supports, and discern possible areas of struggle, distress, and crises present for clients. Additionally, asking about how the presenting problem is a challenge; whether there are identity concerns; and if relationships and connections are disrupted, in jeopardy, or severed can assist with identifying needed client supports. Through holistically understanding client concerns social workers can better support their spiritual healing.

ACTIVITY BREAK 4
We invite you to visit the links and videos on spiritual assessments below. First, assess yourself then practice with a peer or mentor prior to incorporating these tools with a client.

> **Spiritual Assessments**
>
> 1. Spiritual Assessment in Health Care (TheSesame12, 2013)
>
> 2. SSOPP Spiritual Assessment Interview (Spiritual Competency Academy, 2021)
>
> 3. LaRocca-Pitts spiritual assessment models (Association of Professional Chaplins, n.d.)

Hodge (2015) provided an overview of various visual assessment approaches, including spiritual lifemaps, genograms, ecomaps, and ecograms. Spiritual listening, as noted above, involves curiosity and empathy to deeply understand the perspective of the client. The social worker demonstrates a willingness to be with a client in their reality which can reduce isolation and the worker can encourage the client to engage in new perspective taking. The spiritual attunement process includes listening for implicit meanings, subordinate storylines (alternative stories hidden within the narrative), and spiritual narratives.

ACTIVITY BREAK 5
Visit the links in the text box to view the visual assessment tools. First, assess yourself, then practice with a peer or mentor prior to incorporating these tools with a client.

> **Visual Assessment Approaches**
>
> 1. Spiritual Lifemap (Limb & Hodge, 2007)
>
> 2. Spiritual Genogram (Hodge, 2001)
>
> 3. Spiritual Ecomap (Hodge & Limb, 2014)
>
> 4. Spiritual Ecogram (Limb & Hodge, 2011)

Conducting implicit and explicit spiritual assessments assists with establishing the relevance of spirituality for the helping plan. The treatment plan and goals are collaboratively created with the client to identify the next steps and strategies for action.

Spiritual Interventions

There are many types of spiritual interventions that can be included in treatment for clients. Within evidence-based practice frameworks, spiritual components can enhance a holistic approach to care.

ACTIVITY BREAK 6

We invite you to try one of the following interventions. Then consider how you might incorporate these into your work. Feel free to journal after each practice.

Spiritual Interventions

1. Create a spiritual space in your office (images, books, flags, tapestries, singing bowls, crystals etc.).
2. Incorporate rituals such as choosing a virtue, value, relationship, angel, or other oracle card at the end of each session. This can foster deeper meanings to what has been discussed.
3. Develop continuing bond activities in grief work such as creating memory books, writing messages and burning them in a ritual or putting them in a lake or river, or creating a pillow out of a piece of clothing or blanket belonging to the deceased.
4. Use bibliotherapy to allow a client to read scriptures, engage in prayer, or create mantras.
5. Engage in music, dance, chanting, or creative movement.
6. Engage in a Mandala Exercise (Boynton & Margolin, 2022), spiritual art, or writing.
7. Consider joining a spiritual support or activity group.
8. Visit a sacred site, or go on a pilgrimage.

Contemplative Interventions

Contemplative daily activities can support social workers in their own self care and grounding, as well as assist with co-regulation (see Cmind, 2021). They can also be discussed and integrated with clients as helpful coping strategies. Active contemplative practices include yoga, Tai Chi, Qi Gong, dance, walking a labyrinth, and sports. Expressive contemplative activities include art, journalling, poetry, storytelling, musical activities, meditative chanting, and visualization. Spending time in nature, engaging in "green exercise" or mood walks (see Mind your Mind, 2024) and forest bathing can also be contemplative and regenerative. Forest bathing is the English translation of the Japanese therapy Shinrin yoku (Kotera et al., 2020). This practice involves walking in nature, typically through a forest. By engaging sight, smell, taste, sound, and touch to appreciate and delight in the surrounding beauty, inhale pure oxygen, and receive negative ions which are beneficial to the body. When spending time in nature the nervous system rests, rejuvenates, and heals. This move from a sympathetic to a parasympathetic state is why Shinrin yoku significantly reduces the effects of vicarious trauma (Kotera et al., 2020), which field education students often experience. More information on this topic can be found in Chapter 3 in this book.

Other important interventions such as self-compassion, forgiveness, and gratitude can open one's heart. Spiritual practices that include prayer, rituals, scripture, inspirational reading, or pilgrimages are also helpful in awakening one to our spiritual interconnectedness. There is a plethora of literature and online resources to boost creativity and inspiration, develop empathy and compassion for others; improve focus, attention, and concentration; reduce stress, anxiety, and depression; and combat fatigue and burnout. Spiritual interventions are a means of honouring and caring for oneself in authentic ways. Deeper spiritual practices can lead to insights and strengthened intuition (which is deemed as the art of social work practice), that have the potential to truly transform thoughts, feelings, and actions. We have both found meditation as a daily practice has greatly benefitted our overall health and wellbeing; enhanced our authenticity; and deepened our relationships to others, nature, and the Universal Consciousness that lives all around us.

Meditation is an ancient practice that is found across the globe. It can be employed as a self-care strategy for social workers and an intervention for clients. It enables one to become aware of and release unwanted thoughts and beliefs and experience the accompanying sensations and feelings as a natural consequence of balancing their body, mind, heart (Margolin, 2014). There are different types of meditation, from those that engage a mindfulness practice while sitting or walking, to focusing on an object or a flame, to practicing quiet stillness or emptiness, to focusing on spiritual words or phrases, to chanting affirmations and mantras, to rhythmic motions such as swaying, rocking, or circling. Meditation can also be combined with the use of a mandala (a circular design used to focus) and a mantra (a sacred sound or word) (Boynton & Margolin, 2022). Many individuals find listening to songs an uplifting and mindful practice (see Mraz, 2012).

Meditating on the breath supports concentration on our essential life force. Inhaling and exhaling is a natural meditation that occurs whether we are aware of it or not (Sen, 2016). It enables one to tune out stress and worry and the critiquing inner voice of judgment. The main task in meditation is to be with and feel the breath rejuvenate and cleanse the body with the inhalation, and to expand, and to release with the exhalation as the breath disperses into the atmosphere. Proclamation (Mahavakya) Meditation, an ancient Vedanta system from India, is one mantra meditation system found to have promising preliminary results with students (Margolin, 2014). This system brings together four great words or mantras to empower individuals to attune to their Creative Consciousness (Sen, 2016). It is well suited as an educational practice to support PTG (Sen & Margolin, 2021). According to Margolin and Sen (2022), students reported that Mahavakyam Meditation enabled concentration; tranquility and balance; elevated mood; enhanced personal and professional relationships; and a recognition of the causal connection between thoughts, emotions, and circumstances.

Tools for Hope: Creative Expressive Practices

Creative expressive practices such as art, dance, play, and movement often facilitate deeper meaning-making for students. They are particularly important for trauma, grief and loss work with clients for spiritual coping, expression, emotional processing and reappraising worldview, and a resource in fostering PTG and transcendent meaning making (Boynton & Vis, 2011; Vis & Boynton, 2008). Creative practices and processes offer strategies to support safety, healing, and create space, and self-transcendence (Margolin, 2019). We are creative by nature and develop a sense of self and the world through symbolic play in childhood and active or creative imagination in adulthood. Poetic engagement and writing provide another path to connect to one's deep feelings and to make meaning (Wiebe & Margolin, 2012). Natalie Rogers, originator of Person-Centred Expressive Arts Therapy (PCEAT), and daughter of Carl Rogers, built upon her father's work and focused on creative engagement as a therapeutic tool (Rogers 2011, 2012, 2015, 2019).

Tuning into Spirit/Consciousness

We recommend starting important meetings with a simple ritual, ceremony, or mindful practice to prepare to engage and interact in a good manner. Examples include a quiet meditation or reflection or symbolically laying down worries and concerns from the day and placing them in the garbage or an imaginary basket or container that can be later picked up if required.

Visualization

Visualization practices can be grounding and centering. Van der Kolk (2014) conveyed that the body holds on to trauma memories; physiological responses can be triggered, making the body think that the trauma is still present. What is not often considered is that the body can also hold on to positive memories with related physiological responses. These memories activate sensory and somatic experiences within the body. Thus, our mind and body can be a container for positive and spiritual experiences, which can be accessed when needed.

ACTIVITY BREAK 7

We invite you to try the following practices and consider how you might incorporate these into your work. Feel free to journal after each practice.

Visualization Practices

1. Visualize and imagine a past event that brought feelings of love and connection. Fully embrace the memory along with all that you see, hear, touch, smell, taste, and feel.

2. Close our eyes and imagine a wave in the ocean. Feel the wave rise up and splash back down. Notice the wave merging back into the whole ocean. Do this a few times. Now consider, can you separate the wave from the ocean? Similarly, can you separate yourself from all that is around you?

3. Observe an ice cube melting in the water. Imagine you are that ice cube becoming one with the whole universe.

4. Clearly visualize a deep driving desire and feel your passion arising. Imagine it already exists. What do you notice? What do you see? How do you feel? Fully embrace the imagined experience.

5. Find an object that holds meaning or has a spiritual significance for you. Notice what the object evokes within you. Does it transport you to another time and place? Do you feel a strong connection to the object or something beyond?

Transcendence

Maslow's (1971) hierarchy of needs includes transcendence where an individual transcends or moves beyond the ego, and it also includes peak or flow experiences that are spiritual in nature. One might see the sacredness in all things and in simple daily encounters. Through considering spirituality and fostering client spiritual development we support them to grow and transmute their harrowing life events, we consciously engage in promoting PTG and transcendence. Margolin and Sen (2022) discussed the power of a purpose or vision to support transcendence from trauma.

Our model is informed by Tedeschi and Calhoun's (2018) framework on PTG. They found that individuals who encountered traumatic events experienced PTG in five areas: 1) appreciating life more fully and changes in one's priorities; 2) identifying personal strengths and a renewed self-perception; 3) welcoming changes to relationships and a greater sense of connection, feeling compassion and a greater understanding for others who are suffering; 4) accepting new possibilities, new interests, and activities; and 5) embracing spiritual and existential change. These five areas are related to spirituality as they involve connectedness, meaning, and purpose. Therefore, it is only prudent to include spirituality as a core area of social work to support growth and transcendence from adversity, as well as personal self-transcendence and spiritual awakening and transformation. When we hold transcendence of self as a process and a potential outcome of our work with others, and for ourselves, we can awaken to our authentic way of being.

Becoming Spiritual Influencers

Students often don't realize that they are not only learners in the practicum setting but change agents as well. Students bring new frameworks, theories, concepts, research, and applicable practice insights they have been learning in the classroom to social workers in the field that have likely been out of the intensive academic environment, and spirituality is no exception in this knowledge translation. With the advent of spiritually focused social work literature and research, students have an opportunity to become spiritual influencers in their practicum sites and upon being hired. The first way this can be achieved is by sharing concepts about spirituality and social work with their supervisor and colleagues and starting a dialogue about those concepts. Students can also bring readings on spiritual assessment and treatment to supervisory or agency meetings and explore the possibility of sharing the material and newfound knowledge with agency staff. If students notice a positive response, they can further discuss personal challenges, insights, and moments of growth with their own spirituality and invite others to speak about their meaning-making. This sets the stage to invite creative brainstorming about how agency staff can ethically bring important aspects of themselves, or practices and rituals into their work without bracketing out core aspects of self as so many have been taught to do in the name of professionalism.

Students are encouraged to consider practicum projects that enhance spiritual integration in the workplace such as reviewing the agency policy manual to scan for policies, procedures, and protocols for safety and consensually including client and counsellor spirituality in service delivery. They could advocate for spiritual spaces for contemplation or to practice rituals and ceremonies. Enhancing one's own competencies in assessment and treatment or community practice (depending on the setting) are routine in social work practicum learning plans. Students can further this learning by overtly committing to develop their competencies around spiritual, cultural, religious, and sacred work and by inspiring others by sharing their learning. They may offer to conduct a workshop on a spiritually informed and focused therapeutic practice with staff and co-facilitate with another practicum student, staff member, or their supervisor to provide opportunities for the agency community to experiment with spirituality in safe ways.

Consciously working from spiritual concepts such as safety, humility, gratitude, exquisite empathy, positivity, and nonjudgement increases the intensity with which students can bring these qualities of ideal social work practice into relationships with clients, and mentors. When students see themselves as spiritual influencers they begin to inquire into the spiritual gaps, and in that inquiry, can discover creative solutions and invite other workers into the wonderful discovery of spiritual evolution and transformation. This can begin a process of supporting holistic strength-based ways of relating and supporting one's own and others' self-transcendence. Spiritually influencing students have a wonderful opportunity to shape the culture of the agency or organization and can begin to adopt spiritually inclusive practices. In this way, student spiritual influencers fully role model integrating spirituality into practice.

Recommendations and Suggested Learning Goals for Field

The practicum learning plan is a document that Canadian schools and departments of social work incorporate into field education to assist in the evaluation of student learning through practicum. This document is based on a collaborative learning approach where learning is student-driven and guided by agency supervisors and faculty. Students model and demonstrate a commitment to holistic wellness when they include spirituality in field education. The following sample, which aligns with the Canadian Association of Social Workers (CASW; 2005) Code of Ethics and the Alberta College of Social Workers (ACSW; 2019) Standards of Practice, is offered to inspire students to incorporate spiritual goals into their learning plans.

ACTIVITY BREAK 8

Review the practicum learning objectives below. Choose any that fit or resonate with you and incorporate them into your own learning plan.

Table 11.1: Examples of Spiritual Goals in the Practicum Learning Plan

SOCIAL WORK PRACTICE AREAS	LEARNING OBJECTIVES TO BECOME A SPIRITUAL INFLUENCER	PRACTICAL TASKS TO REACH OBJECTIVES TO BECOME A SPIRITUAL INFLUENCER
PROFESSIONAL SOCIAL WORK IDENTITY	Familiarize onself with the spiritual content in the guiding principles, policies, and protocols of the agency.	a. Read the policy manual with an eye to seek out spiritually focused policies, procedures, and protocols. b. Observe and learn about the culture of the agency and spiritual philosophy if present.
	Learn to build respectful relationships and deep connections with agency supervisors and staff.	a. Conduct information interviews with agency supervisor and other workers and ask how they integrate their personal and professional lives in terms of their values, beliefs, and worldview. Ask how this has influenced their work and relationships with colleagues and clients. b. Ask about their experiences in including spirituality in working with clients. c. Have discussions about spiritual self-care.
	Learn to build authentic and deep respectful relationships with clients.	a. Meet clients where they are in terms of their spiritual worldview. b. Practice exquisite empathy. c. Conduct a spiritual assessment and ask about spirituality in relation to treatment. d. Create a spiritually safe environment that might include objects, images, sayings, books, pamphlets, etc.
	Understand one's own spiritual or holistic worldview in relation to social work practice.	a. Read spiritual, philosophical, and religious literature to learn about your worldview; jot down quotes or mantras that especially resonate with you and keep them visible in your workspace to see throughout the day. b. Seek out media that inspires and empowers you.
	Foster conscious, healthy relationship with a spiritual dimension of self.	a. Practice awareness and mental calmness during all practicum activities throughout the day. b. Focus on being with my breath without controlling it. c. Create a sacred place in my home that I contemplate, reflect, write, meditate, and/or envision my goals and aspirations. d. Prioritize my wellness by making time each day to visit my sacred place. e. Entertain myself and unwind from the day with positive uplifting content. f. Complete a holistic wellness wheel activity and make a plan (see LaRocque, 2021). g. Practice loving-kindness.

Table 11.1: (*continued*)

SOCIAL WORK PRACTICE AREAS	LEARNING OBJECTIVES TO BECOME A SPIRITUAL INFLUENCER	PRACTICAL TASKS TO REACH OBJECTIVES TO BECOME A SPIRITUAL INFLUENCER
GENERALIST PRACTICE	Develop skills and abilities to conduct a spiritual assessment.	a. Read literature on engaging clients in spiritual conversations to find out if discussing spirituality, religion, or philosophy is important for them. b. Observe and job shadow other counsellors and debrief to learn about their process of integrating spirituality into their work. c. Read client files, with supervisor consent, where spirituality has been part of treatment. d. Attend and observe counselling group sessions that have a focus on spiritual inclusion. e. Learn to assess for trauma. f. Watch YouTube videos or listen to spiritually-focused content on assessment and intervention.
	Gain knowledge on spiritual frameworks and language	a. Speak with clients about spiritual concepts such as humility, gratitude, exquisite empathy, positivity, nonjudgement; together, brainstorm goals to foster these qualities in themselves. b. Spend time with spiritual leaders or elders, ask questions.
	Learn skills in culturally, holistic, or spiritually sensitive interventions.	a. Read current and related literature. b. Develop awareness of various religions, faiths, and philosophies. c. Consult with agency and faculty supervisor. d. Observe and shadow other counsellors and debrief to learn about their treatment process and integration of spirituality. e. Learn trauma-informed spiritual interventions. f. Attend and observe counselling group sessions with a focus on spiritual inclusion.
REFLECTIVE PRACTICE	Develop self-reflective skills for spiritual development.	a. Keep a journal and write for 10 to 15 min at the end of each practicum day on spiritual strengths and areas of development. b. Contemplate areas I felt stuck or challenged and focus on growing from those challenges. c. Speak with a peer or person I trust about personal spiritual insights from practicum. d. Attend weekly supervisory meetings prepared with questions and topics concerning spiritual development. e. Contemplate personal questions in Activity Breaks above.

SOCIAL WORK PRACTICE AREAS	LEARNING OBJECTIVES TO BECOME A SPIRITUAL INFLUENCER	PRACTICAL TASKS TO REACH OBJECTIVES TO BECOME A SPIRITUAL INFLUENCER
COMPETENCE WITH DIVERSITY	Engage with spiritual leaders or elder.	a. Consult with spiritual leaders or elders to learn about spiritual teachings. b. Engage in cultural ceremonies, develop awareness of community resources that support deep meaning-making (e.g., arts collectives, Habitat for Humanity, charitable groups). c. Watch related YouTube presentations and those offered in this chapter.
SOCIAL POLICY AND SOCIAL JUSTICE	Agency Policy Research Project Recommend spiritual content for agency manual. Reflect on how to increase social justice advocacy.	a. Read the manual(s) and relevant spiritual literature. Inquire into the following: Is the spiritual dimension of health reflected in the agency's mission and vision statements, in the policy manual, within worker relationships and interactions, and/or in assessment and treatment practices? b. Inquiry could occur through readings as well as information interviews and focus groups with social workers and faculty and agency supervisors to seek their perspectives, and then compile and put forth recommendations. c. Reflect on client and supervisor, mentor interactions. Ask: Could I have brought a more inclusive lens to our interactions Are there ways I left out aspects of the client's spiritual identity? What can I do in our next session that I can acknowledge that aspect?

Our Parting Message

We believe that spirituality should be embedded throughout the social work curriculum, and it is a central aspect of field practice. We continue to work at creating this vision and develop webinars and podcasts. With the model presented in this chapter, we have equipped you with initial tools to enhance your knowledge, skills, and attitudes for developing a spiritually sensitive practice approach and becoming a spiritual influencer. We hope student, faculty, and supervisor readers alike will find this chapter a useful catalyst for continuing to discover their own spiritual worldview, related values and beliefs, and embrace cultivating daily spiritual disciplines for flourishing in the social work profession.

REFERENCES

Ainsworth, M. D. S. (1977). Social development in the first year of life: Maternal influences on infant-mother attachment. In J. M. Tanner (Ed.), *Developments in psychiatric research: Essays based on the Sir Geoffrey Vickers Lectures of the Mental Health Foundation* (pp. 1–20). Hodder & Stoughton.

Alberta College of Social Workers (2019). *Standards of practice.* https://acsw.in1touch.org/document/2672/DOC_FINALACSWStandardsOfPractice_V1_1_20200304.pdf

Association of Professional Chaplins. (n.d.). LaRocca-Pitts spiritual assessment models. https://www.apchaplains.org/

Boynton, H., & Margolin, I. (April, 22, 2022). *Centering ourselves with consciousness to serve others and self-heal* [Video]. Youtube. https://www.youtube.com/watch?v=LRQT_e3yh3o&t=1013s

Boynton, H. M., & Vis, J. (2011). Meaning Making, spirituality, and creative expressive therapies: Pathways to posttraumatic growth in grief and loss for children. *Counselling and Spirituality, 30*(2), 137–159.

Boynton, H. M. (2016a). Children's spirituality: A component of holistic care in child welfare. In R. Neckoway and K. Brownlee (Eds.), *Child welfare in rural remote areas with Canada's First-Nations Peoples: Selected reading* (pp. 165–189). Centre of Education and Research on Positive Youth Development.

———. (2016b). *Navigating in seclusion: The complicated terrain of children's spirituality in trauma, grief and loss* [Unpublished doctoral dissertation]. University of Calgary.

———. (2022). Spirituality and possibilities for posttraumatic growth in children. In H. M. Boynton and J. Vis (Eds.), *Trauma, spirituality and posttraumatic growth in clinical social work practice* (pp. 23–38) [Manuscript submitted for publication]. University of Toronto Press.

Boynton, H. M., & Vis, J. (2017). Spirituality: The missing component in trauma therapy across the lifespan. In B. Crisp (Ed.), *Routledge handbook of religion, spirituality and social work* (pp. 193–201). Routledge.

Boynton, H. M., & Mellan, C.J. (2021). Co-creating authentic sacred therapeutic space: A spiritually sensitive framework for counselling children. *Religions, 12*(7), 524. https://doi.org/10.3390/rel12070524

Boynton, H. M., & De Vynck, E. (2022). *Spiritual and cultural attunement in social work practice*, Canadian Society for Spirituality and Social Work and the American Society for Spirituality and Social Work [Video]. YouTube. https://www.youtube.com/watch?v=SIV7_iPOj60

Boynton, H. M., & Margolin, I. (2022). *Centering ourselves in consciousness*, Canadian Society for Spirituality and Social Work and the American Society for Spirituality and Social Work [Video]. YouTube. https://www.youtube.com/watch?v=LRQT_e3yh3o

Boynton, H.M., & Vis, J. (Eds.). (2022). *Trauma, spirituality, and posttraumatic growth in clinical social work practice.* University of Toronto Press.

Buber, M. (1958). *I and thou.* (R.G. Smith, Trans). Charles Scribner's and Sons. (Originally work published 1937).

Canda, E., Furman, L. D., & Canda, H. (2020). *Spiritual diversity in social work practice: The heart of helping* (3rd ed.). Oxford University Press.

Canda, E. & Smith, D. (Eds.). (2001). *Transpersonal perspectives on spirituality in social work.* The Haworth Press.

Carneiro, É.M., Navinchandra, S. A., Vento, L., Timóteo, R. P., & De Fátima Borges, M. (2019). Religiousness/Spirituality, resilience and burnout in employees of a public hospital in Brazil. *Journal of Religion and Health, 58,* 677–685. DOI: 10.1007/s10943-018-0691-2

CMind. (2021). *The Tree of Contemplative Practices [Illustration].* The Center for Contemplative Mind in Society. https://www.contemplativemind.org/practices/tree

Crisp, B. R. (Ed.). (2017). *The Routledge handbook of religion, spirituality and social work.* Taylor & Francis.

Diego-Cordero, R., Ávila-Mantilla, A., Vega-Escaño, J., Lucchetti, G., & Badanta, B. (2022). The role of spirituality and religiosity in healthcare during the COVID-19 pandemic: An integrative review of the scientific literature. *Journal of Religion and Health, 61,* 2168–2197. https://doi.org/10.1007/s10943-022-01549-x

Dezorzi. L. W., & Crossetti, M. G. O. (2008). Spirituality in self-care for intensive care nursing professionals. *Rev Latino-am Enfermagem, 6*(2), 212–217.

Gardner, H. (2020, July 8). Existential intelligence: Why now? *Mi Oasis*. Howard Gardner's Official Authoritative Site of Multiple Intelligences. https://www.multipleintelligencesoasis.org/blog/2020/7/8/a-resurgence-of-interest-in-existential-intelligence-why-nownbsp

Graham, J. R., Coholic, D., & Coates, J. (2006). Spirituality as a guiding construct in the development of Canadian social work: Past and present considerations. *Critical Social Work, 7*(1), 1–43. https://ojs.uwindsor.ca/index.php/csw/article/download/5774/4713?inline=1

Hodge, D. R. (2001). Spiritual genograms: A generational approach to assessing spirituality. *Families in Society, 82*(1), 35-48. https://doi.org/10.1606/1044-3894.220

Hodge, D. R., & Limb, G. E. (2014). Spiritual assessment and latter-day saints: Establishing the preliminary validity of spiritual eco-maps. *Journal of Social Service Research, 40*(3), 367-380, https://doi.org/10.1080/01488376.2014.893947

Franco, D., & Lopex, M. (April 22, 2022). *SSSW & CSSSW: Spirituality, cultural diversity, and social work* [Video]. Youtube. https://www.youtube.com/watch?v=SIV7_iPOj60

Freeman, D. R. (2007). Spirituality and the calling of social work students. *Social Work and Christianity, 34*(3), 277–297.

Gillis, L. M. (2013). The ABC's of self care. *Homeless Hub*. The Canadian Observatory on Homelessness. https://www.homelesshub.ca/resource/abcs-self-care

Hart, M. A. (2002). *Seeking Mino-Pimatisiwin*. Fernwood Publishing.

Hirsbrunner, L. E., Loeffler, D. N., & Rompf, E. L. (2012). Spirituality and religiosity: Their effects on undergraduate social work career choice. *Journal of Social Service Research, 38*, 199–211. https://doi.org/10.1080/01488376.2011.645411

Hodge D. R. (2013). Implicit spiritual assessment: an alternative approach for assessing client spirituality. *Social Work, 58*(3), 223–230. https://doi.org/10.1093/sw/swt019

Hoskins, M. L. (1999). Worlds apart and lives together: Developing cultural attunement. *Child and Youth Care Forum, 28*(2), 73–85. https://doi.org/10.1023/A:1021937105025

Kotera, Y., Richardson, M., & Sheffield, D. (2020). Effects of shinrin-yoku (forest bathing) and nature therapy on mental health: A systematic review and meta-analysis. *International Journal of Mental Health and Addiction, 20*(1), 337–361. https://doi.org/10.1007/s11469-020-00363-4

Kvarfordt, C., & Sheridan, M. (2010). Predicting the use of spiritually-based interventions with children and adolescents: Implications for social work practice. *Currents: New Scholarship in the Human Services, 9*(1), 1–30. https://cdm.ucalgary.ca/index.php/currents/article/view/15885

Kvarfordt, C. L., & Herba, K. (2018). Religion and spirituality in social work practice with children and adolescents: A survey of Canadian practitioners. *Child and Adolescent Social Work Journal, 35*(2), 153–167. https://doi.org/10.1007/s10560-017-0513-5

Limb, G. E., & Hodge, D. R. (2007). Developing spiritual lifemaps as a culture-centered pictorial instrument for spiritual assessments with Native American clients. *Research on Social Work Practice, 17*(2), 296-304. https://doi.org/10.1177/1049731506296161

Limb, G. E., & Hodge, D. R. (2011). Utilizing spiritual ecograms with Native American families and children to promote cultural competence in family therapy. *Journal of Marital and Family Therapy, 37*(1), 81–94. https://doi.org/10.1111/j.1752-0606.2009.00163.x

LaRocca-Pitts, M. (2012). *FACT, A chaplain's tool for assessing spiritual needs in an acute care setting*. Association of Professional Chaplains. https://doi.org/10.1080/10999183.2012.10767446

LaRocque, A. (2021). *Understanding the wellness wheel*. Canadian Mental Health Association. https://cmha.calgary.ab.ca/blog/understanding-the-wellness-wheel/

Margolin, I. (2014). Collage as a method of inquiry for university women practicing Mahavakyam Meditation: Ameliorating the effects of stress, anxiety, and sadness. *Journal of Religion & Spirituality in Social Work: Social Thought, 33*(3/4), 254–273. https://doi.org/10.1080/15426432.2014.930632

———. (2019). Breaking free: One adolescent woman's recovery from dating violence through creative dance. *American Journal of Dance Therapy, 41*(2), 170–192. https://doi.org/10.1007/s10465-019-09311-9

Margolin, I., & Jones, A. (2023). Nine Women: Collages of Spirit-Collages of Self. *Qualitative Inquiry, 30*(1). https://doi.org/10.1177/10778004231176103

Margolin, I., & Sen, T. (2022). Post-traumatic growth across the lifespan: Pathways back to spirit. In J. Vis and H. M. Boynton (Eds.), *Trauma, spirituality and posttraumatic growth in clinical social work practice* (pp. 197–211). University of Toronto Press.

Maslow, A. H. (1971). *The farther reaches of human nature*. Penguin Books.

Mayaka, B., & Truell, R. (2021). Ubuntu and its potential impact on the international social work profession. *International Social Work, 64*(5), 649–662. https://doi.org/10.1177/00208728211022787

Mindyourmind. (2024). *Mind your mind blog*. https://mindyourmind.ca/blog/mood-walks-walking-better-mental-health

Mraz, J. (2012, October 15). *Living in the Moment*. Directed by Derec Dunn & Shannon Toumey [Video]. YouTube. https://www.youtube.com/watch?v=YUFs_1vKYlY

Oxhandler, H. K., & Pargament, K. I. (2014). Social work practitioners' integration of clients' religion and spirituality in practice: A literature review. *Social Work, 59*(3), 271–279. https://doi.org/10.1093/sw/swu018

Oxhandler, H. K., Parrish, D. E., Torres, L. R., & Achenbaum, W. A. (2015). The integration of clients' religion and spirituality in social work practice: A national survey. *Social Work, 60*(3), 228–237. https://doi.org/10.1093/sw/swv018

Oxhandler, H. K., & Ellor, J. W. (2017). Christian social workers' views and integration of clients' religion and spirituality in practice. *Social Work and Christianity, 44*(3), 3–24. https://www.nacsw.org/Publications/SWC/SWC44_3Sample.pdf

Oxhandler, H. K., & Giardina, T. D. (2017). Social workers' perceived barriers to and sources of support for integrating clients' religion and spirituality in practice. *Social Work, 62*(4), 323–332. https://doi.org/10.1093/sw/swx036

Pandya, S. P. (2018). Students' views on expanding contours of social work practice through spirituality. *Journal of Religion & Spirituality in Social Work: Social Thought, 37*(3), 302–322. https://doi.org/10.1080/15426432.2018.1485072

Pearce, M. J., Pargament, K. I., Oxhandler, H., Vieten, C., & Wong, S. (2019). A novel training program for mental health providers in spiritual competencies. *Spirituality in Clinical Practice, 6*(2), 73–82. https://doi.org/10.1037/scp0000195

Rogers, N. (2019, January 7). *Person-centered expressive arts therapy with Natalie Rogers* [Video]. Youtube. https://www.youtube.com/watch?v=AtaFR2J2uEI

Rogers, N. (2015, December 5). *An IEATA Tribute to Natalie Rogers* [Video]. Youtube. https://www.youtube.com/watch?v=9SDJbs4zTCk

Rogers, N. (2012, November 9). *Expressive Arts Therapy Video with Natalie Rogers* [Video]. Youtube. https://www.youtube.com/watch?v=sd62Al_NsYU

Rogers, N. (2011). *The creative connection for groups: Person-centered expressive arts for healing and social change*. Science and Behavior Books.

Saleeby, D. (2013). Introduction: Power in the people. In Saleeby, D. (Ed.), *The Strengths Perspective in Social Work Practice* (6th ed., pp. 184–193). Pearson Higher Ed.

Seidlitz, L., Abernethy, A. D., Duberstein, P. R., Evinger, J. S., Change, T. H., & Lewis, B. L. (2002). Development of the spiritual transcendence index. *Journal for the Scientific Study of Rligion, 41*, 439–453. https://doi.org/10.1111/1468-5906.00129

Sen, T. (2016). *Ancient secrets of success: The four truths revealed*. Omnisun.

Sen, T. & Margolin, I. (2021, May). Exploring Mahavakyam Ancient Secrets Meditation with Female Future Social Workers. Maternal Health Canada. Maternal Infant Health Canada - Healthy Seminars [Video]. YouTube. https://youtu.be/VQqrNnKEc40

Siegal, D. (2022, August 18). *Culture of empathy builder*. Centre for Building a Culture of Empathy. http://cultureofempathy.com/References/Experts/Daniel-Siegel.htm.

Spiritual Competency Academy. (Feb. 12, 2021). *The SSOPP spiritual assessment instrument* [Video]. Youtube. https://www.youtube.com/watch?v=nUYLhEZGn-8

Spiritual Competency Academy. (April 8, 2022). Screening Strengths Organized Personal Problems (SSOPP) Spiritual Assessment Interview. https://spiritual-competency-academy.thinkific.com/

Tedeschi, R. G., Shakespeare-Finch, J., Taku, K., & Calhoun, L. G. (2018). *Posttraumatic growth: Theory, research, and applications* (1st ed.). Routledge.

TheSesame12. (2013, March 7). *Spiritual Assessment in healthcare* [Video]. Youtube. https://www.youtube.com/watch?v=SCO4a7cj5B8

Tygielski, S. (2022, June 17). *The power of sustainable self-care*. Mindful: healthy mind, healthy life. https://www.mindful.org/the-power-of-sustainable-self-care/

van der Kolk, B. A. (2014). *The body keeps the score: Brain, mind, and body in the healing of trauma*. Viking.

Vis, J., & Boynton, H. M. (2008). Spirituality and transcendent meaning making: Possibilities for enhancing posttraumatic growth. *Journal of Religion and Spirituality in Social Work: Social Thought, 27*(1–2), 69-86.

Wiebe, S., & Margolin, I. (2012). Poetic consciousness in pedagogy: An inquiry of contemplation and conversation. *In Education: Exploring Our Connective Education Landscape, 18*(1), 23-36. https://doi.org/10.37119/ojs2012.v18i1

Wigglesworth, C. (2012). *SQ21: The twenty-one skills of spiritual intelligence*. Select Books.

Wigglesworth, C. (2014, January 12). *The roadmap to nobility: Cindy Wigglesworth at TDxLowerEastSide* [Video]. Youtube. https://www.youtube.com/watch?v=mX9adE0FSaw

Wilber, K. (1997). An integral theory of consciousness. *Journal of Consciousness Studies, 4*(1), 71–92. https://www.newdualism.org/papers/K.Wilber/Wilber-JCS1997.pdf

———. (1998). *The eye of spirit*. Shambhala.

Wright, S. G. (2005). *Burnout: A spiritual crisis*. Nursing Standard Essential Guide. Harrow, UK: RCN Publications.

Yeshiva University. (2021). Practical applications of the culturagram to social work. https://online.yu.edu/wurzweiler/blog/practical-applications-culturagram-social-work

Zohar, D. (2018). *Spiritual intelligence: A new paradigm for collaborative action*. The Systems Thinker. https://thesystemsthinker.com/spiritual-intelligence-a-new-paradigm-for-collaborative-action/

NOTES:

NOTES:

NOTES:

NOTES:

12

Advancing Social Work Field Education in Healthcare

Patricia L. Samson, Janet McFarlane, Debra Samek, Hilary Nelson, and David B. Nicholas

Field education plays a critically important role in professional social work education. Yet in recent decades, the field of social work has been impacted by disciplinary and structural shifts affecting practice in healthcare settings. Healthcare social workers have grappled with greater workload demands amidst the continuing need to offer field education; the volume of available field placements has not kept pace with student interest and need. To address this challenge in our jurisdiction of Alberta, Canada, field placement efficiencies and innovations have been sought through collaborative efforts of healthcare social workers and university-based social work educators. Novel field education approaches have been developed and trialed in our region. This chapter highlights these innovations and their impact. We provide students with a general background on the role of social work in healthcare and how this influences field education opportunities, followed by a description of examples of innovation that have been locally implemented. You will gain an understanding of the complexities involved in this field of practice and how creative innovations are being implemented to support students in obtaining quality work-integrated learning opportunities in this milieu.

Social Work in Healthcare: Background and Context

Health, when envisioned broadly, includes social connection, spirituality, cultural considerations, financial stability, emotional well-being, and quality of life (Hutchison et al., 2011; Schrecker et al., 2010). While these activities are in line with the orientation of other healthcare professions, social workers introduce complementary skills and values through the pursuit of person-centered (or patient-centered) care (Canadian Association of Social Workers [CASW], 2005; National Association of Social Workers [NASW], 2008). Patient-centered care is a health-system term for person-centered care; care is focused on the patient/person as the priority. As such, social workers tend to shift from an expert voice to a recognition and honoring of the voice of the patient as a key tenet in their professional stance. This challenges the traditional medical model or reductionist orientations to healthcare. The traditional *medical model* of practice views physicians as the primary driver of care, from diagnosis to treatment planning and implementation (Anderson, 1995). It entails a hierarchical view of the team, where priority is usually given to medical practitioners (doctors, nurses, etc.) and the primary focus of care is on treating the acute illness/presenting medical issue (Anderson, 1995; Haegele & Hodge, 2016). In contrast, social work contextualizes the medical condition within consideration of the whole person to amplify patient voices and perspectives, and this approach is viewed as integral to quality care of patients.

It is recognized that there are gaps in contemporary healthcare, as one need only turn on the news to hear reports of the 'crisis' facing our Canadian healthcare system. According to Purnell et al. (2016), gaps include disparities and inequitable access to quality healthcare based on factors such as race, gender, ethnicity, level of social supports, geographic location, and income. The social determinants of health (SDH) encompass the underlying societal issues that contribute to/perpetuate disease, morbidity, and mortality rates across regions — locally, nationally, and internationally (World Health Organization [WHO], 2008). Socioeconomic factors significantly shape our understanding of the concepts of health and health equity (Braveman & Gottlieb, 2014); marginalized populations experience multifaceted gaps in relation to access and equity in the healthcare system. The noted gaps can be proactively addressed by hallmarks of social work practice, including person and family-centeredness and anti-oppressive practice. Social work roles in healthcare settings include support, system navigation, crisis management, mediation and conflict resolution, discharge planning, and advocacy (Beddoe, 2011; Craig & Muskat, 2013; Gibbons & Plath, 2009; Holliman et al., 2001; Judd & Sheffield, 2010). It is noteworthy that there is limited scholarship on the role of social work in healthcare over the last several years, largely due to the continual shifts in the scope of practice for interdisciplinary teams in the rapidly changing health context (Ashcroft et al., 2018). Social workers act as one of the most continuous healthcare providers on the multidisciplinary healthcare team by providing consistency and continuity of care throughout the patient journey, often advocating for unmet patient needs. There are systemic challenges for social workers in the healthcare system, including excessive workload demands and a hierarchical disciplinary structure (Beddoe, 2011; Whitehead, 2007). Healthcare staff, such as physicians or nurses, hold decision-making authority regarding care pathways (Mizrahi & Abramson, 2000), which risks social workers at times being viewed and treated as unequal partners (Beddoe, 2011; Keefe et al., 2009).

Beddoe (2011) suggests that the history of social work in healthcare can be seen to locate social work as a "guest" in a system of care often dominated by medical practitioners. Keefe et al. (2009) put forth the notion that the role of the social worker should be more clearly defined, in work and in relation to others on the healthcare team. A history of mistrust and role confusion exists in the care delivery system (Craig & Muskat, 2013), which can create disciplinary isolation and an under-utilization of social workers (Ashcroft et al., 2018; Craig & Muskat, 2013). Greater understanding of the role and expertise of social work is warranted (Craig & Muskat, 2013).

There is tremendous value in the role of social work for addressing psychosocial needs and SDH barriers for those in need of care. Social work is integral to the health of Canadians and the overall healthcare system in terms of optimal patient experiences and outcomes. Social workers contribute detailed knowledge about community resources in assisting patients to navigate services (Holliman et al., 2001). Disciplinary preparation and values heighten care delivery through varying patient and system impacts such as improved quality of life and a reduction in readmission rates (Bronstein et al., 2015; Gibbons & Plath, 2009; Jencks et al., 2009; Keefe et al., 2009).

A review of the relevant literature identifies a range of areas of inquiry and a need for building capacity in social work healthcare delivery. Social work practice is highlighted as a key contributor to healthcare system improvement. The proven and potential initiatives in the scope of social work practice warrant capacity-building efforts to advance the role of social work amidst pressing resource gaps and other challenges to enhance the overall quality of healthcare practice.

Field Education in Social Work in Healthcare

Field education is integral to professional education. Practicums and service-learning opportunities within social work education are based on a learning paradigm founded on a student-centred approach rather than a hierarchical or utilitarian one (Barr & Tagg, 1995). The learning paradigm engenders collaborative learning spaces amidst and between students and instructors to cultivate student success. Teachers are facilitators (Barr & Tagg, 1995) in genuine learning environments and create safe spaces for students to navigate real-life scenarios from the practice context (Preez, 2012). Teaching and learning in social work involve a consolidative framework of theories, values, knowledge, and skills needed to support the development of professional competence for graduates (Larrison & Korr, 2013). These professions are built on a relational model, where relationships are central components to education and practice and exemplify notions of partnership and reciprocity in an authentic manner (Folgheraiter, 2007; Hartick-Doane & Varcoe, 2007).

Pedagogical approaches often employed in social work education are anchored in the practice theory of experiential learning and include problem-based learning (PBL), case-based learning (CBL), simulation, and practice-based activities including field practicums (Illingworth & Chelvanayagam, 2017) in the social work practice milieu. Kolb (1984) identifies four genres of experiential learning through which new knowledge, skills or attitudes are achieved, for example concrete experience, reflective observation, abstract conceptualization, and active experimentation. In this Kolb's model of experiential learning, learning is detailed in a recurrent fashion by integrating thoughts, emotions, perceptions, and behaviour in ways that are persistently being recreated (Kolb, 1984). Problem-based learning and CBL deliver students real-life examples to work through in a practice context where students are encouraged to think critically and reflect on the learning experiences provided. Learning opportunities that afford these real-life experiences provide genuine learning spaces for students to integrate theory onto practice (Samson, 2018).

Ingraining the ability to work collaboratively in graduating professional social work students is one way to address the siloed approach to healthcare provision through engendering the necessary skills to navigate multi-professional teams in providing quality care (McLoughlin et al., 2018). Healthcare, when delivered by a collaborative interprofessional team, improves patient health outcomes, particularly for populations and individuals who are underserved or have complex social needs (McLoughlin et al., 2018). An interprofessional healthcare team holds diverse knowledge and skills that can lead to more effective and holistic client-centered services (Green & Johnson, 2015). Students who are involved in healthcare practicums have opportunities to work with professions from a range of disciplines, depending on the practicum context. In a hospital setting, students may attend interdisciplinary team meetings, liaise with community practitioners and agencies, work with nursing or physical/occupational therapists and the like in supporting patients in navigating the healthcare system. Students may also have opportunities to engage in family meetings and liaise with other community supports depending on the patient context in supporting treatment and recovery plans.

Considering Field Education in Social Work in Healthcare

Historical underfunding and limited infrastructure in healthcare have created challenges for field educator preparedness and in prioritizing practicums within social work teams. Along with these changes, increasing population challenges and complexities have confronted social workers in their daily work. Increased populations creating greater needs and changing community demographics have been reflected in healthcare, and the importance of social work in promoting health and well-being has been amplified. These changes, including in recent years the COVID-19 pandemic and its unmasking of societal resource challenges at community and societal levels, are requiring us to redefine and re-imagine the field education landscape. As an essential component of professional education to support students transitioning into professional careers, field practicums provide the venue where students apply theory onto practice (Bogo, 2015; Taylor Institute, 2022). Practicums are a mandatory part of the social work curriculum and are embedded in the accreditation standards set forth by the Canadian Association for Social Work Education (CASWE; 2017).

Students in field practicums are supervised by practice-based field instructors (FIs; Bogo, 2006), who provide mentorship and opportunities for students to partake in experiential learning. However, in a climate of continuing funding retrenchment, there are headwinds facing the delivery of healthcare-based field education. Reduced funding has contributed to the urgency for strong educational opportunities yet also constrains resources. In addition to shrinking placement options, FIs themselves face an increased workload and/or job losses in the current economic and political climates across Canada and other nations, amidst reorganization of human service and education delivery systems. These challenges in the field context do not bode well for creative, energized field education experiences for either FIs or students. Yet within such adversity, educators and FIs are invited to re-envision ways to support students in the practice milieu that optimally expose students to real-world experiences to aid in the development of needed practice skills. For the past several years in Alberta health-system social work leaders, social work educators and researchers, and students have been working together in a community-university partnership to generate new ideas and ways to better support students, both in practicum experiences and opportunities for future employment in the healthcare system upon graduation. Activities have included the development of Social Work in Health, a course that has seen educators and social work practitioners in the healthcare context co-teach students in the classroom; this provides an excellent venue for students to learn theory related to practice in the healthcare field and ways to bring it to life via employing the on-the-ground experience of social work practitioners. The learnings from this course can help ground students who may choose to pursue a health-based field practicum opportunity in the future.

The conventional field practicum approach of a single preceptor/field educator per student (comprising one student working solely with one field instructor throughout the entirety of the field placement) may no longer be viable for all students/field placements. Multiple factors have rendered this approach untenable as the only field education option, including an exponentially growing volume of social work trainees and schools across jurisdictions (including online programs) and a disconnect between classroom and field-based learning. Field practicum placement coordinators now place over 250 students/year in most Canadian social work programs in the face of dramatically reduced budgets that notably have been deeply felt in post-secondary educational institutions (Ayala et al., 2018). These financial constraints contribute to diminished field placement access and a reported disconnect of field experience/practice relative to classroom learning (Ayala et al., 2018; Samson et al., 2021). Of further demand in field education is the multifold increase in competing co-op programs. As of 2015, over 1,000 social work programs in Canada, in addition to other professional programs, such as nursing, occupational therapy and psychology, offer practica (Ayala et al., 2018). These programs compete for the same placements, especially in addiction and mental health; the net result is diminished capacity and availability of practicums (Ayala et al., 2018).

In response to these changes, including disciplinary and sectoral (healthcare) struggles, social work education in healthcare must adapt to offer effective, integrated education more efficiently for practice entry. A recent pilot of a rotational supervision practicum model was trialed at the Master of Social Work (MSW) level for a small cohort of students (Samson et al., 2021). This model involved students rotating through multiple fields of practice in the hospital setting, engaging in a new practice area every six weeks. This provided an opportunity for students to achieve broader exposure to the hospital-based healthcare system and to have experience working in a variety of departments, including the emergency room, gerontology, and oncology. While this model will be explored in more detail in the material that follows, it serves as a great example of creativity and innovation aimed at supporting students in developing entry-level social work practice skills. Innovation is a necessity for optimizing educational opportunity, enriching student experience and impact, and preparing students for healthcare practice. Novel approaches for field practicums are needed to adapt with the healthcare system in ways that are supported by and integrated into theoretical content taught in social work education.

Advancement of Field Education Training and Student Experience

Substantial advancement of field education in social work has emerged largely because of attempts to adapt and improve field education processes. Accordingly, new models are being trialed. The following section is focused on innovations that have been trialed to advance social work field education in healthcare. Multiple innovations are offered in the hope that these ideas may offer new insightsand options for student field placement advancement in other jurisdictions and contexts. New models and ideas to advance field education benefit students by potentially creating more practicum opportunities in the healthcare field more broadly. Rotational models can expand learning venues and strengthen capacity to bring on more FIs, hopefully generating more practicum opportunities for students. Providing students access to continuing education events and models for healthcare staff provides increased learning opportunities for students that are discipline specific to social work. Co-teaching among and between social work practitioners in the healthcare system and social work educators provides real-life expertise and learning moments for students that extend beyond theoretical conceptions and include application to practice in meaningful ways that can help support transformative learning for students in this milieu.

In the following sections, we detail some of these innovations, which include integrated rotational models, student-led communities of practice (CoP), student learning series, student and field educator orientations, promotion of rural or remote opportunities, and development of integrated classroom content, below.

Integrated Rotational Model

Although not new, the *integrated rotational model* may be a desirable alternative to traditional single instructor field placement models for students, FIs, and organizations. This approach offers an alternative to the traditional practicum model by replacing a student placed in a practicum with a single preceptor for its entirety. Rather, a group of students rotate from supervisor to supervisor, offering students exposure to a variety of social workers' areas of expertise, styles of practice, and opportunities for the student to apply/practice skills gained in classroom and field learning. This approach arguably allows students to ascertain, develop, assimilate, and trial their emerging approach to practice in diverse contexts, and potentially enhances the application of theoretical learning from the classroom to the field (and vice versa). Different approaches to learning can be incorporated in this type of integrated model, such as CBL where students can perhaps follow a specific patient from one department to the next as they navigate their healthcare journey. This serves as a specific example of Kolb's (1984) experiential learning theory and how it can be applied to practice through different strategies (i.e., CBL). Practice-based learning (learning that occurs in the field) provides students with hands-on, real-life experiences that help them learn how to apply theory in the practice context.

Despite these potential benefits, this approach has not been widely applied or tested in healthcare social work settings in Canada or internationally. However, preliminary literature and pilot work by this team are conveying the potential importance of considering this approach in healthcare field education. A few pilots have been conducted (Dawson et al., 2017; Muskat et al., 2017), including one done by this team (Samson et al., 2021). Moreover, this approach has been implemented within gerontological social work placements in the United States, yielding benefits for trainees who have gained greater opportunities and greater depth in classroom and field learning (Birkenmaier et al., 2012; Gough & Wilks, 2012). Within our western Canadian healthcare context, social workers have been trialing a variety of rotational practicum models, where learning activities are scaffolded—building upon one another—to support student learning in the field.

Emergent Outcomes from Rotational Field Education Approaches. Although more research is needed, and is indeed underway, findings to date are beginning to shape themes regarding benefits from rotational field placements for students and FIs. According to Samson et al. (2021), benefits to students include broadened exposure and experience; FIs benefit from greater collaboration across hospital sites and eased workload demands associated with shared field supervision and instruction. Critical to these gains in field education has been the innovative leadership of key stakeholders who collaborate in the development and implementation of new field models. This includes healthcare managers, field education leads, individual FIs, and faculty members. The next section of the chapter presents the benefits, key considerations, and limitations of the integrated rotational model for field supervisors and students.

BENEFITS TO FIELD SUPERVISORS

Rotational supervision models offer some advantages for FIs including:

- Reduces the time commitment for field placement supervisors and provide workload balance. For example, a rotational model allows for a division of labor between two or more supervisors.

- Prepares healthcare students for employment. Working between a variety of sites, programs, and/or portfolios uniquely prepares students for casual pool work and/or temporary assignments, which are common transition steps into the healthcare career path.

- Re-engages healthcare social work staff in student field education and their commitment to advancing the profession. Shorter supervisory time commitments and a collaborative supervision model that distributes the administrative and supervisory tasks can be more sustainable.

- Continuing Competency Program credits. Agreements between post-secondary institutions and social work professional organizations allow for a division of total continuing competency credits allocated for practicum supervisor placements among more than one supervisor, which could build FI capacity.

BENEFITS TO STUDENTS

- Provides students with multiple supervisory perspectives to develop their own social work practice.

- Expands opportunities and organizational exposure.

- Provides an experience that mirrors the multiple roles and responsibilities of healthcare social workers.

- Increases opportunities to build a network of relationships and contacts within the organization, site, program and/or portfolios.

- Prepares students for entry level roles where social workers often work between multiple programs, units, sites, and/or portfolios.

CONSIDERATIONS IN DELIVERING AN INTEGRATED ROTATIONAL MODEL

1. Optimizes student compatibility or fit within their role. A rotational placement is likely to appeal to a student who enjoys a fast-paced environment, adapts easily to change, and is comfortable in a shared supervision model. Rotational models require a student who is flexible, open to feedback, has a keen work ethic, and is eager to contribute feedback to the field supervisor team.

2. Standardized student orientation to the organization and discipline in addition to site-, unit-, program- and/or portfolio-specific orientation.

3. Standardization of field supervision roles and responsibilities across placements.

4. Development of student learning plans that includes alignment with rotational placement learning objectives across all placement experiences.

LIMITATIONS OF AN INTEGRATED ROTATIONAL MODEL

- Short rotations can limit learning opportunities and provide insufficient time to thoroughly understand an area of practice.

- Rotations that take students to multiple geographic locations may pose challenges for them in locating their workspaces and limiting relational opportunities (with peers, supervisors, other members of the healthcare team., etc.) due to frequent changes.

- Integration seminars that support field practicums can vary widely in relation to student experiences. Seminars that serve primarily as debriefing sessions may not fully support bridging theory onto practice by in-depth exploration of clinical and practice issues that link to skill development. (Samson et al., 2021)

Overall, rotational models offer some unique learning opportunities for students who are interested in healthcare-based integrated learning opportunities. Important things to consider are being aware of what you need to feel prepared to enter this type of field education experience. Perhaps taking a Social Work in Health course, if one is available at your school, will help ground your expectations for this type of environment and provide a venue for you to become familiar with some of the language, policies, procedures, and patient issues you may encounter in this setting. Engaging in fulsome orientations to the practicum setting and clear communication with your FI and integration seminar instructor, are important considerations.

Social Work Student Community of Practice

The social work student (SWS) community of practice (CoP) is a peer-led initiative developed for students by students. The intent of the CoP is to provide a community of support and learning for Bachelor of Social Work (BSW) and MSW students in healthcare placements across Alberta. The CoP is structured with the collaborative learning circle principles of distributive leadership, collective wisdom, and group strengths to engage in meaningful group and individual development. Distributive leadership is a leadership model that shares power collaboratively among people rather than having a singular person in an authoritative position; it incorporates "collegial sharing of knowledge, practice and reflection" (Keppel et al., 2010, p. 166). Objectives of the social work studentCoP include networking opportunities, organization and resource navigation support, examination of the critical role social workers hold in healthcare, and peer-to-peer support.

Virtual meetings are held bi-weekly and are facilitated by a team of two students and a field supervisor. Each session has a theme identified by the collective as a priority practice topic. The sessions combine videos, practice reflection opportunities, exploration of and connection to the core clinical activities and competencies of healthcare social workers, and resource networking opportunities where students can build connections to and learn about community services, supports, etc. Participation is optional and attendance varies from session to session. Students are encouraged to discuss what they learn and questions that arise with their field supervisors on the session topics as a strategy to support scaffolded learning.

Student Learning Series

Within healthcare in Alberta, social workers have identified core clinical activities along with associated technical competencies intended to support clarity for the role of social workers in diverse healthcare settings and increase consistency in social work practice. Many of these core clinical activities and competencies are applied generically across programs, units, and portfolios. Standard education has been developed in relation to some core clinical activities and is available to social work students. To augment the available social-work-specific education, it made sense to begin developing additional education that would be available to all social work students within the province, regardless of program, supporting student orientation to the health context, skill development, education standardization, and the field supervisor's workload.

The student learning series is an optional monthly webinar offering several topics, including social determinants of health, decision making capacity, grief and loss, social work and health care ethics, transitioning from student to employee, a harm reduction approach to practice, and a social work psychosocial assessment This complementary learning is in addition to mandatory organizational training that all students are required to complete prior to arriving at their placement. Mandatory training sessions are consistent with what new employees undertake: orientations to health and safety expectations, policies and procedures that govern practice in the organizational setting, etc. The webinars are intended to focus on social-work-specific skills and competencies development.

Student Orientation Guide

Small, innovative student field education projects, such as the ones outlined in this chapter, can quickly and efficiently begin to create positive momentum and change for students in the healthcare practicum. Engagement in project work can aid students in their learning, growth, and development as they transition from students to emerging social work practitioners. Shifting the overall context from crisis to sustainability for social work student placements will take time and a coordinated approach. Partnering with post-secondary institutions, regulatory colleges, and internal organizational departments are key to developing sustainable models, both in the healthcare context and beyond. However, structural change is only one component, and there are multiple opportunities for small, micro change to create momentum for larger change. In addition to projects already outlined, the *Student Survival Guide* illustrates the immediate and secondary impact that small-scale projects can have.

The *Student Survival Guide* is a student-led project that was adapted from social work student orientation materials developed by healthcare social workers. The guide brings together social-work-specific learning topics and resources identified as foundational to student orientation and learning from both staff and student perspectives. The guide highlights the needed utility of the document and clearly aligns with the orientation and learning priorities of other organizational departments, such as the student placement team, human resources, and the organization's workforce planning goals. Due to the momentum generated, the stage was set to embark on larger organizational discussions to align this work and partner on the development of organization-wide student orientation and learning pathways across the local healthcare spectrum. Small "just do it" projects can be the momentum that drives bigger change.

Orientation Development for Social Work in Healthcare Trainees and Field Instructors

Further innovation has been focused on student orientation. The collaborative effort of university faculty members and health-based social workers resulted in the development and delivery of a healthcare field education orientation for students at the start of the semester, as well as ongoing training on core social work topics throughout practicum field instruction. The intent of the student orientation is to support students in navigating a healthcare practicum from the lens of lived experience from students who have gone through practicums in this setting. This orientation is a work-in-progress that is evolving as subsequent cohorts of students engage in health-based practicums. Generally, topic areas covered include networking; training; workshops and knowledge building; essentials for communication, professional practice, and the role of allied health in health care; supervision topic areas; building a sense of community among students; and examining healthcare as a potential career path.

Training for students includes extensive workshops on clinical ethics, decision-making and capacity, and financial assessment. For FIs, a healthcare-focused orientation is offered with a workshop on how to teach critical thinking. This training offers "on-the-ground" practice guidance in the aim of engaging, informing, and supporting field instructors; streamlining student field-based training; and optimizing student and field supervisor experience. Quarterly three-hour sessions have been offered, and evaluation has determined strong endorsement of these capacity-building sessions, with particular benefit identified by students; feedback shows strong support for these sessions from students due to increased knowledge, awareness, and clinical intervention skills these opportunities afford.

Promoting Rural and Remote Field Education Opportunities

Students interested in rural practice were offered the opportunity to participate in a rural cohort practicum experience. In rural settings, there are often interested FIs but limited numbers of students interested in, or able to take advantage of, rural placement opportunities. Barriers such as housing, additional financial burden, and isolation were identified and mitigated through partnerships with Alberta Health Services (AHS) housing, recruitment, rural operational leaders, and a funder agency, the Rural Health Professions Action Plan (RhPAP). This field education opportunity has offered diverse learning experiences, including heightened provincial social work training modules on topics such as decision-making and ethics, and has deepened field education experiences for students, which have, in turn, augmented FI training requirements. Additionally, through work with the RhPAP, students have been oriented into the local community to address the potential experience of loneliness and isolation and to strengthen their knowledge of the community and available resources and services. This opportunity for rich placement experiences has proactively addressed recruitment needs particular to rural communities.

As a broader recruitment strategy, this field education approach is directly linked to job opportunities for social workers in healthcare within rural regions upon graduation. Future opportunities exist to expand this approach for social work students both as a discipline-specific cohort, but also as an interdisciplinary cohort. For this approach to be successful and ultimately scaled up and spread, consideration will need to be given to the scheduling of placements within a semester (possibility of block placements) and a method of instructional delivery for concurrent courses and integrative seminars will need to be developed.

Developing Classroom Content in Tandem with Field Education Advancements

Advancing innovation in field education takes a team effort between stakeholders in social work education, including academics and researchers; facilitators in the field education office and healthcare settings; practicing social worker leaders; and most importantly, students. Over the last several years, we have sought to deeply reflect on the degree of complementarity of our university BSW-level social work in healthcare training in the classroom to assess its fit with field needs and the field education offered. To that end, we have examined integral elements for successful healthcare practice; hence, key learning objectives and pedagogical approaches. Building from key learnings emerging from our work, we have redeveloped (and are continuing to redefine) social work classroom education to better complement key needs and learnings in the field context. The Social Work in Health course addresses the practice of social work in healthcare, reflecting the healthcare needs of Canada's population. It provides an overview of the structure of the healthcare system, the SDH, and the role of the social work profession in this context. Key concepts pertinent to healthcare are explored in this course including interprofessional teams, patient-centered care, care transitions, advanced care planning, ethical decision-making, assessment, intervention, documentation, continuous quality improvement and the skills required for social work efficacy. The course serves as a foundation to support entry-level practice for students new to this field, which can be built upon in the real-life context of practice when students commence field learning.

Our collaborative team, which includes those from academic, field, and student perspectives, continues to seek opportunities to find synergies to further advance social work in healthcare. A key learning from early pilot projects is the need for field, students, and faculty members to work closely together in co-creating opportunities and new ideas for continually moving forward. The power of *us* emerges as we work and think holistically together on these concepts — university, field, field education, student life, classroom learning, research, *and* teaching and learning — rather than isolated in our silos. This has and will continue to move us further forward in thinking about new ideas to address the emerging crises in accessing field education, and importantly, guide us as we seek to move to a more seamless educational pathway into social work in healthcare. Throughout our journey, this process has reflected our collective quest to address the questions of how we can better invite and inspire students into healthcare-based social work and how we can prepare them for this career and support them educationally in the field. Other examples of field innovation could be explored and shared; however, these samples we have shared here are possible innovation. Reflections in Moving Forward: Key Issues to Consider in Advancing Field Education

At the core of our collaborative work in healthcare to support field education, this work is a process of re-envisioning opportunities and ways of delivering field education given current financial, political, etc. realities. Steps for moving forward in improving social work education in our jurisdiction have required collectively moving forward together. Our experience invites the continuing development of strong partnerships as innovation requires trust and collaboration between the field and the academy. The following is a list of some key considerations that can guide field education development through systematic change. Important elements include clarity of mandate and aims, consideration of options and the activities needed to advance those options, reflection on the fit of options with students' interest and professional goals, balance of what is needed in the field and what optimizes student learning and growth (a key is not just making the placement the best learning opportunity possible for a given student, but also the sustainability of the placement options), consideration of field instructors' supervisory needs and fit of a given model or approach, recalibration of student learning contracts to fit for other ways of orchestrating placements.

This may require a different template and orientation in conveying and determining field placement success (e.g., language from "client" to "participant," or "team member" to "partner"), Strong communication in clearly discerning, aiming for, and communicating expectations, and Being bold and creative. Think about how placements can offer a "win/win" outcome, for example, student learning *and* what is viable given the pressures on field instructors in busy field practice environments.

Our preliminary work on advancing field education in healthcare has shown us that long-term commitment is productive; indeed, it has been generative and team-building to us as group of social workers in the field and academia. Striving for innovation in field education in healthcare is a work in progress — perhaps that work is never complete! Yet as a team working together, new ideas can be birthed and trialed — ideas that may lead to more options and opportunities. From our experience, the effort to work together for innovative change is pressing and critically important to the advancement and recruitment within social work in healthcare, particularly given the critical importance of the field practicum in social work education.

Questions to Consider When Choosing Social Work in Healthcare

As a social work student (or as future or current social worker) in healthcare, you have unique insights that can contribute to the development and evaluation of this field context. We would like to end this chapter with some questions to consider. These questions invite you to consider your engagement with healthcare social work and develop ideas for social work field education.

1. What excites you about social work in healthcare as a career opportunity?

2. What personal and professional strengths do you have that would benefit social work in healthcare?

3. What supports, resources or networking opportunities would help you grow and thrive in this area of social work?

4. What opportunities are available at your university for collaborative work?

5. Are there any changes to social work education that you think would complement skill development for practice readiness?

6. Do you have any innovative ideas, and what could you do to help implement them?

RESOURCES

Samson, P., Nicholas, D., Jones, C., Hilsen, L., Samek, D., Mielke, K., Holtzman, S., Walley, B., Manas, M., & Deol, M. (2020, July 15-19). *Contributing to the global agenda: Building social work capacity in healthcare* [Workshop]. The International Federation of Social Workers (IFSW) Conference — The 2020 to 2030 Social Work Global Agenda: Co-Building Social Transformation (virtual international conference venue). https://www.youtube.com/watch?v=t1KdOAcox00

REFERENCES

Anderson, R. M. (1995). Patient empowerment and the traditional medical model: a case of irreconcilable differences? *Diabetes Care, 18*(3), 412–415. https://doi.org/10.2337/diacare.18.3.412

Ambrose-Miller, W. Ashcroft, R. (2016). Challenges Faced by Social Workers as Members of interprofessional collaborative healthcare teams. *Health and Social Work, 41*(2), 101–109. https://doi.org/10.1093/hsw/hlw006

Ashcroft, R. B., McMillan, C., Ambrose-Miller, W., McKee, R., and Brown, J. (2018). The emerging role of social work in primary healthcare: A survey of social workers in Ontario family health teams. *Health and Social Work, 43*(2), 109–117. https://doi.org/10.1093/hsw/hly003

Ayala, J., Drolet, J., Fulton, A., Hewson, J., Letkemann, L., Baynton, M., Elliott, G., Judge-Stasiak, A., Blaug, C., Tetreault, A., &Schweizer, E. (2018). Field education in crisis: Experiences of field education coordinators in Canada. *Social Work Education: The International Journal, 37*(3), 281–293. https://doi.org/10.1080/0261547 9.2017.1397109

Barr, R. B., & Tagg, J. (1995). From teaching to learning—A new paradigm for undergraduate education. *Change: The Magazine of Higher Learning, 27*(6), 12–26. https://doi.org/10.1080/00091383.1995.10544672

Beddoe, L. (2011). Health social work: Professional identity and knowledge. *Qualitative Social Work, 12*(1), 24–40. https://doi.org/10.1177/1473325011415455

Birkenmaier, J., Curley, J., & Rowan, N. L. (2012). Knowledge outcomes within rotational models of social work field education. *Journal of Gerontological Social Work, 55*(4), 321–336. https://doi.org/10.1080/01634372.201 1.625596

Bogo, M. (2006). Field instruction in social work: A review of the research literature. *The Clinical Supervisor, 24*(1/2), 163–193. https://doi.org/10.1300/J001v24n01_09

Bogo, M. (2015). Field education for clinical social work practice: Best practices and contemporary challenges. *Clinical Social Work Journal, 43*(3), 317–324. https://link.springer.com/article/10.1007/s10615-015-0526-5

Braveman, P., & Gottlieb, L. (2014). The social determinants of health: It's time to consider the causes of the causes. *Public Health Reports, 129*(1_suppl2), 19–31. https://doi.org/10.1177/00333549141291S206

Bronstein, L., Gould, P., Berkowitz, S., James, G., & Marks, K. (2015). Impact of a social work care coordination intervention on hospital readmission: A randomized controlled trial. *Social Work, 60*(3), 248–255. https://doi.org/10.1093/sw/swv016

Canadian Association of Social Workers. (2005). *Standards of practice and ethics.* https://casw-acts.ca/en/51-standards-practice-and-ethics

———. (2005). *Code of ethics.* https://www.casw-acts.ca/sites/default/files/documents/casw_code_of_ethics.pdf

Craig, S. L., & Muskat, B. (2013). Bouncers, brokers, and glue: The self-described role of social workers in urban hospitals. *Health and Social Work, 38*(1), 7–16. https://doi.org/10.1093/hsw/hls064

Dawson, L., Jones, R., Maingot, C., Niv, H., & Parrish, L. (2017). Social work practicum placements in pediatric outpatient chronic care: Exploring rotational placements. *Canadian Social Work, 19*(1), 98–107. https://web.p.ebscohost.com/ehost/pdfviewer/pdfviewer?vid=0&sid=7be1c5f1-dd35-4a9e-99b0-98bcd515eca0%40redis

Folgheraiter, F. (2007). Relational social work: Principles and practices. *Social Policy and Society, 6*(2), 265–274. https://doi.org/10.1017/S1474746406003526

Gibbons, J., & Plath, D. (2009). Single contacts with hospital social workers: The clients' experiences. *Social Work in Healthcare, 48*(8), 721–735. https://doi.org/10.1080/00981380902928935

Gough, H., & Wilks, S. (2012). Rotational field placements: Integrative review and application to gerontological social work. *Social Work Education, 31*(1), 90–109. https://doi.org/10.1080/02615479.2010.549222

Green, B.N., & Johnson, C.D. (2015). Interprofessional collaboration in research, education, and clinical practice: working together for a better future. *Journal of Chiropractic Education, 29*(1), 14–36. https://www.ncbi.nlm.nih.gov/pmc/articles/PMC4360764/

Haegele, J. A., & Hodge, S. (2016). Disability discourse: Overview and critiques of the medical and social models. *Quest, 68*(2), 193–206. https://doi.org/10.1080/00336297.2016.1143849

Hartick-Doane, G., & Varcoe, C. (2007). Relational practice and nursing obligations. *Advances in Nursing Science, 30*(3): 192–205. https://doi.org/10.1097/01.ANS.0000286619.31398.fc

Holliman, D. C., Dziegielewsk, S.F., & Datta, P. (2001). Discharge planning and social work practice. *Social Work in Healthcare, 32*(3), 1–19. https://doi.org/10.1300/j010v32n03_01

Hutchison, B., Levesque, J. F., Strumpf, E., & Coyle, N. (2011). Primary healthcare in Canada: Systems in motion. *Milbank Quarterly, 89*, 256–288. https://doi.org/10.1111/j.1468-0009.2011.00628.x

Illingworth, P., & Chelvanayagam, S. (2017). The benefits of interprofessional education 10 years on. *British Journal of Nursing, 26*(14), 813–818. https://doi.org/10.12968/bjon.2017.26.14.813

Jencks S., Williams M., & Coleman E. (2009). Rehospitalizations among patients in the Medicare fee-for-service program. *New England Journal of Medicine, 360*, 1418–1428. https://www.nejm.org/doi/full/10.1056/nejmsa0803563

Judd, R. G., & Sheffield, S. (2010). Hospital social work: Contemporary roles and professional activities. *Social Work in Healthcare, 49*(9), 856–871. https://doi.org/10.1080/00981389.2010.499825

Keefe, B., Geron, S. M., & Enguidanos, S. (2009). Integrating social workers into primary care: Physician and nurse perceptions of roles, benefits, and challenges. *Social Work in Healthcare, 48*(6), 579–596. https://doi.org/10.1080/00981380902765592

Keppell, M., O'Dwyer, C., Lyon, B., & Childs, M. (2010). Transforming distance education curricula through distributive leadership. *Australasian Journal of Educational Technology, 26*(8), 165–178. https://doi.org/10.14742/ajet.1017

Kolb, D. A. (1984). *Experiential Learning: Experience as the source of learning and development.* Prentice-Hall.

Larrison, E. T., & Korr, W. S. (2013). Does social work have a signature pedagogy? *Journal of Social Work Education, 49*(2), 194–206. https://doi.org/10.1080/10437797.2013.768102

McLoughlin, C., Patel, K. D., O'Callaghan, T., & Reeves, S. (2018). The use of virtual communities of practice to improve interprofessional collaboration and education: findings from an integrated review. *Journal of interprofessional care, 32*(2), 136–142. https://doi.org/10.1080/13561820.2017.1377692

Mizrahi, T., & Abramson, J. S. (2000). Collaboration between social workers and physicians: Perspectives on a shared case. *Social Work in Health Care, 31*(3), 1–24. https://doi.org/10.1300/J010v31n03_01

Muskat, B., Craig, S. L., & Mathai, B. (2017). Complex families, the social determinants of health and psychosocial interventions: Deconstruction of a day in the life of hospital social workers. *Social Work in Health Care, 56*(8), 765–778. https://doi.org/10.1080/00981389.2017.1339761

National Association of Social Workers. (2008). *NASW code of ethics (guide to the everyday professional conduct of social workers.* NASW. https://www.socialworkers.org/About/Ethics/Code-of-Ethics

Preez, P. (2012). The human right to education, the ethical responsibility of curriculum, and the irony in safe spaces. In C. Roux, (Ed.), *Safe spaces: Human rights education in diverse contexts* (p. 51–62). Sense Publishers.

Purnell, T. S., Calhoun, E. A., Golden, S. H., Halladay, J. R., Krok-Schoen, J. L., Appelhans, B. M., & Cooper, L. A. (2016). Achieving health equity: closing the gaps in health care disparities, interventions, and research. *Health Affairs, 35*(8), 1410–1415. https://www.healthaffairs.org/doi/pdf/10.1377/hlthaff.2016.0158

Samson, P. L. (2018). Critical thinking in social work education: A Delphi study of faculty understanding. Unpublished doctoral dissertation. University of Windsor, Canada. https://scholar.uwindsor.ca/etd/7395

Samson, P., Gloeckler, T., & Nicholas, D. (2021 July, 12). *Rotational practicum/supervision model: A MSW pilot project.* Final Research Report.

Schrecker, T., Chapman, A., Labonté, R., & De Vogli R. (2010). Advancing health equity in the global marketplace: How human rights can help. *Social Science and Medicine, 71*, 1520–1526. https://doi.org/10.1016/j.socscimed.2010.06.042

Taylor Institute. (2022). *Experiential learning resources for teaching and learning continuity.* https://taylorinstitute.ucalgary.ca/resources/experiential-learning-continuity

World Health Organization. (2008). *Social determinants of health* Report of a Regional Consultation Colombo, Sri Lanka, 2–4 October 2007. WHO Regional Office for South-East Asia. https://apps.who.int/iris/bitstream/handle/10665/206363/B3357.pdf

NOTES:

NOTES:

NOTES:

Interprofessional Education and Practice in Social Work Field Education

Kelly Allison and Grant Charles

Most social and health issues are complex. Addressing them requires a coordinated, collaborative approach from a wide range of health professional groups (e.g., physicians, nurses, social workers) and community social service professionals (e.g., child welfare professionals, child and youth care workers, probation officers). However, this collaboration often does not happen. A major criticism of both the health and human services systems is that different professions working within them operate in silos disconnected from the work of each other (Costello et al., 2018). This individualized way of working decreases collaboration and communication between and within the systems. As a result, services users often do not get the full support that they need or deserve. There are many reasons for professions working independently of each other, but one of the key reasons is that many professionals lack the knowledge, skills, attitudes, and values for effective interaction between the professions working in the health and human service sectors (Charles et al., 2010; Salhani & Charles, 2007). This disconnection with other professions begins in the foundational training for each of the professions in post-secondary institutions and continues through field learning in practicums and, upon graduation, into practice.

In this chapter, we seek to counter siloed professional behavior and enhance interprofessional effectiveness by presenting the concepts of interprofessional education and practice. We identify the consequences of not working well together, describe the different forms of professional education and practice in our current work environments, articulate a rationale for why social workers should engage in interprofessional and collaborative practice, and describe the main concepts that define interprofessional education and practice. We hope that by understanding the rationale for, and outlining necessary skills for effective interprofessional collaborative practice, social work students entering the field will have foundational knowledge to intentionally begin to understand other professions, analyze the interprofessional practice they observe, and begin to develop competencies that will enhance their future practice.

One of the main goals of field education is to learn about the profession of social work and how social workers operate in the world (Bogo & Vayda, 1998; Bogo, 2010). While this holds true at all levels of social work education, it is particularly important in the first field placements. Field education is one of the primary methods through which social work students develop a sense of professional identity and learn to become social workers (Oliver, 2013; Maynard et al., 2015; Smith et al., 2015). Practicums provide the opportunity to apply what students have learned in the classroom about the social work profession's values, knowledge base, and skills (Bogo & Vayda, 1998; Bogo, 2010).

This development of a professional identity is, by its nature, a time of reflection and inward focus whereby students begin to integrate what they have been learning in the classroom with the realities of practice in the real world (Wiles, 2013; Ben Shlomo et al., 2012). When social work students begin to look outward, it is not uncommon to compare themselves with other health and human service professions. They, in part, figure out who they are by trying to figure out who they are not. This comparison can lead to a better understanding of their own profession and the other health and human service professions if done with a goal of learning to work more effectively together.

Unfortunately, increased interprofessional effectiveness is often not what results from this comparison with other professions (Glaser, 2016; Mizrahi & Abramson, 2000). In an attempt to elevate their own work and their developing sense of professional identity, social work students can sometimes criticize and downplay other professions. Contributing to this negative appraisal is the fact that students often view other professions through stereotypes portrayed in media or in society. Rather than learning to work well with other professions based upon their strengths and knowledge, this lack of true understanding of others serves to create barriers to collaborating effectively with them. Other professions can also experience the same trap of stereotyping the social work profession and misunderstanding and judging social workers. This lack of genuine appreciation of each other's roles and scope of practice creates a disconnect between what various professionals are trying to achieve with the service users with whom they are working. While each profession believes that they are doing best for the service users, poor collaboration with their professional partners can limit their effectiveness and potentially create problems.

While this may simply sound like a case of professional rivalry, there can be significant, grave consequences to service users because of this lack of collaboration and understanding between professions. It is well documented that there are significant negative service user outcomes associated with poor communication, cooperation, and understanding between the professions in the health and human services (Kohn et al., 2000). In North America, it has been estimated that thousands of people die each year through errors occurring in healthcare practice due to poor communication, coordination, and/or professional cooperation (Kohn et al., 2000; Romanow, 2002). Deaths also occur in the human service sector due to poor co-ordination and communication between professions. The Alberta Child Advocate (2022) has investigated numerous child deaths caused at least in part because professionals have failed to work effectively together. In addition to deaths, many service users have suffered injury or received ineffective or inadequate help and support because of the difficulties between the professions working together. The numbers of people being poorly served is staggering (Kohn et al., 2000). Poor service user outcomes and inadequate service continue to be problems despite an increased awareness in the health and human service systems of the benefits of interprofessional collaboration to service user safety and the quality of care provided.

To understand the reasons why health and human service professions struggle to work well together, we have identified several barriers to interprofessional collaboration and communication. Organizational structure and culture can impede professions working together when there is hierarchical decision making, a lack of time for collaboration, or when professionals are not in the same physical space, making communication more difficult (Ambrose-Miller & Ashcroft, 2016). Professions also have different values and philosophies of working (Drinka & Clark, 2000; Loxley, 1997; Miller et al., 2001), role insecurity, and a fear of their professional roles being encroached upon by other professions (Loxley, 1997; Miller et al., 2001; Hornby & Atkins, 2000). These concerns can lead to territoriality, and the need to protect professional knowledge (Geva et al., 2000; Hornby & Atkins, 2000; Miller et al., 2001). Power differences between the professions and fear of potentially losing their job can also contribute to poor collaboration (Geva et al., 2000; Hornby & Atkins, 2000). Many of these barriers to collaborative practice developed in reaction to the historical oppression by some of the professions to the others (Charles et al., 2010).

These barriers to professional collaboration are often replicated within university settings (Paul & Peterson, 2001; Charles et al., 2010): Students can be conditioned through practice stories from faculty to feel misunderstood and underappreciated by their colleagues in the health and hum services profession even before they start their placements. This can result in a suspicion of the motivations of other professionals; a devaluing of other profession's knowledge, skills, and worldviews; and a corresponding sense of territoriality to protect one's own turf. This makes it easy for individual professions to justify to themselves why their worldview is the best, or why another profession "doesn't get it". An unintended consequence of this dynamic is that it becomes difficult to accept one's own profession's role in the provision of ineffective or harmful services to people using the helping systems. If social work students assume their professional worldview is right and those of other professions are wrong, it becomes easier to blame other professions for systemic problems and take little or no responsibilities for the contributions of the profession of social work in these problems..

The Origins of Barriers Between the Professions

Many of the current barriers to collaborative practice can be traced back to the historical development of the health and human services professions (Charles & Alexander, 2014; Charles, Dharamsi & Alexander, 2011; Charles & Dharamsi, 2010). The way the professions were established and the early settings in which they worked still influence how they interact. Service delivery was straightforward in the later parts of the 19th century when the first health and human services began as formal professions. Many of the health professions (medicine, pharmacy, and nursing) only interacted in acute hospital settings. Their roles were hierarchical in nature, and well defined with little role overlap. There was little thought to understanding the roles or worldviews of the other professions. The healthcare system was quite simplistic in how it functioned in addressing physical health issues. However, there were major gaps in service delivery as the few existing professions did not have the expertise to meet the complex needs of service users. With the evolution of our understanding of health, the need for diverse health professions expanded necessitating interprofessional collaboration.

The motivation to meet the full range of needs of service users eventually lead to the establishment of the over sixty health and human service professions currently practicing in Canada.

> To get an idea of some of the health and human services professionals in Canada review this list adapted from the BC Health Professionals List of Regulated Professionals and the National Organization for Human Services https://docs.google.com/document/d/1P4JLC1 L0NyXxyvlQJOOqQnxMssK11eAnBTZ4qaEGf_Q/edit
>
> BC Health Regulators. (2022). *Regulated Health Professionals*. https://bchealthregulators. ca/health-regulation-in-bc/regulated-health-professions/
>
> National Organization for Health and Human Services. (n.d.). *What is Human Services*. https://www.nationalhumanservices.org/what-is-human-services

The need to improve service through the proliferation of new professions has resulted in a far more complex system than had previously existed. It is increasingly uncommon for a service user to only interact with a single service provider from a single profession. Service users often interact with a team or teams of professionals who are supported behind the scenes with even more members of other professions. While this means that service users may receive more effective interventions than in the past, it also means that the opportunities for poor communication and collaboration have multiplied. The likelihood of role confusion between professions has also increased. The complexity of teams and systems and the number of professionals now needing to communicate, coordinate, and cooperate can lead to dire consequences for clients (Charles et al., 2010).

The method of training health and human service students lays the foundation for poor communication and collaboration between the professions (Charles & Alexander, 2014). The current pedagogical approaches can reinforce the barriers between the professions rather than break them down. Most professions use what can be called a modified apprenticeship model of training. This model stems from the earliest days of the professions when students did their training almost entirely in practice settings such as a hospital. Education and training eventually expanded to include classroom learning in post-secondary institutions, although the core beliefs underpinning the training did not change. Apart from skills and knowledge transfer, professional training involves the indoctrination and socialization of the students into their individual professions (Hall, 2005). This promotes pride in one's own profession and an understanding of one's own professional culture but does little to promote an understanding of other professions. In most professional programs, limited information is taught about the roles and scope of practice of the other professions with whom they will be working with daily.

Interprofessional education and practice counters this lack of information by offering a practical framework within which the numerous health and human service professions can interact with each other to deliver the best level of care.

Why Interprofessional Practice?

The primary purpose of interprofessional practice is to improve the quality of care and service delivery for service users. Key benefits of effective interprofessional practice are reduced intervention errors that lead to poor services, less harm to patients and lower death rates (D'Amour et al., 2005). These benefits should be sufficient reasons to improve our relationships with other professions. However, improving interprofessional knowledge and collaboration also benefits individual professions.

In a study at the University of British Columbia in 2003, students from various professions took part in an intensive field learning experience where they came together to do their practicums in rural healthcare centres (Charles et al., 2011). While each of the students completed profession-specific placement requirements, they were also provided time for structured and unstructured interprofessional learning opportunities. Students from the different professions reported a significant increase in their understanding and appreciation of other professions (Charles et al., 2006; Charles et al., 2008).

There were several benefits noted by the social work students (Charles et al., 2011). The first was that they gained a deeper understanding of the scope of practice of social work by explaining to others the roles and world view of their profession. Teaching other students about their own profession helped them appreciate the unique strengths and contributions of social worker, especially in group and team settings. Their profession-specific training in group processes helped the social work students make significant contributions to resolve conflicts and mediate difficult situations in a way that benefited all team members.

This interprofessional experience allowed social work students the opportunity to educate students from other professions regarding the value of their profession in an applied way (Charles et al., 2011). By demonstrating specific skills to social work practice, articulating their systems perspective, and demonstrating their commitment to social justice, social work students were able to help the other students expand their understanding of the value of the profession of social work (Charles et al., 2011).

The social work students also became less judgemental and more informed in their critiques of the other professions (Charles et al., 2011). By working collaboratively alongside the other students and seeing the struggles these students experienced, social work students were able to better understand the complexities of those professions rather than just viewing them through stereotypes. This led to deeper dialogue and even greater understanding and appreciation of other professions.

To improve outcomes for service users, Interprofessional education and practice has been developed to counter the traditional and siloed ways professions are typically trained and practice (Kelly et al., 2020). This is not to say that all aspects of professional education should be interprofessional in nature. We need practitioners who have specialized knowledge and skills and continue to require profession-specific training approaches. However, we also need to continue to increase our ability to effectively work together across our traditional practice boundaries and barriers. Interprofessional education and practice offers a means by which students can learn to better appreciate the contributions and worldviews of the other professions. The next section of the chapter examines key interprofessional concepts and competencies.

Definitions

To help explain the rationale for interprofessional practice and education, the following definitions may be helpful.

Unidiscipline (Uniprofessional) Education and Practice

When members of a single profession work and learn together almost exclusively with other members of their own profession, this is considered unidiscipline education and practice (Charles and Alexander, 2014). Most professional education at universities take place in a unidiscipline context. While unidiscipline professionals may occasionally interact with people from other professions, their primary point of contact is with members of their own profession. For example, child protection teams in many jurisdictions are a uniprofessional practice as they tend to be solely made up of social workers.

Multidisciplinary (Multiprofessional) Education and Practice

Multidisciplinary practice occurs when two or more professions work along side each other in the same setting, often supporting the same client or patient, but their work is primarily independent of other professions (Charles & Alexander, 2014). Some outpatient clinics operate using a multidisciplinary model where professions such as social workers and occupational therapists may be co-located in the same general office space but have little professional contact with each other. Multidisciplinary education occurs when students from various professions learn together in classrooms by attending the same lectures together. In multidisciplinary education, students are not engaged in learning together, but are focused solely on mastering the course content from their own professional perspective.

Interdisciplinary Education and Practice

Interdisciplinary work and education draw upon and integrate knowledge from several disciplines (Charles & Alexander, 2014). The various professionals often come to appreciate the skills and knowledge base of the other professions in the setting, but there is no deliberate effort to understand the worldview of their colleagues. There can be role overlap and some blurred discipline boundaries in interdisciplinary practice. An example of such overlap is a mental health clinic where different professions, such as social work, psychology, nursing, and medicine, work together with both overlapping and distinct roles. Interdisciplinary courses are common at many universities. For example, a child development course might use knowledge derived from psychology, nursing, and medicine. Multidisciplinary courses incorporate knowledge from several academic disciplines or professions, although the class setting is usually either unidisciplinary (such as social work students in a social work program) or multidisciplinary.

Interprofessional Education and Practice

Interprofessional education and practice is a process whereby two or more professions interact purposefully to learn with, from, and about each other with the goal of improving, collaboration, and the quality of care (Charles & Alexander, 2014; Charles et al., 2015; Charles et al., 2010). The key component of interprofessional practice is taking the time to learn about the culture, knowledge base, and worldview of the other professions through interacting with them rather relying on any positive or negative stereotypes students may have of them. This requires active and engaged conversations with members of the other professions to understand how their histories, values, beliefs, attitudes and customs drive their professional interactions with service users and members of other professions. Ideally, this process of learning with, from, and about the other professions in the classroom would begin prior to entering field placements. By having classes on practice topics with members of other professions, it would be possible to have structured conversations about the specific differences and similarities in how different professions approach care delivery. Although scheduled interprofessional education is becoming more common in many universities through specific learning modules students participate in together, there are still limited interprofessional learning opportunities due to scheduling conflicts and expanding uniprofessional curriculum demands. Unfortunately, this means that much of the learning about other professions continues to primarily happen in field placements rather than in the classroom.

Transdisciplinary Approaches

Interprofessional practice and collaboration can move beyond the integration of professional knowledge and roles and begin to work from a transdisciplinary approach (Choi & Pak, 2006). When teams work from a transdisciplinary model, they often use a common theoretical and practice framework, such as harm reduction, that has been developed from the knowledge of multiple disciplines. As teams transcend discipline boundaries, each discipline may experience role release, where they acknowledge that others can do some of their professional roles, and role expansion, where they begin to take on roles that were, at one time, viewed as outside their scope of practice (Choi & Pak, 2006). An example of a transdisciplinary approach is the Assertive Community Treatment Team in Vancouver, BC where a psychiatric nurse might offer group therapy and a social worker may administer emergency naloxone to a client.

Core Concepts and Competencies Related to Interprofessional Practice

There is a developing body of research exploring some of the key concepts embedded in effective interprofessional collaboration. The following are some of the core ideas related to interprofessional collaboration.

Collective Ownership of Goals

A defining element of teamwork is collective action toward a common goal (D'Amour et al., 2005; Saint-Pierre et al., 2018). Collaborative practice involves several professionals analyzing problems, identifying goals, and assuming joint responsibility for actions toward meeting those goals (Hall, 2005). Iachini et al. (2018) also recognize goal evaluation as an element of effective collaboration. Frequently cited goals of professionals working together is improved services and outcomes for service users (Ambrose-Miller & Ashcroft, 2016; Philips & Walsh, 2019; Lutfiyya et al., 2019).

Shared Information and Tasks

Sharing encompasses many factors in interprofessional collaboration, including sharing information, sharing tasks and responsibilities, and sharing decision making (D'Amour et al., 2005). Information sharing can be a vital component of the continuity of care for service users. However, as confidentiality is a key ethical imperative for social workers, student should always understand their ethical and legal requirements regarding information sharing (Canadian Association of Social Workers [CASW], 2005).

Sharing also relates to how professional responsibilities and tasks are divided and distributed (D'Amour et al., 2005). There is a recognition that the scopes of practice for different professions can overlap (e.g., psychologists, nurses, and social workers can all provide emotional support for service users and families). Shared responsibilities and tasks allow professionals who work together to coordinate and allocate specific tasks to certain professionals or to recognize the contribution of several professionals to the same task (D'Amour et al., 2005; Morely & Cashell, 2017).

Finally, a key aspect of sharing is shared decision making. Collaborative practice is most effective when there is mutual input from multiple disciplines in case planning or when decision making incorporates the perspectives of several professionals (Sainte-Pierre et al., 2018).

Partnership

Partnership can describe both the quality of relationships between professionals working together and the outcomes of the relationships. Partnerships are often described as professionals having collegial relationships that are authentic, open, and constructive (D'Amour et al., 2005; Morley & Cashell, 2017). Partnerships can also encompass the idea that newly created professional activities can be the result of working together (Bronstein, 2003; Iachini et al., 2018). An example from one of the author's own practice is the newly developed protocols or policies that resulted from emergency physicians and social workers collaborating with child protection teams in Vancouver, British Columbia (2016) regarding youth in care who came to the emergency room intoxicated. A new protocol was developed that ensured the safety of youth being discharged from hospital and was not onerous on child protection social workers.

Interdependency

When thinking about how social workers might work together with other professions, interdependency is crucial to effective collaboration (D'Amour, 2005, Iachini et al., 2018). Defined as "the state of being dependent on another" (Meriam-Webster, 2022), interdependency recognizes that social workers need to rely on other professionals to help them address complex social issues and meet the needs of the clients they serve. Interdependence requires cooperation; each discipline has an awareness of the roles and contributions of other professions and respect for and value the knowledge and skills that other professions can contribute to service delivery (D'Amour et al., 2005, Morley & Cashell, 2017).

Power

Power is related to different professionals' influence on the behaviour of others, decision making about patient care or how service delivery unfolds in a health care setting (Nugus et al., 2010). Power struggles sometimes exist between health professionals from different hierarchical, social, and economic levels within organizations and/or across organizational boundaries when interprofessional collaborations involve more than one organization (Karam et al., 2018). Overt differences in power exist when governance models or structural issues give more decision-making power to one professional over another or when there are compensation practices that reward one profession over others (Ambrose-Miller & Ashcroft, 2016). However, power between professions can also be covert where the centrality of one profession is unspoken yet known by all. An example of this is the implicit understanding among team member's that the doctor's schedule takes precedence for meetings or rounds (Ambrose-Miller & Ashcroft, 2016). Power that is dominated by one profession, involves communication that is often unidirectional and where decisions involve little input from other professions is thought to be a competitive style of power (Nugus, et al, 2010).

However, power on interprofessional teams can also be intentionally distributed and collaborative allowing for the empowerment of all members of a team (Ambrose-Miller & Ashcroft, 2016; D'Amour et al., 2005). Collaborative power encourages interdependent participation of team members and input into decision making, recognizes each professions' distinctive knowledge and encourages negotiated leadership within the team (Nugus et al., 2010). Teams exercising collaborative power tend to have less interpersonal conflict (Almost et al., 2016).

A Framework of Interdisciplinary Collaboration

As healthcare is a setting where many different professions interact and work together for the benefit of service users and families, there is a growing body of research regarding interprofessional collaboration in healthcare contexts. Several studies have identified core skills and needed for effective interprofessional collaboration and teamwork in healthcare settings, including cooperation, assertiveness, effective communication, the ability for professions to work autonomously, and the ability of team members to co-ordinate tasks and decision-making (D'Amour et al., 2005; Hall, 2005).

The Canadian Interprofessional Health Collaborative (CIHC) is a group of health organizations, educators, researchers, professionals, and students from across Canada. In 2010, a CIHC working group created an interprofessional competency framework that can help social workers and other health disciplines conceptualize the key skills and competencies necessary to collaborate. Although this framework was developed specifically for healthcare, its concepts are applicable to other social work settings where interprofessional collaboration is needed.

The framework outlines six core competencies that require the development and integration of attitudes, behaviors, values, and judgments necessary for collaborative practice (Canadian Interprofessional Health Collaborative [CIHC], 2010). The six core competencies are:

- Role clarification,
- Patient/service-user/ family/community centered care,
- Interprofessional communication,
- Team functioning,
- Interprofessional conflict resolution, and
- Collaborative leadership.

In the next section we outline the key components of this framework and expand upon them to help students think about interprofessional collaboration in other settings.

Role Clarification

Role clarification means that social workers can both describe their own role and scope of practice as well as the role and scope of practice of other professions they work with (CIHC, 2010). They understand their unique knowledge, skills, and roles and have a good understanding of how their roles interface with the knowledge, skills, and roles of other professions in contributing to the care of service users. (CIHC, 2010).

According to the CIHC (2010), role clarification can be demonstrated by:

- Being able to describe your own role and the role of others.
- Recognizing and respecting the diversity of roles, responsibilities, and competencies of other professions on the team.
- Being able to perform your own role in culturally respectful ways.
- Communicating roles, skills, and knowledge using appropriate language.
- Accessing the knowledge and skills of others through consultation.
- Considering the roles of others when determining your own professional and interprofessional role.
- Integrating roles seamlessly into models of service delivery.

Patient/Service- User/Family/Community-Centered Care

Social workers and other professionals can prioritize and value the voices and engagement of patients, service-users, families, and communities in the design or implementation of their care and service delivery (CIHC, 2010). Service users are seen as the expert in their own lives and are given access to information, knowledge, or skills in a respectful way so they can become partners in their care or service delivery. To be service user-centered, professionals listen carefully to the expressed wishes, needs, and goals of service users; this information is central to care or service delivery plans (CIHC, 2010).

The Institute for Patient and Family Centered Care (1992) identifies four key concepts of service user and family centered care.

1. **Dignity and respect**: listening and honoring service user and family perspectives and choices. Service user and family knowledge, values, beliefs, and cultural backgrounds are incorporated into the planning and delivery of care.

2. **Information sharing**: communicating and sharing complete, timely and unbiased information with service users and families in ways that are affirming and useful. Service users and families are given accurate information to effectively participate and make decisions in their own care.

3. **Participation**: encouraging and supporting service users and families to participate in care and decision-making at the level they choose.

4. **Collaboration**: working with service users and families in designing policy, developing, implementing, and evaluating programs, designing facilities and professional education.

You can watch the video Patient and Family Centered Care at PHC produced by Providence Health Care in Vancouver to have a better understanding of the meaning of service user and family centered care.

Providence Health Vancouver. (2016, April 26). *Patient & family centred care at PHC* [Video]. YouTube. https://youtu.be/lqfcfuwtj4g

---

Interprofessional Communication

Effective communication skills are central to social work practice and essential for professionals working collaboratively (Ambrose-Miller & Ashcroft, 2016; Hall, 2005; Richards et al., 2005). This competency means that professionals prioritize respectful, authentic, and trusting relationships with their colleagues (CIHC, 2010). They can actively listen to one another, using verbal and nonverbal communication skills, and confirm their understanding with the speaker. Good communication requires transparency and communication technology that enhances shared decision making and collaboration (CIHC, 2010).

For more information about the National Interprofessional Competency Framework, developed by the Canadian Interprofessional Health Collaborative, please follow this link: CIHC_IPCompetencies_Feb1210r.pdf - Google Drive

Canadian Interprofessional Health Collaborative [CIHC]. (2010). *A national interprofessional competency framework*. University of British Columbia.

Team Functioning

Sometimes collaborative practice takes place within loosely defined networks, while other times it takes place in organized interprofessional teams. Groups of professionals working together in teams need to have some understanding of group dynamics and team development processes (CIHC, 2010). Social workers have training in group processes that can be beneficial to teamwork. Guidelines for ensuring respectful and ethical discussions, shared decision-making processes that consider confidentiality, and interprofessional ethics are important for aspects of effective team functioning.

Interprofessional Conflict Resolution

Conflict is a natural and expected aspect of professionals working together. In fact, disagreements can be valuable in teams helping professionals working together to make better decisions (Almost et al., 2016). Although expected, conflict needs to be addressed respectfully and constructively for effective collaborative practice (CIHC, 2010). Conflict needs to be differentiated from other behavior such as bullying, harassment, ostracism, or violence where there is intent to intimidate, threaten, insult, humiliate, exclude, or harm another (Almost et al., 2016). Whereas conflict can have positive outcomes, the previous types of behaviours always have negative outcomes and should be formally reported.

Role ambiguity, power hierarchies and differences in goals between professionals can be potential sources for disagreements and conflict (Ambrose Miller & Ashcroft, 2016; CIHC, 2010; D'Amour et al., 2005). All team members need to ensure that they create environments that are safe for diverse opinions to be expressed. All professionals should be provided space to share their perspective, even if that perspective is in opposition to others. Teams and groups should have processes and strategies in place to address conflict as it arises, analyze the source of conflict, and take steps to find solutions. Communication is essential to effective interprofessional conflict resolution.

Collaborative Leadership

When professionals work on structured teams, collaborative leadership means that the team applies leadership principles that are both task and relationship oriented (CIHC, 2010). Collaborative leadership means that leadership can be shared amongst members and that the group uses the expertise of their members at various times for different tasks. Individual members take accountability for their actions, responsibilities, and roles. Collaborative leadership requires a climate for collaboration and attending to the relationships among members so there are effective processes for discussion, negotiation, and decision making (CIHC, 2010).

Understanding Other Professions

It takes time to learn about other professions — it does not simply involve having one or two conversations with others. Understanding the complexities of the culture and worldviews of others and how this translates into practice, beliefs, and actions is a dynamic and ongoing process that requires reflection. The University of British Columbia's model of interprofessional education reflects the belief that there are optimal learning times for health and human services students and practitioners to incorporate the key concepts of interprofessional education and practice (Charles et al., 2010). These optimal points of learning are dependent upon peoples' stage of professional identity development and their readiness to learn and develop new perspectives on professional interaction. The UBC model of interprofessional education outlines three stages involved in this process (Charles et al., 2010):

Stage 1 – Exposure: Exposure lays the foundation for an advanced understanding and integration of the key concepts and competencies (role clarification, patient/service user/family/community-centered care, interprofessional communication, team functioning, interprofessional conflict resolution, collaborative leadership) of interprofessional practice. While students primarily focus on the development of their own professional identity, they are also provided with the opportunity to learn about the worldviews and roles of other health and human service professions: students learn that there can be multiple perspectives on any number of practice issues. These different perspectives are not right or wrong but are simply reflective of the world and practice views of the other professions. This exposure primarily occurs within the classroom setting prior to or during the first practicum. This is often a parallel learning experience where students take classes with members of other professions or are in field placement with them.

The Second Stage: Immersion. This stage of learning is collaborative, rather than parallel, where students learn from other professions. At this stage, students need to be able to maintain their own foundational professional identity while simultaneously be open to accepting that there are other valid worldviews, values and beliefs as they begin to learn about other professions. Students can gain an interprofessional worldview within which the student incorporates and understands the multiple perspectives of other professions, as well as the role and contributions they make to service user care. This is achieved through the provision of opportunities for ongoing structured and unstructured interactions with people from other professions. These interactions help students learn about the strengths and challenges of other professions and to contribute to other students better understanding social work. This requires thoughtful reflection on the dynamics of these moments of learning with members of other professions.

The Third Stage: Mastery. The mastery stage often occurs at advanced levels of training and education. In the mastery stage, students or practitioners incorporate the key concepts of interprofessional practice into their everyday professional lives. Mastery occurs when one has a well-developed sense of who they are as members of their own profession and of the role of social work within the helping systems. This usually only happens when students or practitioners have had significant practice experience and advanced professional training to interact from a place of competency with members of other professions. The goal of the mastery stage is to develop advanced-level critical thinking skills and a high degree of self-reflection that allows a deeper understanding of the contribution of one's own and the other professions within the health and human service delivery systems. Advanced learning experiences available through graduate programs and senior level placements or considerable experience in practice are often required to achieve mastery.

Conclusion

It is imperative that communication and collaboration between health and human service professions is improved to increase the likelihood that service users will get the care and support they need (Charles, 2011). Social work students and practitioners need to purposefully take the time to learn about and appreciate the contribution and struggles of the other professions. The first step in this process is to begin to see other professions as allies and not enemies. This requires that individual professions move away from their own positions of arrogance of believing and maintaining that their own profession's worldview is the only valid one. Social workers need to learn to see the practice world through multiple perspectives as well as their own.

Social work students and practitioners can develop competencies that will enable them to interact and work more effectively with other professions. Being able to articulate their own role and scope of practice as well as understand the role of others is essential. Learning effective communication skills, group development processes, and conflict resolution skills can enhance interprofessional collaboration. Finally, learning how to prioritize the service user's voice in their own care and service delivery, as well as developing leadership skills that are both task and relationship oriented will help social workers collaborate with other professions more effectively. Current service systems are far too complex; they will only change for the better if professionals change the way we interact with each other (Rubin et al., 2018). The best way to improve our levels of effectiveness and collaboration is to learn with intentionally and actively, from, and about the other professions.

Discussion Questions

1. What stereotypes, assumptions or biases do we have about other professions we work with? What stereotypes, assumptions or biases might other professions have about social workers? How might these stereotypes impede interprofessional collaboration?

2. What core competencies for interprofessional collaboration might social work students and social workers have that is unique to our professional training? How might social workers use these skills for enhancing collaboration with others?

3. Where do you see barriers to interprofessional practice in your practicum setting? What key concepts of interprofessional collaboration are evident in practice? Where do you see opportunities for social work students in practicums to enhance their knowledge and understanding of other professions?

4. Read the following case example and answer the questions below.

You are an in-patient hospital social worker. Jake is a 55-year-old patient who has been in hospital for acute depression for the past 5 days, and the team wants to discharge him tomorrow because there is a shortage of beds and they need to admit new patients. Jake has experienced chronic depression with acute episodes requiring urgent hospitalization for the past 30 years. He lives alone and has limited social supports, and is single and does not have any children. Jake is currently on disability financial support as he often cannot work when he is depressed. The physician has increased the dosage of his antidepressant, but this has shown only a mild improvement in his mood. The attending physician is advocating that this improvement is sufficient to have Jake be discharged tomorrow, but Jake is unsure he is ready for discharge.

You feel that Jake could benefit from being connected to more supports in the community before being discharged and this will reduce his likelihood of needing acute care in the near future. You are confident that you could arrange these supports within another day or two.

1. What action would you take as Jake's social worker?

2. What skills in interprofessional collaboration would be useful in this scenario?

REFERENCES

Almost, J., Wolff, A. C., Stewart-Pyne, A., McCormick, L. G., Strachan D., & D'Souza, C. (2016). Managing and mitigating conflict in healthcare teams: An integrative review. *Journal of Advanced Nursing, 72*(7), 1490–505. https://doi.org/10.1111/jan.12903

Ambrose-Miller, W., & Ashcroft, R. (2016). Challenges faced by social workers as members of interprofessional collaborative health care teams. *Health & Social Work, 41*(2), 101–109. https://doi.org/10.1093/hsw/hlw006

Ben Shlomo, S., Levy, D., & Itzhaky, H. (2012) Development of professional identity among social work students: Contributing factors. *The Clinical Supervisor, 31*(2), 240–255. https://doi.org/10.1080/07325223.2013.733305

Bogo, M. (2010). *Achieving competence in social work*. University of Toronto Press.

Bogo, M., & Vayda, E. J. (1998). *The practice of field instruction in social work* (2nd ed.). University of Toronto Press.

Bronstein, L. R. (2003). A model for interdisciplinary collaboration. *Social Work, 48*(3), 297–306. https://doi.org/10.1093/sw/48.3.297

Canadian Association of Social Workers. (2005). *CASW Code of Ethics and Scope of Practice*. https://casw-acts.ca/en/Code-of-Ethics

Canadian Interprofessional Health Collaborative. (2010*). A national interprofessional competency framework*. University of British Columbia. https://drive.google.com/file/d/1Des_mznc7Rr8stsEhHxl8XMjgiYWzRIn/view

Charles, G. (2011). Reflective response: Interdisciplinary and interprofessional collaboration: Essential for the doctoral advanced practice nurse. In M. Dreher and M. E. Smith Glasgow (Eds.), *Role development for doctoral advanced nursing practice* (pp. 351–356). Springer.

Charles, G., Bainbridge, L., Copeman-Stewart, K., Tiffin, S., & Kassam, P. (2006). The Interprofessional rural program of British Columbia (IRPbc). *Journal of Interprofessional Care, 20*(1), 40–50. https://doi.org/10.1080/13561820500498154

Charles, G., Bainbridge, L., Copeman-Stewart, K., & Kassam, R. (2008). The impact of an interprofessional rural healthcare practice education experience on students and communities. *Journal of Allied Health, 37*, 127–131.

Charles, G., Bainbridge, L., & Gilbert, J. (2010). The University of British Columbia model of interprofessional education. *Journal of Interprofessional Care, 24*(1), 8–18. https://doi.org/10.3109/13561820903294549

Charles, G., & Dharamsi, S. (2010). Service learning, interprofessional education and the social work placement: The case for combining the best of all worlds. In E. Ralph, K. Walker and R. Wimmer (Eds.), *The practicum in professional education: Canadian perspectives* (pp. 69–88). Detselig Press.

Charles, G., Dharamsi, S., & Alexander, C. (2011). Interprofessional field education: Reciprocal learning for collaborative practice. In J. Drolet, N. Clark, and H. Allen (Eds.), *Shifting sites of practice: Field experience in Canada* (pp. 253–263).

Charles, G., Birring, V., & Lake, S. (2011). What's in it for us?: Making the case for interprofessional field education experiences in social work. *Journal of Teaching in Social Work, 31*(5), 579–593. https://doi.org/10.1080/0884 1233.2011.615265

Charles, G., & Alexander, C. (2014). An introduction to interprofessional practice in social and health care settings. *Relational Child and Youth Care Practice, 27*(3), 51–55.

Charles, G., Alexander, C., & Oliver, C. (2015). Overcoming isolation: Making the case for the development of blended service learning and social work interprofessional field education experiences to improve university-community engagement. *Currents: Scholarship in the Human Services, 13*(1), 1–17. https://cjc-rcc.ucalgary.ca/index.php/currents/article/view/15949

Choi, B., & Pak, A. (2006). Multidisciplinarity, interdisciplinarity and transdisciplinarity in health research, services, education, and policy: 1. Definitions, objectives, and evidence of effectiveness. *Clinical and Investigative Medicine, 29*(6), 351–364.

Costello, M., Prelack, K., Faller, J., Huddleston, J., Adly, S., & Doolin, J. (2018). Student experiences of interprofessional simulation: Findings from a qualitative study. *Journal of Interprofessional Care, 32*, 95–97. https://doi.org/10.1080/13561820.2017.1356810

D'Amour, D., Ferrada-Videla, M., San Martin Rodriguez, L., & Beaulieu, M. D. (2005). The conceptual basis for interprofessional collaboration: core concepts and theoretical frameworks. *Journal of Interprofessional Care, 19*(sup1), 116–131. https://doi.org/10.1080/13561820500082529

Drinka, T. J. K., & Clark, P. G. (2000). *Health care teamwork: Interdisciplinary practice and teaching*. Auburn House.

Geva, E., Barsky, A., & Westernoff, F. (2000). Developing a framework for interprofessional and diversity informed practice. In E. Geva, A. Barsky, and F. Westernoff (Eds.), *Interprofessional practice with diverse populations: Cases in point* (pp. 1–28). Auburn House.

Glaser, B. (2016). Interprofessional collaboration and integration as experienced by social workers in health care. *Social Work in Health Care, 55*(5), 395–408. https://doi.org/10.1080/00981389.2015.1116483

Hall, P. (2005). Interprofessional teamwork: Professional cultures as barriers. *Journal of Interprofessional Care, 19*(supl), 188–196. https://doi.org/10.1080/13561820500081745

Hornby, S., & Atkins, J. (2000). *Collaborative care: Interprofessional, interagency and interpersonal* (2nd ed.). Blackwell.

Iachini, A. L., Bronstein, L. R., & Mellin, E. (2018). *A guide for interprofessional collaboration.* Council on Social Work Education Press.

Institute for Patient and Family Centered Care: Transforming health care through partnerships. (n.d.). *Patient and family centered care.* https://www.ipfcc.org/about/pfcc.html

Karam, M., Brault, I., Van Durme, T., & Macq, J. (2018). Comparing interprofessional and interorganizational collaboration in healthcare: a systematic review of the qualitative research. *International Journal of Nursing Studies, 79*, 70–83. https://doi.org/10.1016/j.ijnurstu.2017.11.002

Kelly, P. L., Heyman, J. C, Tice-Brown, D., & White-Ryan, L. (2020). Interprofessional practice: Social work students' perspectives on collaboration. *Social Work in Health Care, 59*(2), 108–112. https://doi.org/10.1080/00981389.2020.1719565

Kohn, L. T., Corrigan. J. M., & Donaldson, M. S. (2000). To err is human: Building a safer health system. *Institute of Medicine, Committee on Quality of Health Care in America.*

Loxley, A. (1997). *Collaboration in health and welfare: Working with difference.* Kingsley.

Lutfiyya, M., Chang, L., McGrath, C., Dana, C., & Lipsky, M. (2019). The state of the science of interprofessional collaborative practice: A scoping review of the patient health-related outcomes based on literature published between 2010 and 2018. *PLoS One, 14*(6), 1–18. https://doi.org/10.1371/journal.pone.0218578

Maynard, S. P., Mertz, L. K. P., & Fortune, A. E. (2015). Off-site supervision in social work education: What makes it work? *Journal of Social Work Education, 51*(3), 519–534. https://doi.org/10.1080/10437797.2015.1043201.

Merriam-Webster. (n.d.). Interdependence. In *Merriam-Webster.com dictionary.* https://www.merriam-webster.com/dictionary/interdependence

Miller, C., Freeman, M., & Ross, N. (2001). *Interprofessional practice in health and social care: Challenging the shared learning agenda.* Arnold.

Mizrahi, T., & Abramson, J. (2000). Collaboration between social workers and physicians: Perspectives on a shared case. *Social Work in Health Care, 31*(3), 1–24. https://doi.org/10.1300/J010v31n03_01

Morley, L., & Cashell, A. (2017). Collaboration in health care. *Journal of Medical Imaging and Radiation Sciences, 48*(2), 207–216. https://doi.org/10.1016/j.jmir.2017.02.071

Nugus, P., Greenfield, D., Travaglia, J., Westbrook, J., & Braithwaite, J. (2010). How and where clinicians exercise power: Interprofessional relations in health care. *Social Science & Medicine, 71*(5), 898–909. https://doi.org/10.1016/j.socscimed.2010.05.029

Office of the Child and Youth Advocate Alberta. (2022). *Mandatory reviews into child death: April 1, 2021 – September 30, 2021.* https://www.ocya.alberta.ca/adult/publications/investigative-review/

Oliver, C. (2013). Social workers as boundary spanners: Reframing our professional identity for interprofessional practice. *Social Work Education, 32*(6), 773–784. https://doi.org/10.1080/02615479.2013.765401

Paul, S., & Peterson, C. Q. (2001). Interprofessional collaboration: Issues for practice and research. *Occupational Therapy in Health Care, 15*, 1–15. https://doi.org/10.1080/J003v15n03_01

Phillips, J. D., & Walsh, M. A. (2019). Teaming up in child welfare: The perspective of guardians ad litem on the components of interprofessional collaboration. *Children and Youth Services Review, 96*, 17–26. https://doi.org/10.1016/j.childyouth.2018.11.016

Providence Health Care Vancouver. (2016, April 26). *Patient and family centered care at PHC.* [Video]. YouTube. https://www.youtube.com/watch?v=lqfcfuwtj4g

Richards, S., Ruch, G., & Trevithick, P. (2005). Communication skills training for practice: the ethical dilemma for social work education. *Social Work Education, 24*(4), 409–422. https://doi.org/10.1080/02615470500096928

Romanow, R. J. (2002). *Building our values: The future of health care in Canada—Final report.* Commission on the Future of Health Care in Canada. https://publications.gc.ca/collections/Collection/CP32-85-2002E.pdf

Rubin, M., Cohen Konrad, S., Nimmagadda, J., Scheyett, A., & Dunn, K. (2018). Social work and interprofessional education: integration, intersectionality, and institutional leadership. *Social Work Education, 37*(1), 17–33. https://doi.org/10.1080/02615479.2017.1363174

Saint-Pierre, C., Herskovic, V., & Sepúlveda, M. (2018). Multidisciplinary collaboration in primary care: a systematic review. *Family Practice, 35*(2), 132–141. https://doi.org/10.1093/fampra/cmx085

Salhani, D., & Charles, G. (2007). The dynamics of an interprofessional team: The interplay of child and youth care with other professions within a residential milieu. *Relational Child and Youth Care Practice, 20*(4), 12–20. https://www.researchgate.net/publication/273694211_The_dynamics_of_an_interprofessional_team_The_interplay_of_child_and_youth_care_with_other_professions_within_a_residential_treatment_milieu

Smith, D., Cleak, H., &d Vreugdenhil, A. (2015). "What are they really doing?" An exploration of student learning activities in field placement. *Australian Social Work, 68*(4), 515–531. https://doi.org/10.1080/031240 7X.2014.960433

Wiles, F. (2013) "Not easily put into a box": Constructing professional identity. *Social Work Education, 32*(7), 854–866. https://doi.org/10.1080/02615479.2012.705273

NOTES:

NOTES:

NOTES:

The Transition From School to Work, From One Work Setting to Another: Guided by Curiosity

Karen Lok Yi Wong

In this chapter, I share my experiences of how curiosity guided my transitions from school to work and from one work setting to another. I am sharing my experiences because I expect that many readers of this book are social work students, and they will experience the transition to practitioners in the future. To support my personal experiences of transitioning to professional social work practice, I first review literature on the topic of transitions. It helped me know what work has already been done on this topic and how my experience could add to the work already done. I then explain the curiosity approach and refer to my experiences as examples to explain how curiosity guided my transitions. I explain how I applied curiosity to overcome challenges during transitions by searching for answers, asking questions, observation, and reflection. Because of curiosity, I reached a deeper understanding of the challenges I faced and issues I encountered during my transitions. With this approach, I was able to turn stress and fear of transitions into interest to explore the unknown. This chapter can be used as a support for social work students and social workers who experience challenges during transitions.

Literature on Transitions

Glassburn (2020) interviewed recent Master of Social Work graduates about their transition from school to work. The main challenges these graduates faced during the transition were pressure to get a job as soon as possible, lack of knowledge about how to negotiate for their salary, lack of orientation at workplaces, realization of the gap between expectation and reality, overwhelmedness about things they did not know, lack of workplace supervision, emotions management, and compassion fatigue or burnout (Glassburn, 2020). The author suggested that more opportunities for orientation and supervision support graduates transitioning from school to work.

Tham and Lynch (2019) interviewed recent social work graduates. According to these graduates, the main challenges of transitioning from school to work included lack of workplace training and having an unorganized or even chaotic introduction to the workplace (Tham & Lynch, 2019). The authors recommended revisiting social work education curriculum to improve student preparation for the transition to work.

Richards-Schuster et al. (2016) conducted a survey to understand the challenges of recent social work graduates' transition to work. The main challenges was the discrepancy between what they imagined at school and what they can do in reality to practice social justice (Richards-Schuster et al., 2016). The authors recommend letting students see real-world injustices while at school; connecting students with recent graduates; and helping students develop skills in relationship building, reflection, cultural and educational humility, and self-care.

The literature shows that social work students encounter challenges transitioning from school to work. A common challenge is that social work students feel unprepared when they transition into a job . For myself, the challenges of transitions happened not only when moving from school to work but also from one workplace to another. Literature suggests that there are many ways to overcome the challenges (Glassburn, 2020; Richards-Schuster et al., 2016; Tham & Lynch, 2019). From my experience, one way was through being curious: I turned my fear and stress being in a new place into curiosity. To my understanding, there is little literature about using curiosity to cope with the challenges of transitions, which is the central theme of this chapter. However, even though literature about overcoming transition challenges through curiosity is limited in social work, there is literature on this area in other disciplines such as Nursing (Sun et al., 2023) and Vocational Studies (Koen et al., 2012). The literature in other disciplines talked about how curiosity helped overcome transition challenges and ease the transition process.

Curiosity Approach

When I was training to be a social worker, I was introduced to and inspired by literature of different social work approaches. An article that still profoundly influences me today after years of practice is 'Not-Knowing' and 'Assumption' in Canadian Social Services for Refugees and Immigrants: A Conversational Inquiry into Practitioner Stance by DeFehr et al. (2012). Even though the article is about practitioners working with refugees and immigrants, I believe that it has implications to practitioners working with other populations and settings, too. The authors described the approach they were using but did not give a specific name to it. However, I understand that the approach is built around the practitioner's curiosity. For easier reference, I will call this the "curiosity approach."

According to DeFehr et al. (2012), the curiosity approach refers to the genuine curiosity about people around us, including understanding their perspectives and strengths. Practitioners do not make assumptions, and instead, they work from the stance that they want to know more about the people they are working with. This includes clients, colleagues, and community partners. Coming from curiosity, we ask people what they think instead of assuming we know what they think. This prevents us from making assumptions and thus helps to avoid misunderstanding. Moreover, curiosity also refers to curiosity about the world. We think about an issue or a challenge in the world from different angles. We consider these issues and challenges from new perspectives. We think deeper about them instead of just seeing their surfaces.

Examples of Transitions Guided by Curiosity

I used the curiosity approach several times to guide my transitions from school to work and from one workplace to another. There are many ways to put our curiosity into practice. For example, I search for answers, ask questions, observe, reflect. I will explain how I apply these strategies in the examples that follow.

SETTING 1: SENIOR COMMUNITY CENTRE

My first social work job was in a senior community centre. One of my roles was providing information and referral services, which are services that clients come to the centre and ask for information and support for, such as tax filing service, benefit applications, and bus pass application. One common reason seniors came to my centre was that they needed certain government resources that they were entitled to but could not apply for them by themselves. This was especially the case when they needed to apply for resources online because, while some were tech-savvy, many seniors were not able to go online.

My colleagues, our clients, and I called government departments to ask what we could do. The government departments answered, "go online, there is no other way." This was shocking for me as a new social worker. At school, we learned about equity (Ife, 2008; Solas, 2008). People come from diverse backgrounds, and because of these backgrounds, some are in more advantaged positions while some are in less advantaged positions — they are not on a level playing field. Accommodation is therefore needed so that people can access equal opportunities. However, the reality told me that society was not accommodating. The government department's response showed that the government did not practice equity.

Many new social workers feel shocked when they realize the discrepancy between what they imagined at school and what they can do in reality to practice social justice (Glassburn, 2020; Richards-Schuster et al., 2016). I began to be curious about my clients and their situations. I asked them, colleagues, and community partners why my clients could not go online. I concluded that there were several reasons. First, some had no financial resources except a public pension, which they had to use for necessities, including food and housing could not afford the technology. Second, some had limited or no technological literacy. Classes and devices on the market often did not consider the needs of senior users. Third, some did not feel comfortable using the technology, and they did not have or could not ask their family or friends to help. There were volunteer programs in the senior community centre, but it was hard to retain volunteers due to limited funding. I reflected on what the implications were that older adults needed to access online to apply for the resources, but they could not go online. At school, I learned that a human need can be interpreted as a human right (Ife, 2008, 2012). In other words, access to technology is a human rights issue. I later collaborated with seniors and research and community partners to conduct a study and publish a report and an article on advocating for seniors' access to technology and related information and services as a human right (Wong et al., 2021a, 2021b).

SETTING 2: LONG-TERM CARE

I later moved to work in long-term care. Residents, families, and team members in long-term care came to me for different things because they believed what they came to me with was within my role as a social worker. However, gradually I felt that something was not right. I worked overtime several hours every day. Yet, I did not know that I should say no when others came to me. I realized that the root problem was that I did not know what my role was. At school, I was taught about the roles of social workers, such as counselling, resource connection, and advocacy. During my first job, I was clear about what my role was because my employer made it clear to me and others on my team. Therefore, I was shocked by not knowing my role in the new setting. It appeared that everything was included within my role, from screening admission packages of new residents to cleaning the belongings of residents who passed away. I felt stressed not knowing my role as it seemed that everything fell on my shoulders. Instead of just feeling stressed and fearing not knowing my role, I was curious to explore what my role was. I asked myself, "What are the social worker's roles in long-term care?" I was the only social worker in the facility, so I did not have another social worker to ask. Therefore, I had to search for answers. I asked residents, families, and colleagues what they thought my role was and should be. I searched for job postings of social workers in other long-term care facilities that included the roles of social workers. I attended conferences and exchanged views with other participants from healthcare and social services located throughout Canada. I even conducted a research project (Wong, 2021) where I interviewed social workers in long-term care about what they thought their roles were and learned that social workers' roles in long-term care depend on the contexts because of the differences in the resident population, family population, team structure, and more. However, as social workers in long-term care, we share a common scope of practice grounded in our fundamental professional values: self-determination, relationship building, and advocating for social justice. We define our job according to these values.

SETTING 3: HOSPITAL

I later moved to work in acute care in a hospital where professionals use terms that people outside healthcare do not necessarily understand. For example, abbreviations are common. I was shocked as I realized that I did not know many of the terms being used because I was not taught them in school. In my previous work setting in long-term care, even though it was a healthcare setting, these terms were not used. I tried to guess the terms from the context and searched for the answers. However, I still could not understand all of them. At one point, I was curious about myself, "What don't I just ask my colleagues what the terms mean?" I reflected that this was related to my fear of being seen as incompetent or bothering other colleagues. I did not want to look stupid by asking people simple questions, and I did not want to bother my colleagues in a fast-paced work setting. However, I could not do my job properly without understanding what the terms meant because I was responsible for the best interests of my clients. For the sake of my clients, I asked my colleagues what the terms meant; I soon realized that some of my colleagues also did not understand the terms. When I asked my questions, I unintentionally helped the speakers who used the terms understand that not everyone understood what they were saying. This facilitated a culture of using simple language and facilitated interdisciplinary collaboration.

The hospital I worked in was in a multicultural and aging community in Vancouver, British Columbia. The primary language used in healthcare services in Vancouver is English. However, clients came from diverse cultural and language backgrounds. My previous work settings had clients from diverse cultural and language backgrounds, but the environment of this hospital was even more diverse. Working with the cultural and language diversity was a challenge to me at first because many of my clients spoke limited English, sometimes because of cognitive deterioration. When my colleagues and I asked these clients whether they had further questions, they usually said no. However, we did not want to make assumptions that the clients understood our question, and we were curious whether and to what extent the clients understood what we said. Therefore, we asked the clients, "Would you please tell me how you understand what I said?" We realized that they did not understand, or they understood in different ways from what we told them. I reflected on how we could improve communication. Interpretation did not entirely resolve the problem Because sometimes clients continued to not understand or they misunderstood what we said even if there was an interpreter present. We came to realize that sometimes the gap was more than language — it was a gap in culture. We do not have a definite answer on how to improve the communication. However, my curiosity guided me to think deeper about spending more time to clarify my intent when we come from different language and cultural backgrounds.

I learned from my colleagues that clients from certain cultural groups are more likely to decline home-care resources after discharge from the hospital. Homecare refers to professionals going to the home of clients to provide care. My colleagues attributed the decline to culture. Patients of some cultural groups prefer to receive care from their families. While I thought this was reasonable, I was curious to explore this further. Therefore, when patients or their families declined the resources, I asked them for the reasons. Indeed, many of them were open to home care resources. However, they and their families had limited English abilities. They worried that if they could not communicate with the professionals, the situation would be worse than not having the home-care resources. This made me think about whether we have enough language and culturally appropriate home care resources in our healthcare system. I also started raising the lack of language and culturally appropriate home care resources among my healthcare and social work colleagues.

Conclusion

I used examples from my experiences to show how curiosity guided my transitions from school to work and from one workplace to another. My experiences taught me that I felt shocked with the new challenges every time I moved to a new setting. However, curiosity helped me to reduce my anxiety working in a new setting. Also, it helped me to go deeper with the new challenges. It helped me turn my stress and fear of transitions into interests to explore the unknowns.

I applied curiosity by different strategies: searching for answers, asking questions, observation, and reflection: I observed why my clients could not go online when I graduated from school and practiced in the senior community service centre. I searched for what the roles of social workers were when I transitioned to long-term care. I asked my colleagues what medical terms meant when I first started working in the hospital. I constantly reflected about my practice and things I observed. My reflection led me to take actions, such as research and advocacy.

How do we nurture curiosity? I found networking with other people helpful. Talking to people helps me to learn about their perspectives which broadens my understanding of and nurtures my curiosity of people. I also found continuous education helpful; learning new ideas keeps me curious about the world. It helps me acknowledge that the world is changing daily, so my curiosity should never stop.

Note: This chapter was based on the author's lecture when she received the Inspiring Social Worker Award 2021 co-organized by the British Columbia Association of Social Workers and the University of British Columbia.

Discussion Questions

1. What does curiosity mean to you?
2. Why is curiosity important in social work practice?
3. How could curiosity guide your transitions?
4. How could curiosity guide your practice?
5. How could you cultivate your curiosity in practice?

REFERENCES

Defehr, J., Adan, O., Barros, C., Rodriguez, S., and Wai, S. B. (2012). "Not-knowing" and "assumption" in Canadian social services for refugees and immigrants: A conversational inquiry into practitioner stance. *International Journal of Collaborative Practices*, *3*(1), 75–88.

Government of Canada. (2022). Employment and Social Development Canada. https://www.canada.ca/en/employment-social-development.html

Ife, J. (2008). Comment on John Solas: "What are we fighting for?" *Australian Social Work*, *61*(2), 137–140. https://doi.org/10.1080/03124070801998392

Ife, J. (2012). *Human rights and social work: Towards rights-based practice*. Cambridge University Press.

Koen, J., Klehe, U.-C., & Van Vianen, A. E. M. (2012). Training career adaptability to facilitate a successful school-to-work transition. *Journal of Vocational Behavior*, *81*(3), 395–408. https://doi.org/10.1016/j.jvb.2012.10.003

Lynn Glassburn, S. (2020). Where's the roadmap? The transition from student to professional for new Master of Social Work graduates. *Qualitative Social Work*, *19*(1), 142–158. https://doi.org/10.1177/1473325018807746

Richards-Schuster, K., Ruffolo, M. C., Nicoll, K. L., Distelrath, C., Galura, J., and Mishkin, A. (2016). Exploring Challenges Faced by Students as they Transition to Social Justice Work in the 'Real World': Implications for Social Work. *Advances in Social Work*, *16*(2), 372–389. https://doi.org/10.18060/18526

Rossiter, A. (2006). The "beyond" ethics in social work." *Canadian Social Work Review*, *23*(1/2), 139–144.

Solas, J. (2008). Social work and social justice: What are we fighting for? *Australian Social Work*, *61*(2), 124–136. https://doi.org/10.1080/03124070801998384

Sun, C., Xing, Y., Wen, Y., Wan, X., Ding, Y., Cui, Y., Xu, W., Wang, X., Xia, H., Zhang, Q., & Yuan, M. (2023). Association between career adaptability and turnover intention among nursing assistants: The mediating role of psychological capital. *BMC Nursing*, *22*(1), 29. https://doi.org/10.1186/s12912-023-01187-y

Tham, P., and Lynch, D. (2019). "Lost in transition?" — Newly educated social workers' reflections on their first months in practice. *European Journal of Social Work*, *22*(3), 400–411. https://doi.org/10.1080/13691457.2017 .1364701

Wong, K. L. Y. (2021). How do social workers working in long-term care understand their roles? Using British Columbia, Canada as an example. *Journal of Gerontological Social Work*, *64*(5), 452–470. https://doi.org/10. 1080/01634372.2021.1900479

Wong, K. L. Y., Sixsmith, A., and Remund, L. (2021a). In Community—Information and Referral Services for Seniors in British Columbia: Past Learnings and Learnings since COVID-19. https://www.sfu.ca/content/ dam/sfu/starinstitute/Documents/In%20Community%20-%20Information%20and%20Referral%20 Services%20for%20Seniors%20in%20British%20Columbia_Report.pdf.

Wong, K. L. Y., Sixsmith, A., & Remund, L. (2021b). "Older adults' access to information and referral service using technology in British Columbia, Canada: Past learnings and learnings since COVID-19." In M. Pomati, A. Jolly, and J. Rees (Eds.), *Social Policy Review 33: Analysis and Debate in Social Policy* (pp. 161–180). Policy Press.

NOTES:

NOTES:

Conclusion: Transformations and Transitions in Field Education

Grant Charles and Julie Drolet

While it is obvious that social work field education is in crisis it should be acknowledged that one of the things that can come out of difficulty is transformation. This book is primarily about transformation.

There are many transformations and transitions happening in social work education. Field education has been changing in response to shifts in practice settings, the pandemic, and technology. Students go through a transformation as they move from being a student to being a practitioner.

This book seeks to serve in both change capacities. The book highlights key concepts about field education system change as well as serving as a support to students as they enter their placements. It helps to serve as a bridge between the classroom and placements as students transition between the two. The book builds upon the foundational knowledge provided in the classroom by helping to expand upon what the students have learned while also providing new ways of being and interacting in the field and the profession.

This concluding chapter poses a number of questions to help you review each chapter and use what you learned during your transition into field placements.

Introduction

List a key message you took from this chapter.

_____
_____
_____
_____
_____
_____

List two ways you will use what you learned in this chapter in your practicum.

_____
_____
_____
_____
_____
_____
_____
_____
_____
_____

Chapter 1: Tips for Starting a Field Practicum

List a key message you took from this chapter.

_____
_____
_____
_____
_____
_____

List two ways you will use what you learned in this chapter in your practicum.

_____
_____
_____
_____
_____
_____
_____
_____
_____

Chapter 2: Making Space for Wellness in Field Education

List a key message you took from this chapter.

_____

_____

_____

_____

_____

_____

List two ways you will use what you learned in this chapter in your practicum.

_____

_____

_____

_____

_____

_____

_____

_____

_____

_____

_____

_____

Chapter 3: Trauma- and Resilience-Informed Practice for Self-Care Among Social Work Students

List a key message you took from this chapter.

_____

_____

_____

_____

_____

_____

List two ways you will use what you learned in this chapter in your practicum.

_____

_____

_____

_____

_____

_____

_____

_____

_____

Chapter 4: Remote Field Instruction and Supervision

List a key message you took from this chapter.

_____
_____
_____
_____
_____
_____

List two ways you will use what you learned in this chapter in your practicum.

_____
_____
_____
_____
_____
_____
_____
_____
_____
_____

Chapter 5: Integrating Research into Social Work Field Education – Beginning with your Learning Contract

List a key message you took from this chapter.

_____
_____
_____
_____
_____

List two ways you will use what you learned in this chapter in your practicum.

_____
_____
_____
_____
_____
_____
_____
_____
_____

Chapter 6: Research As Daily Practice as an Agency Asset

List a key message you took from this chapter.

_____

_____

_____

_____

_____

_____

List two ways you will use what you learned in this chapter in your practicum.

_____

_____

_____

_____

_____

_____

_____

_____

_____

_____

_____

Chapter 7: Maneuvering the Macro: A Guide to Macro-Level Field Placements

List a key message you took from this chapter.

_____

_____

_____

_____

_____

_____

List two ways you will use what you learned in this chapter in your practicum.

_____

_____

_____

_____

_____

_____

_____

_____

_____

_____

Chapter 8: Developing a Theoretical Framework for Practice

List a key message you took from this chapter.

_____
_____
_____
_____
_____
_____

List two ways you will use what you learned in this chapter in your practicum.

_____
_____
_____
_____
_____
_____
_____
_____
_____

Chapter 9: Striving for Equity, Diversity, and Inclusion in Social Work Field Education

List a key message you took from this chapter.

_____
_____
_____
_____
_____

List two ways you will use what you learned in this chapter in your practicum.

_____
_____
_____
_____
_____
_____
_____

Chapter 10: Addressing Discrimination Against Minority Groups in Social Work Practice and Field Education

List a key message you took from this chapter.

_____
_____
_____
_____
_____
_____

List two ways you will use what you learned in this chapter in your practicum.

_____
_____
_____
_____
_____
_____
_____
_____
_____
_____

Chapter 11: Becoming a Spiritual Influencer Through the Heart and Soul of Field Education

List a key message you took from this chapter.

_____
_____
_____
_____
_____

List two ways you will use what you learned in this chapter in your practicum.

_____
_____
_____
_____
_____
_____
_____
_____
_____

Chapter 12: Advancing Social Work Field Education in Healthcare

List a key message you took from this chapter.

_____

_____

_____

_____

_____

_____

List two ways you will use what you learned in this chapter in your practicum.

_____

_____

_____

_____

_____

_____

_____

_____

_____

_____

Chapter 13: Interprofessional Education and Practice in Social Work Field Education

List a key message you took from this chapter.

_____

_____

_____

_____

_____

_____

List two ways you will use what you learned in this chapter in your practicum.

_____

_____

_____

_____

_____

_____

_____

_____

_____

_____

Chapter 14: The Transition from School to Work, From One Work Setting to Another

List a key message you took from this chapter.

_____
_____
_____
_____
_____
_____

List two ways you will use what you learned in this chapter in your practicum.

_____
_____
_____
_____
_____
_____
_____
_____
_____
_____

The next questions move from a focus on each chapter to a more micro approach using the collective knowledge from the book.

Thinking about these key messages you have taken from the chapters, discuss what they may have in common.

_____
_____
_____
_____
_____
_____
_____
_____
_____
_____
_____
_____
_____
_____
_____

How might the barriers associated with the crisis that is currently occurring have a negative impact upon your learning experience in placement?

_____
_____
_____
_____
_____
_____
_____
_____
_____
_____
_____
_____
_____
_____
_____
_____
_____
_____

Take one or more of these barriers that were identified in the book and come up with a plan to mitigate the issue for yourself.

_____
_____
_____
_____
_____
_____
_____
_____
_____
_____
_____
_____
_____
_____
_____
_____
_____
_____

List three messages from the book that brings you optimism about changes happening in field education.

_____
_____
_____
_____
_____
_____
_____
_____
_____
_____
_____
_____
_____
_____
_____
_____
_____
_____
_____
_____

How might you take the knowledge from the book to help instigate change within your placement and in the profession?

_____
_____
_____
_____
_____
_____
_____
_____
_____
_____
_____
_____
_____
_____
_____
_____
_____
_____
_____

The purpose of this book is to help prepare students for placement and to facilitate change within social work field education. This change is needed for a number of reasons including in response the current crisis within our field education system. However, it goes beyond the ongoing crisis that was occurring pre-pandemic and worsened in response to the conditions brought about in response to COVID-19. The book also hopes to contribute to the changes that are occurring within social work as we seek to rectify harms and move towards a profession based upon social justice.

NOTES:

Reflective Journal Workbook

www.ingramcontent.com/pod-product-compliance
Lightning Source LLC
Chambersburg PA
CBHW080355030426
42334CB00024B/2883